THE POLITICS OF WORKING-CLASS EDUCATION IN BRITAIN, 1830–50

THE POLITICS OF WORKING-CLASS EDUCATION IN BRITAIN, 1830–50

D. G. Paz

Manchester University Press

© Denis G. Paz 1980

Published by
Manchester University Press
Oxford Road, Manchester M13 9PL

British Library cataloguing in publication data

Paz, D. G.
  The politics of working-class education in
  Britain, 1830–50.
  1. Labor and laboring classes – Education –
  Great Britain – History – 19th century
  2. Education and state – Great Britain – History
  – 19th century
  I. Title
  371.9'67   LC5056.G7

  ISBN 0–7190–6811–5

Computerised Phototypesetting
by G.C. Typeset Ltd., Bolton, Greater Manchester

Printed in Great Britain
by
Unwin Brothers Limited
The Gresham Press, Old Woking, Surrey, England
A member of the Staples Printing Group

Contents

Contents

Preface

The growth of government intervention in people's lives is a major theme in the history of Victorian Britain. During this period the State grew increasingly involved in the regulation of activities previously left to private or local initiative: working conditions; the building and maintenance of railways; education at all levels from elementary to professional and university 'training; municipal amenities such as sewers, gas, and water; health and safety standards in emigrant ships; welfare for the unemployed, sick, orphaned, and aged. One major governmental concern was the education of working-class children. In the period 1830–50 the State's financial commitment grew from a meagre £20,000 to £125,000 per annum, a new and large department of state was created, and the very question of whether the State should dabble in education became a matter of high policy, if not yet of confidence. This transformation deserves explanation.

In the past, one studied social history by leaping from Act of Parliament to Act of Parliament, as Eric Midwinter puts it, like a mountain goat leaping from peak to peak. Nowadays the approach is more sophisticated, using local studies, comparative and quantitative techniques, 'history from below', and the study of cumulative administrative processes.[1] This last approach has animated my research.

Mine is a political and administrative study of the origins and growth of State activity in British education. Other questions such as the nature of working-class education and its impact on children are certainly worth pursuing, but it is dangerous to study the results of government policy before knowing what that policy was. I further limited the study to the score of years from the Great Reform Bill to the death of Peel. The first event marks the font of reform, from which proceeded all further developments. The second marks a valid point of termination. The initial State educational policy did not fix the nature or direction of subsequent policy; these at first remained open questions. By 1850 the State's educational activities had assumed the form that they were to retain until at least 1870. By 1850, moreover, the terms of debate over the State's role in education had changed. The three themes of Victorian social reform—health, education, and crime—had been defined. Civil service reform and the slow decline of patronage began a transformation in the character of civil servants. Advanced Liberals abandoned non-denominational for secular education as the Lancashire Public School Association began its public and parliamentary agitation.[2]

Within this framework I attempt to discover how and when and why policy on this particular social issue emerged, and to show how the limits of practicable State intervention set themselves early on in the story. I identify the parties responsible for the development of State intervention from the modest grant of 1833 to a large, permanent bureaucracy, and place this development in the still obscure framework of the 'nineteenth-century revolution in government'.

In doing so, I do not assume as a point of departure that 'histories of government with no perception of the state as an agency of social domination' (by 'a capitalist ruling class') 'are fundamentally flawed, myopic . . . and trivialize or misrecognize their content . . .'.[3] Rather, I seek to determine *precisely* what government policies and expenditures were, and then work back to learn how and by whom those policies were shaped. The results suggest that the social control hypothesis might stand some reappraisal.

Acknowledgements

I have to acknowledge the gracious permission of H.M. the Queen for access to papers at the Royal Archives. Transcripts of Crown copyright records in the Public Record Office appear by permission of the Controller of H.M. Stationery Office. For permission to use copyright papers I thank the Marquess of Lansdowne; the Earl Grey; the Earl of Halifax; the Earl of Harrowby; the Earl Spencer; the Earl of Wharncliffe; the Lord Shuttleworth; Sir Richard Acland, Bt.; Sir William Gladstone, Bt.; Sir Fergus Graham, Bt.; the Reverend Canon R. T. Holtby (General Secretary of the National Society for Promoting Christian Education); James B. Gordon, Esq.; the Librarian, Exeter City Library; and the Local Historian, Shrewsbury Library. The Shaftesbury manuscripts are quoted by permission of the Trustees of the Broadlands Archives. For access to the Aldam papers, and for hospitality, I thank Major William Warde-Aldam. In addition, I thank the staffs of the Round Room, Public Record Office; the Students' Room and State Paper Room, British Museum; the National Register of Archives; and all the other national libraries, county record offices, city, university, and denominational archives that I consulted, for their kindnesses. But I wish particularly to thank the young ladies of the Department of Palaeography and Diplomatic, University of Durham, whose massive infusions of tea helped me survive the coal strike of 1972.

For substantive comments on my draft, I thank J. L. Alexander, Lucy Brown, Liam Hunt, Susan Wood Paz, and Jacob M. Price. I also thank R. H. Cameron, M. R. D. Foot, J. M. Goldstrom, Brian Harrison, John Houlding, John Hurt, Richard Johnson, Henry Roper, James J. Sack, and J. C. Sainty.

Parts of this book appeared earlier in the *British Journal of Educational Studies* and the *Journal of British Studies*; I thank their editors for permission to republish. Part of Chapter VIII was presented to F. M. L. Thompson's seminar at the Institute of Historical Research; I thank the members of his seminar for their comments.

A Fulbright Scholarship at the London School of Economics, 1971–73, and a Faculty Research Grant from the Horace H. Rackham School of Graduate Studies, University of Michigan, 1976, supported most of the research for this book. Its writing was made possible by my parents, whose sacrifices helped to support my graduate education. I am more grateful to them than they shall ever know for whatever success I might have in my pursuit of Clio.

Clemson University, 1979   D.G.P.

List of abbreviations

AHR	*American Historical Review*
BJES	*British Journal of Educational Studies*
BM, Add. MS.	British Museum, Additional Manuscript
CRO	County Record Office
DNB	*The Dictionary of National Biography*
Edin. Rev.	*Edinburgh Review*
EHR	*English Historical Review*
Hansard	*Hansard's Parliamentary Debates*
JMH	*Journal of Modern History*
JRL	John Rylands University Library of Manchester
Mirror	*Mirror of Parliament*
NCE	New College, Edinburgh
NL	Newberry Library
NLI	National Library of Ireland
NRA	National Register of Archives
NRA(S)	National Register of Archives (Scotland)
PP	*Parliamentary Papers*
PPL	*House of Lords Papers*
PRO	Public Record Office
RA	Royal Archives
SRO	Scottish Record Office
UCL	University College, London
WLCL	William L. Clements Library, University of Michigan

Chapter I

CONTEXTS

All political questions have pre-histories that are essential for a clear understanding of subsequent developments, and education is no exception. The great nineteenth-century religious revival, the rise of denominational school societies, the State's willingness to cure social ills through legislation, and the creation of 'modern' and efficient methods of administration all supply the necessary contexts in which to view the education question. They both prepared the ground for the State's first initiative in working-class education and dictated the path that the State subsequently took.

I   RELIGIOUS

For a moment just before the French revolution, traditional religious distinctions seemed to have eroded under the impact of Enlightenment rationalism. Reason replaced revelation as the touchstone of belief, and interdenominational co-operation increased in philanthropic endeavours. The French revolution put an end to this and encouraged the growth of denominationalism. Latitudinarianism, it seemed, did not satisfy a Romantic age and led to irreligion and the excesses of the cult of reason. Methodism is a useful example. During Wesley's life the movement maintained that its adherents were good Anglicans, limited the power and authority of preachers and class leaders, and scheduled prayer meetings so as not to conflict with services at the parish church. But from the 1790s Wesleyan Methodism came under pressure from radical and lower-class revivalist movements and responded by tightening denominational lines. And the symbol of its new denominationalism was the creation of a clergy who donned gowns to preach and who celebrated the holy communion. Most other

Nonconformist sects faced similar attacks and generally reacted in a similar manner. The economic troubles and consequent political activity after 1815 exacerbated the matter.[1]

The rise of denominationalism led to the greatest conflict between the sects and the Establishment since the mid-seventeenth century, one in which the Establishment was on the defensive. The clash began at the local level during the 1820s, when the Church attempted to use its legal powers to enforce the collection of tithes and cess. In return, northern Dissenters used their power at the polls to elect hostile vestries; a few became gaol martyrs for non-payment of Church rates. The repeal of the Test and Corporation Acts and the passage of Catholic emancipation ushered in a period of intense conflict at the national level between the Church and its enemies. These legislative events, coupled with the publication of Wade's *Extraordinary Black Book* and the passage of the Great Reform Bill, ushered in a period of reform in Church as well as in State. Just as the Church had been too weak to beat down its attackers in the 1820s, so militant Dissent could not eliminate the Establishment a decade later, or even retain its own unity. Civil and religious issues intertwined to form the great political questions of the 1830s and '40s, and only our secular age leads us to separate and compartmentalise the two.[2]

The Church of England responded positively to the warfare. Anglicans, seeing that reform to end abuses analogous to those being eliminated in the secular sphere was inevitable, adopted measures like the University of Durham or the Ecclesiastical Commission, lest their enemies do worse. If one must have surgery, let a friendly surgeon do it. In return, churchmen expected a sign that the State still acknowledged a national establishment, that it would give the Church, as Blomfield put it, 'additional opportunities of fulfilling her duties, by providing means of joining in her worship for all who desire it'. But political radicals and militant Dissent did not accept such a trade-off. Hence sharp opposition in Parliament met any attempt to divert government funds to religious ends, and by the end of the 1840s there emerged the Liberation Society — the first modern movement for the separation of Church and State. The State therefore suffered great pressure from powerful forces to take a neutral position.[3]

The Church became militant precisely because Dissent was hostile and the State neutral. Defenders of the Establishment principle believed that the growth of Dissent (and particularly of Methodism) would foster a democratic, anti-monarchical spirit, but the party in power for most of the period before 1870—Whigs and Liberals—did not ally with the Establishment in the defence of society. They were mild reformers who drew significant support from both Dissenters and political radicals. Even the Conservative leaders were practical men, Peel and Disraeli, who sacrificed principle so that the Queen's government might be carried on. The practical effects of this erastianism may be seen in the mission field. Eighteenth century government policy had been to encourage Anglican establishment in British North America and the sugar islands, but the nineteenth century saw a shift of policy. The Canadian clergy reserves were transferred to secular use in 1854; the new African and antipodean colonies had concurrent establishment or none at all. Indeed, the Foreign Secretaries, Palmerston and Aberdeen, even subverted the Bishop of London's authority over chaplains to legations and expatriate colonies. Establishment became a liability when the parties in power were both erastian and latitudinarian; High Church clergy in particular came to distrust Parliament and to emphasise the independent sources of clerical authority in sacerdotalism and the apostolic succession.[4]

Thus the State operated in an atmosphere of mutual hostility and well justified suspicion when it came to intervene in education. Buffeted by the claims and counter-claims of Church and Dissent, the governments of the 1830s and '40s attempted to pursue a moderate erastian policy in a milieu wherein almost any policy inevitably provoked jealousy. Because education was at its heart a religious issue, government policy during this period cannot be understood without taking into account the nineteenth-century revival of denominationalism.

II EDUCATIONAL

During the 1780s the industrial revolution began a socio-economic process that profoundly altered the traditional sources of working-class education. In Lancashire, for instance, new trades and the expansion of old ones sparked a growing demand for child labour and destroyed apprenticeship, the traditional way of affording

technical education. Simultaneously population growth swamped
the old endowed and charity schools, which hitherto had supplied
the needs of the area. Similar conditions obtained in other urban
and industrial districts. The Sunday school movement, dame
schools, and ephemeral private-venture academies attempted to
provide part-time or daily instruction, but they varied widely in
quality and were often under-equipped and under-capitalised; nor
were they teaching enough children to read and write. Around that
time the Anglican Andrew Bell and the Quaker Joseph Lancaster
developed independently a method that promised cheap and
efficient instruction for large bodies of pupils. Their method,
monitorialism, was a system of instruction wherein the master
taught each lesson to a group of able students (monitors) who in
turn taught the rest of the children. They differed in two respects.
Bell kept discipline with corporal punishment while Lancaster used
rewards coupled with public ridicule; Lancaster was
undenominational while Bell was Anglican.[5]

Lancaster's work in London attracted the interest of
philanthropists, aristocrats, and at last the King. A committee of
philanthropic Dissenters assumed the business side of his
enterprise, and incorporated in 1814 as the British and Foreign
School Society. Although it had the patronage of Henry Brougham
and the Russell family, the vast majority of its supporters and
officers were Dissenters, and its cardinal rule was the teaching of
the Scriptures without any sectarian exegesis or catechism.
Lancaster's popularity attracted the attention of Sarah Trimmer, a
devout churchwoman and writer of children's books, who
persuaded Bell to come to London to found schools. There he was
taken up by the Hackney Phalanx, a group of High Church,
middle-class Tories, who consciously modelled themselves after the
Clapham Sect. The Phalanx, centred around Joshua Watson, a
former co-publisher of the *Anti-Jacobin Review*, included
Christopher and William Wordsworth, William Van Mildert,
Hugh James Rose, and Robert Southey. These men, who believed
that Bell's method could counteract the spread of seditious Jacobin
ideas among the lower orders, founded the National Society for the
Education of the Children of the Poor in the Principles of the
Established Church in 1811.[6]

Of all great Anglican religious societies, the National Society was
the most closely associated with the High Church. Evangelicals

subscribed, yet they never played a central role; the only Evangelicals who belonged to its governing committee were the Evangelical bishops, as *ex officio* members. The society's place in the religious spectrum was to have profound effects on the history of English education.

Still, voluntary donations were never enough to fund all the schools that were needed. The National Society had an advantage over the British and Foreign, for, as an arm of the Established Church, it could secure a 'King's letter', a declaration issued by the sovereign and read in all churches each year, which authorised special collections for a specific charity. The National Society secured such a letter in 1824; it produced over £28,000, which provided building grants for provincial schools. The windfall lasted until 1832. Thereafter the society had a letter every third year, but each triennium the letter produced less and less, partly because of the economic depression of the 1830s and '40s, partly because the increase in local National schools meant that the claims for donations upon parishioners had multiplied.[7] The school societies' reliance on voluntary donations meant that neither had the wherewithal to found all the needed schools.

III LEGISLATIVE

The conjunction of the school societies' financial weakness and the new problems of the industrial revolution led the State to take an interest in working-class education. The Health and Morals of Apprentices Act, 1802, required apprentices to receive daily instruction in reading, writing, and arithmetic, but its provisions for enforcement were unworkable and it did not touch the vast majority of English children who did work in factories. Samuel Whitbread, the Foxite philanthropist, proposed in 1807 that the poor children of each parish receive two years of education in the three Rs, to be paid out of the poor rate. Whitbread only wanted a declaration from the House of Commons that lower-class education was proper, but his Bill did receive a third reading despite the opposition of conservatives such as the oft-quoted Davies Giddy who feared that education would teach the poor 'to despise their lot in life . . . to which their rank in society had destined them'. Its failure in the House of Lords is attributable to the religious conflict,

not to any anti-educational feeling; the bishops opposed
Whitbread's measure because it did not give primacy to Church
institutions.[8]

These debates had been argued in an eighteenth-century
context, but the end of the Napoleonic wars opened up new
approaches. Henry Brougham raised the education question in the
House of Commons in 1816, and kept it before the country for the
following five years. Brougham's ideas were modest. He proposed
that the Crown investigate charities, and that Parliament offer
grants of public funds, in aid of private contributions, to build
schools in London. His three select committees of 1816–18
produced ample evidence to show that there were not enough
adequate schools to educate England's growing population. In
1818 he again recommended State grants-in-aid to build schools in
urban areas, but rejected any proposals for annual maintenance.
He believed that private resources in large towns were sufficient to
maintain education, once the initial expense, that of building the
schoolhouse, was covered. For rural areas, where support for
education was scanty and the existing schools were usually
Anglican, Brougham recommended a parish school system on the
Scottish model.

Brougham's ideas got nowhere, but thirteen years later the Grey
Ministry returned to his urban proposals.[9] Brougham turned to
extra-parliamentary schemes of education during the next decade,
but others revived the factory question. Oastler, Bull, and others
organised operatives in the provinces, and in the House John Cam
Hobhouse, Thomas Sadler, and Lord Ashley introduced measures
of amendment. Hobhouse wanted to tighten regulations, while
Sadler and Ashley sought the ten-hours clause. But it was clear,
from the evidence of Sadler's select committee and the factory
commission, that any reform of factory legislation must 'have
cognizance', as the commission put it, of the factory children's
education. When the government finally legislated in 1833, it
followed the commission's advice and included an education clause
in the Factory Act.[10]

By then a Whig Ministry committed to reform had come to
power in the first wholesale change of government since 1807 and
had brought the education question once again before the political
nation. The Whigs first faced the issue in the context of Ireland.
Parliament had granted funds since the Union to support voluntary

educational societies, most of which were really Protestant missions; Irish Roman Catholic prelates and leading laymen responded with protests. Parliament reacted to the complaints in the late 1820s with investigations. Thus the Whigs had both data on the state of education and a consensus on the shape that government intervention should take when they created the Irish system of State-operated schools in 1831. That system provided for an unpaid board of education, appointed by the Lord Lieutenant, which paid schoolmasters' salaries, published textbooks, and inspected schools. In religious matters the system was non-denominational; children of all sects joined in combined literary instruction from which all dogmatic material was excluded.[11] Two years later the Whigs addressed themselves to other parts of the empire. The slave emancipation Act also provided for the freedmen's education. They also legislated, as we have seen, for English factory children. Nor did they ignore the vast majority of English children. In the same year that they passed seminal measures for slaves and factory children they launched the first measure for English elementary education, a modest grant of £20,000 to aid the two English school societies to erect schoolhouses. Yet it, too, was seminal, for it was the basis for all subsequent State initiatives.

IV ADMINISTRATIVE

Education was only one of several 'condition of England' questions that exercised the political nation between the introduction of the Great Reform Bill and the death of Sir Robert Peel. That score of years saw a remarkable transformation in British life; it was as if the dyke erected at Waterloo could no longer hold against the liberal ideas of 1789. The industrial revolution and the growth of population created new social problems and exacerbated old ones; the religious revival provided the Victorians with a moral lens through which to inspect their society; the new order after 1830 provided both the means and the language of reform. As with other social problems, the raising of the education question led to the creation of a new branch of government; the cumulative effect of the State's intervention in this and other areas was the 'nineteenth-century revolution in government'. What was this revolution, and how does the education question fit into it? The answer lies in an historiographical debate.

Oliver MacDonagh first raised the issue and offered a model to explain the extraordinary growth of Victorian government. MacDonagh believes that the Victorian age saw a revolution in public administration—'a leap was made to wholly new forms of organization or behaviour which sooner or later affected, and ultimately reshaped the entire society'. The revolution began when an intolerable social evil was discovered and publicised, for 'the ensuing demand for remedy at any price set an irresistible engine of change in motion'. Legislation was passed, but sooner or later the political nation discovered that laws alone were not enough to eradicate the evil, and civil servants were appointed to enforce them. As a result of the reports of these agents, further legislation was passed and a 'superintending central body' of administration, with more civil servants, was established. But civil servants, after the experience of administration, cast off the 'static' idea of merely enforcing the laws for a more dynamic, innovative attitude toward their work; they took upon themselves wide discretionary powers. Hence administration was 'creative and self-generating'; it 'gathered its own momentum as it went along', often without the stimulus of 'master reformers or agitators' or 'master-bureaucrats'; 'a genuine historical process was at work, moulding men and ideas just as it was moulded by them'.[12]

Henry Parris promptly reappraised MacDonagh's reappraisal. He rejects MacDonagh's minimising of Benthamite influence in administration, and advances examples that do not fit MacDonagh's model, examples in which the discovery that legislation was ineffective led not to the appointing of enforcing officers but to more legislation. He further questions MacDonagh's downgrading of the role of master civil servants, and draws the famous distinction between 'professionals' and 'zealots'. The former were men, often lawyers, who could claim some special expertise that qualified them for office. The latter were men who had plans for the betterment of society, which they published whilst in or out of office. Parris offers his own model to explain the growth of Victorian government. The nineteenth-century administrative revolution was a response not only to economic and social change but also to contemporary political and social doctrines. In social-political terms, utilitarianism dominated the period after 1830.

Since utilitarianism's main principle was utility, its application led to the extension of both *laissez-faire* and State intervention. Once special officers had been appointed to administer the law they played a leading role in legislation, including the development of their own powers.[13]

L. J. Hume questions MacDonagh's reading of Bentham, but the most sustained attack has come from Jennifer Hart. She faults MacDonagh for generalising unwarrantably from the facts of emigrant regulations, for dismissing Benthamite administrative models, and for ignoring the 'general climate of opinion'. Further, she rejects the idea of 'intolerability', pointing out that, since the test of intolerability is rectification of the abuse, it is a sign, not a motive, of change. Hart also questions humanitarianism as a cause of social reform, observing that employers failed to take the simplest safety precautions for their workers until stimulated by self-interest. Religion, she believes, was a hindrance to 'social progress'. In the field of education, for instance, religion, or at least squabbles among the Churches, 'retarded the advent' of national education. Last, she condemns MacDonagh for explaining historical change in terms of 'the historical process', for he has written man and free will out of history.[14]

MacDonagh and the 'pragmatic' school have, however, had the better part of the debate. To be sure, David Roberts rejects the entire notion of 'Tory paternalism', but he seems as concerned to counter neo-conservative ideologues of the Eisenhower–SuperMac years as he is to discover the springs of Victorian reform. To him, as to George Kitson Clark, W. L. Burn, and William C. Lubenow, Benthamite ideology and long-term social planning are not central to the evolution of social reform. Rather, they explain that reform in terms of the unco-ordinated, modest, and pragmatic correction of unacceptable social conditions.[15]

Yet, as is often the case in such controversies, neither side's position is completely satisfactory. First, both sides exaggerate the role of ideology in administration. Although most civil servants' attitudes were not coherent enough to deserve the label 'ideology', they did approach daily practical problems with preconceived goals and expectations. Second, the debate reveals gaps in our general knowledge of Victorian administration as well as in the specific differences between the 'new' agencies and the long-established departments. Third, historians must examine the force, role, and fate of anti-government feeling, and must show how periods of administrative action and quiescence relate to party politics. Last, the debate demonstrates the dangers of generalising from insufficient data.[16]

The State's evolving role in working-class education is certainly part of the greater transformation called the 'nineteenth-century revolution in government'. Hence an understanding of the broader historical question should help us to understand the pattern of State involvement in education. At the same time, the education question is a useful case study and empirical test of the broader historical question. This study will explain both. The modest schoolhouse grant of 1833 was the seed from which grew a major department of state. The religious, educational, legislative, and administrative contexts dictated the form that that department took. We now turn to an examination of this grant's transformations in the first twenty years of its life.

Chapter II

THE ORIGIN AND EVOLUTION OF THE TREASURY GRANTS, 1833–38

Historians commonly dismiss the first parliamentary education grant as a mere sop to Radical demands. In this view the Radicals advanced an agenda of measures, of which education was one, when the first reformed Parliament met in 1833. J. A. Roebuck introduced a Bill in July to establish 'the universal and national Education of the whole People'. Although Roebuck did not press his Bill, the government capitulated to Radical clamour in August and proposed a grant of £20,000 for the erection of schoolhouses in England. But the grant was inadequate, and not until 1839 did Lord John Russell satisfy the Radicals' demands. This view is too simple, for the educational events of the 1830s are not mere prolegomena to Russell's reforms. Rather, they have a rich history of their own, and the policy that developed in that decade in large measure dictated the ways in which the State intervened in education in later decades. Hence it is useful to see what governments actually proposed between 1833 and 1838.

I THE BRITISH GRANT

The education issue arose early in the session of 1833, when the Radicals Richard Potter and William Ewart called for the creation of a national system, financed by the confiscation of corrupted endowments and modelled after the Irish school system, established two years before. Several petitions followed, one of which drew a supporting speech from Joseph Hume, the prominent Radical, in April. He castigated the government's failure to persevere in reform and called upon Lord Althorp, Chancellor of the Exchequer, to redeem his character as a reformer by bringing in a root-and-branch measure. Hume also lamented Lord Chancellor

Brougham's seeming abandonment of the education question. Hume had in mind Brougham's speech in the Lords on 14 March, in which he attempted to justify his failure to introduce the education Bill expected of him. Although his committees of 1816–18 had shown that voluntary contributions could not support all the schools needed, he now believed that legislation and State involvement were unnecessary, save in the new industrial towns. He returned to the issue on 31 May, repeating his 'sanguine expectation' that the government would remedy the lack of education in the great towns.[1]

The desired measure appeared on 16 August, when among the miscellaneous estimates appeared the now famous proposal for a grant of £20,000 'in aid of Private Subscriptions for the erection of School Houses, for the Education of the Children of the Poorer Classes in *Great Britain*'.[2] The House approved the appropriation the next day. Lord Althorp defended the estimate as a cautious measure that provided only for single grants to build new schoolrooms where public subscriptions were deficient, and assured the House that the Treasury would 'undoubtedly . . . be very cautious as to the mode in which it is applied'. The Treasury, he explained, would follow the recommendations of the two school societies in dispensing grants, make no awards without adequate local contributions, and require guarantees that schools, once built, would be maintained. The vote, Althorp added, was an experiment that would not be renewed if private contributions declined. But he did not anticipate that, for the government's policy fulfilled the proposals of Brougham's committee of 1818. The Radicals, pointing out that it was no longer 1818, charged that the proposed grant was typically Whig piecemeal reform—it redressed specific abuses but shrank from general schemes. It was inadequate and ineffective, as well; the amount proposed was a pittance, and only the Treasury's favourites would get aid. At the other end of the political spectrum, Sir Robert Inglis accused the government of slipping 'a new system' through the back door and William Cobbett condemned the scheme as 'a French plan—a *doctrinaire* plan'.[3] Lord John Russell concluded the debate in a temporising Whig vein:

until Parliament has it in its power to adopt a more comprehensive system, . . . a grant of this nature may be useful, and may tend much to promote the general welfare, as well as the religion and morality of the country.[4]

The division list reflects Radical opposition to the measure. The Whig front bench solidly supported it, but the Radicals, including Hume and Brotherton, voted against. Their opposition stemmed not from the paltry size of the grant but from their dislike of Whig measures of mere amelioration.[5]

Roebuck's resolution of 30 July only committed the House to consider the question early in the next session, and had no role in the origin of the government grant. Roebuck used the opportunity to sketch the Radical programme for national education: compulsory, non-denominational education after the Prussian model, supervised by a Cabinet-level Minister of Public Instruction. Lord Althorp opposed this approach to the problem, reiterating the policy already suggested by Bougham, to which he committed the government a fortnight later. Although Althorp agreed that English education was deficient, he maintained that the preceding twenty years had seen a remarkable improvement due to private exertions. Since State intervention would certainly inhibit voluntary contribution, other ways of aiding education must be found. Other M.P.s took up the criticism, and in the end Roebuck withdrew the resolutions.[6]

Why did the government intervene in education? The hypothesis that sees the decision as originating within the Ministry is stronger than that which sees it as a simple response to cumulative Radical pressure. The latter assumption has no documentation; it is not enough to point to tracts, articles, and parliamentary speeches that exercised what pressure they could, and then to conclude that the subsequent ministerial move was in response to that pressure. There is no evidence to show that the Ministry considered itself obliged to satisfy Radical demands; in any case such a passive role might fit the Cabinet in 1840, but not in 1833. It would surely be more perceptive to see Hume's attack of 25 April and Roebuck's efforts on 30 July—not to mention the February petitions—as obstructions to ministerial policy rather than as a positive campaign on their own account.

Brougham seems to have been the grant's father. His statements of March and May, in my view, were trial balloons. (Lord

Ellenborough certainly thought they were.[7]) Brougham himself defended the grant as a product of his 1818 committee's recommendations; Althorp's and Russell's use of the same justification provides a further link. In March 1834 Thomas Spring Rice, the Treasury's Financial Secretary, sent Brougham information about the distribution of 'our Education vote'. Brougham claimed the honour in 1835, 1847, 1850, and 1853, and both Melbourne and Russell granted him it.[8] But if Brougham were responsible for the grant, his action was that of a Whig Minister, not that of a Radical leader.

II   THE SCOTTISH GRANT

The government decided to renew the grant in 1834, but changed its terms: the £20,000, appropriated in 1833 for Great Britain, was now limited to England. Radicals supported the vote but the limitation to England drew criticism from some Scottish Members, who urged the government to extend the grant. Spring Rice, who had introduced the appropriation, claimed that Scotland had been excluded because the grant, the year before, had been an experiment; he added, 'it now assumed somewhat of a different character'.[9] This did not satisfy the Scottish M.P. Andrew Johnston, who threatened to call for a division if the Ministry did not extend the grant. His threat drew an explanation from Althorp, who had hitherto left matters to Spring Rice.

The reason why Scotland was not included in the grant last year was simply this; that England not having had any provision at all made for the education of the people, the proposed experiment ought rather to be tried here than in Scotland.[10]

And he firmly refused to commit the government on the question. A second proposal got a more encouraging answer. When Ewart suggested that the State institute normal schools on the Prussian model, Spring Rice expressed his hope that Althorp would authorise him to make a proposal to the House before the session closed.[11]

Two days later Brougham addressed the Lords on the same subject, reaffirming his position of the previous year, that the State should limit its role to the encouragement of schoolhouse construction. He also urged that the government grant an additional £20,000 for the support of normal schools and predicted that the session would not end without something being done.[12] Besides the allusion to Spring Rice's hope that the Ministry would act on his proposal, the Lord Chancellor's speech contains an even more suggestive passage.

> It is not in my contemplation, nor is it any part of the plan, to impose schoolmasters upon any school founded by voluntary contributions. All that is intended, is to appoint a place where those who wish to open schools may send their masters to be instructed in the performance of their functions.[13]

Brougham's talk of 'the plan', of what is 'intended', might refer merely to one of his many plans and means little in itself, but the conjunction of this speech with Spring Rice's comments on normal schools two nights before points to the possibility of co-operation between the two on this issue, and such bodies as the Church of Scotland, the National Society, and the *Times* took these statements as announcements of ministerial plans.[14]

One month later there appeared in the miscellaneous estimates a grant of £10,000 to contribute to the building of schoolhouses in the great towns of Scotland and model schools to train teachers in England. Between the grant's appearance and its passage, John C. Colquhoun, another Scottish M.P., asked leave to introduce a Bill to endow the salaries of Highland teachers. Althorp preferred extending the English grant-in-aid formula to Scotland, but Colquhoun contended that endowment was the best way to supply the needs of Scottish schools. When the House debated the appropriation in August, Althorp announced that the rules used to distribute the English grant would be extended to Scotland. The Treasury renewed the grant in 1836. This time, however, the money for schoolhouses was not restricted to the great towns, and the model schools were to be Scottish rather than English. The grant was repeated in 1837 and 1838, the provision for model schools being dropped in the latter year. The only recorded debate occurred in 1838, when William Gillon questioned the government's use of the funds, for Spring Rice had spent part of the sum appropriated on salaries, not schoolhouses.[15]

The Scottish grant of 1834 was probably a consequence of the English grant of the year before. That State funds were available for England made it more difficult for the Ministry to deny them to North Britain; the only possible answer to Scottish demands was the grant. In their speeches, however, Spring Rice and Brougham dwelt on another topic—model schools; when the grant finally appeared, it provided for such institutions. Could it be that the two men had plans for such a grant? Did they wish to move beyond simply contributing to the erection of schoolhouses?

III   A PARLIAMENTARY ENQUIRY

These grants satisfied few parties. The ministerial Whigs who had produced them now found that the bulk of the money went to the Established Church and they looked to explore further opportunities for State intervention.[16] Their opportunity came when the Radicals, defeated in open debate in 1833, tried in 1834 to use parliamentary investigation as a vehicle for broader legislation.

J. A. Roebuck moved for a select committee to investigate the means of establishing a system of national education on 3 June 1834. His speech, a classic assertion of the liberal credo, is still worth reading today, but the Whigs outmanoeuvred him. Lord Morpeth, soon to become Melbourne's Chief Secretary for Ireland, defended government policy by proposing to restrict the committee's field of enquiry to the parliamentary grant's results. Althorp, posing as an honest broker, devised instructions that combined the substance of Morpeth's with some of Roebuck's trappings, and this was duly passed. The government thus had taken the committee out of the Radicals' hands. Althorp nominated the first committee; although Roebuck moved for the committee's renewal in 1835 and treated it as his, he never once took the chair, while Lord John Russell chaired thirteen of the committee's twenty-four sessions.[17] (Although it should probably be called the 'Russell Committee', I shall use 'Roebuck Committee', the more familiar title.) The committee made no recommendations, publishing only the evidence taken without comment. Although the reports fail to identify the questioners, one may obtain certain insights into what may have been the thinking of some ministerialists on State intervention.

The transcript indicates that the witnesses were chosen and their testimony was guided. James Pillans, Rector of the Edinburgh High School and a classmate of Brougham's at university, was used to explain the French, Prussian, and Scottish systems. His testimony supporting compulsory education and the reform of charitable endowments suggests that Brougham may have been behind his presence. Other witnesses were brought in to prove the Treasury grant's good effects. Henry Dunn, the secretary of the British Society, William Allen, its treasurer, and J. T. Crossley, master of the Borough Road School, agreed that the grant had encouraged private donations, but contended that the State should limit itself to providing matching funds. These representatives received a sympathetic hearing from the committee, and the tenor of the questions suggests that the committee approved of their system, particularly of its religious provisions.[18]

Witnesses from the National Society, on the other hand, underwent hostile questioning. The Rev. William Johnson, superintendant of the Central School in Westminister, William Cotton, a long-time member of the society's General Committee, and the Rev. J. C. Wigram, the society's secretary, all had to answer loaded questions about their treatment of Dissenters and their motives for operating schools.[19]

Supposing that dissenting or Roman Catholic children belonging to any of your schools, were found not to attend at church on a Sunday, would a statement that they had been at any other place of worship be a sufficient excuse?—I apprehend that the rule would leave it to the local managers of the school to decide that.

Would it be a sufficient excuse in the school over which you preside yourself?—We have never had a case arise.

Suppose it were to arise?—I do not think that is a fair question.[20]

Wigram tried to explain why the society could not separate the Church's doctrines and sacraments from practical morality, but his questioners interpreted that position to be mere exclusivity. One suspects that the questioner who asked Wigram if the society excluded from its schools prayers involving points of doctrine probably did not understand his answer, that there was no such thing as a prayer without a doctrine.[21]

The committee, then, was much more sympathetic to witnesses who represented the B.F.S.S.'s unsectarian approach than it was to those who supported Church education. In his second day of questioning, Pillans was led by a questioner to agree that general moral tenets and the central dogmas of Christianity could be inculcated, omitting peculiar sectarian beliefs. Allen agreed that it was easy to teach ethics without dogma, and the Rev. James

Carlisle, an Ulster Presbyterian and commissioner for Irish education, was brought in to show that non-sectarianism worked in practice.[22] The purpose of all this testimony was to discredit the National Society.

The committee's evidence is of interest not only for what it shows about the religious question but also for the hints it gives of future government policy. The anonymous questioners showed a great interest in the inspection of schools. They were concerned as well to raise the educational and social standing of schoolmasters, that the lower classes might show them more respect.[23]

These details are important in the light of Brougham's testimony to the committee, in answer to questions put to him by Russell. Brougham reiterated his opposition to legislation, stressed the need to preserve private contributions, and rejected Prussian compulsory education, so dear to Roebuck, but did name four areas where the State ought to intervene. The Treasury grant should be increased, the endowed charities reformed, public libraries established, and the government should finance a normal school 'connected with some such good school as that in the Borough Road'.[24] Brougham had been allowed to read the transcript of prior testimony before he wrote his answers,[25] and it is tempting to think that he and Russell arranged to answer the questions raised by other witnesses, and to propound their position on government intervention. Certainly Brougham had his own plans for the Roebuck Committee, trying to convince Althorp to turn it into a Royal Commission in 1834. Althorp declined, but Lord Kerry raised the subject again in 1835. Rumours flew and B. F. Duppa, an educational reformer and friend of Brougham's, tried to obtain a place on it. The Tories, however, were against that idea and scotched it as a recommendation of the Roebuck Committee in 1835. Kerry persisted, talking to Spring Rice and Russell, but the idea came to nothing.[26] Yet the incident is of value in indicating the centres of Whig dissatisfaction with the educational *status quo*.

It seems clear that Russell, Kerry, Spring Rice, and Brougham used the committee to strike at both the right and the left. They wished to defeat Radical proposals to nationalise education by vindicating the Treasury system. At the same time, they needed to weaken the National Society's claim to the State's largesse. The emphasis in the evidence on the need for larger grants and for aid to society-controlled normal schools suggests an attack on

Radicalism; the carping and hostility towards the National Society suggests an attack on clerical claims. In short, we see further evidence of the government, or at least of a group within it, pressing on with its own policies, not reacting passively to Radical pressure or indifferent to the whole question.[27]

IV   THE MODEL-SCHOOL GRANT

The Whigs, returned to power in April 1835, found that the short-lived Peel Ministry had intended to renew the £20,000 grant for English schoolhouses. Spring Rice, now Chancellor of the Exchequer, sent it up for adoption in August, and the grant was renewed routinely in 1836 and 1837. It is at this point that the grant may be called annual, for in surviving the change of governments it clearly had the support of both parties.[28] Grants-in-aid tend to create constituencies that press for their renewal; in this case the National Society, which submitted many more applications than the grants of 1833 and 1834 could accommodate, stood ready to profit from a renewed grant under Tory auspices. Thus, in the absence of documentary evidence, it seems reasonable to think that Sir Robert Peel, a friend of the Church to begin with, saw no harm in adopting this Whig policy.

But after the Whigs were back in power, on 10 August 1835, the House approved a different grant without serious debate: £10,000 for model schools in England to train teachers. The explanation for its quiet reception must be sought outside the House. Five weeks before the model-school estimate had been printed, J. C. Wigram of the National Society discussed model schools with the Chancellor of the Exchequer, 'with particular reference to the . . . grant of £10,000'. Spring Rice had probably informed the National Society in advance of the model-school grant, hoping thereby to gain its support.[29] If this were the case, then he was being less than candid, for he did not intend the societies to share in this grant.

The National Society applied for the grant in July 1835. The Treasury replied with thirty-five months of red tape, delay, and claims that the matter was receiving its 'best attention'. There it remained until 14 June 1838, when, in the course of a speech in the Commons, Spring Rice explained why the model-school grant had not yet been spent.

For the two years last past, the Government have made offers for extending improved model schools for the instruction of masters, and neither society, the British or the National, has come forward to accept those offers.[30]

This sparked an indignant reminder from Wigram that Spring Rice had 'expressly and repeatedly stated . . . that [he] did not intend to give assistance to either Society out of the Model-school grant'.[31] A renewal of his application followed. For this, he received an appointment to interview the Chancellor—who stood him up—a Treasury request for concrete plans, and a correspondence of clarification that dragged on until February 1839, when the Treasury announced that it had referred the application to the new Privy Council Education Committee. Wigram duly wrote to that body, but was told that it did not yet exist. In a last attempt he turned again to Spring Rice. The Chancellor replied that the matter was out of his hands, but that, if the Privy Council approved, the Treasury would be pleased to make 'a liberal contribution'. Spring Rice's 'offer' must have infuriated Wigram.[32]

The model-school grant was in a sense the logical consequence of the Scottish grant of the year before, which included a provision for English model schools. Lord Kerry, at the centre of educational policy-making, called it 'a great step. The admission of the principle is a great victory.'[33] The standard account, that of R. W. Rich, credits Brougham directly. Rich believes that the grant was a government response to resolutions moved by Brougham, which the Lords debated on 21 May and 30 June 1835. To be sure, one mentioned training schools, but most called for the reform of charitable endowments. Melbourne, who defended the Ministry's policy in these debates, turned to Spring Rice for advice and warned Brougham that his resolutions ignored the Grey Ministry's record and might lead to religious controversy. Brougham achieved nothing with his resolutions.[34]

Melbourne's conduct in this affair does not show the cynical indifference to education that several scholars have seen in him.[35] The new Prime Minister's main interest was in defending the Whig record. He did not, however, treat the issue, even in private, in a flippant or contemptuous manner. His objections to Brougham's proposals were reasonable and his suggestions constructive. Nevertheless Melbourne was cautious; he wished to avoid religious controversy by co-operating with the societies. Spring Rice would have had to take account of his chief's caution in preparing plans for the model-school grant.

Spring Rice had not intended to allow the training grant to fall into the hands of the National Society. Hence, when he submitted questionaires on teacher training to that society in December 1835 and June 1838, he sent duplicate queries to the B.F.S.S. His own ideas, however, included neither society. Kerry and he discussed model schools throughout 1835, canvassing the questions of the school's location and of whether it should be managed by one or the other of the school societies or by Treasury appointees. Concurrently, he listened to Brougham's ideas on the subject, inviting him to his English home to visit. It seems clear that he wished, as he told Wigram, 'to bring the two Societies under one general rule', by establishing one training school for teachers of both.[36] Yet he never put concrete proposals before the Prime Minister, but merely hoarded the money until 1839, when Lord John Russell tried to spend it on a non-sectarian school. Perhaps Melbourne's conservatism denied Spring Rice the Cabinet approval necessary for such a scheme. Perhaps Spring Rice himself hesitated to act for fear of the Church's reaction.

Thus what Spring Rice did between 1835 and 1839 was to keep the National Society at bay, without alienating it too much, in the hope that he could construct his own plan. This never happened, but he at least succeeded in the narrower goal of keeping the funds out of the National Society's hands.

V SCHOOL INSPECTION

A further significant change in the terms of the schoolhouse grant occurred in 1838. The English grant for that year included a new clause, providing for 'the inspection of the schools already established'. The debate on this appropriation, which took place in Committee of Supply on 9 July, has an air of artificiality about it. Two Whig M.P.s, R. A. Slaney and Thomas Wyse, raised the question of inspection. Slaney, a Shropshire landowner and liberal Whig, represented Shrewsbury for most of the 1830s. Interested in the 'condition of England' question, he made his mark in Parliament as a statistician, speaking often on municipal health, factories, the poor law, and education. The traditional benevolence of a country squire tempered his political economy, saving him from the Gradgrind school. Wyse, active in the Catholic Association, became M.P. for Tipperary in 1830 and played a minor part in the creation of the Irish educational system. In 1832 he lost his seat after breaking with O'Connell over Repeal and did not return to Westminster until 1835, as M.P. for Waterford. During his enforced absence he studied the problem of the industrial revolution's effects on British society, and produced a book, *Education Reform*, in 1836. He concluded that technological changes had transformed radically the nature of society, producing severe dislocations in the relationships of the classes. Education reform was the answer. In the short run, it would prevent revolution; in the long run, it would enable the lower orders to take their place in the governing of society.[37]

Slaney and Wyse complained that the government did not know how its money was being spent because it did not inspect schools, and hoped that the Ministry would do something. Spring Rice thereupon announced that the government had taken steps. He held in his hand, he said, a Treasury minute containing plans for a comprehensive return of all schools that had received State aid. Once the government had surveyed the existing schools it would proceed with its plans for inspection. (The minute in question was probably that of 5 July 1838, which offered £500 to each society to finance a study of the schools that they had recommended for Treasury aid since 1833.)[38]

Richard Johnson has contended that Slaney and his 'party' of progressive reformers were responsible for this provision.[39] But it is unnecessary to look to external pressure groups to explain the government's adoption of inspection for education.

The device of inspection from a central authority had become by 1838 a well known Victorian bureaucratic technique. The inspection of schools, in fact, was a widely accepted goal. The two school societies had talked of a primitive form of inspection as early as 1813, and the British Society had appointed its first inspector of London schools in 1830. Precedents for inspection, both foreign and domestic, also existed by 1838. Sarah Austin's and Leonard Horner's translations of Victor Cousin's reports on the Prussian and Dutch school systems and James Pillans's article in the *Edinburgh Review* on Guizot's reforms in France were well known among educators. At home, anatomy, factory, and prison inspectors and Assistant Poor Law Commissioners had made familiar this administrative tool. The actual inspection of schools, moreover, already existed within the British Empire. The Irish board of education had adopted the Kildare Place Society's inspectorial programme, begun in 1820. In Scotland, the Gaelic School Society maintained a half-time inspector to tour its schools. Finally, Spring Rice himself had instituted the supervision of West Indian schools in 1837.[40]

The introduction of the principle of inspection into the mass of precedents developed in education before 1839 was not due to backbench pressure. Given the lack of evidence linking Slaney or Wyse with the change in the terms of the English grant of 1838, contrasted with the presence of evidence linking Spring Rice to changes in other grants, it seems more probable that the change proceeded from within the government.

VI   WHIG POLICY IN THE 1830s

If we avoid the tendency to gloss over government policy in the 1830s in the rush to reach Russell's educational scheme of 1839, so often seen as a triumph for 'progressive' forces, we can reassess the roles of the various political factions in making that policy.

The part the Radicals played was but a small one. They were defeated in 1833 and 1834, and thereafter remained inactive until shortly before 1839. Their relative ineffectiveness in this as in other questions was due to their inability to organise into a coherent and disciplined parliamentary pressure group, as the Irish, for instance, did later. Given this general weakness, they were unable to push general measures successfully against Tory and Whig opposition. Their marriage to the idea of thoroughgoing reform meant that they wielded little influence in the moulding of educational precedents between 1833 and 1838. They never supported the government's initiatives, and at best served to draw the Tories' fire in debate.

Whig politicians indeed had connections with radical societies and doctrinaire groups. Althorp supported Ricardian and Huskissonian economics against monopolies and indirect taxes; along with Russell and Spring Rice, he belonged to Brougham's Society for the Diffusion of Useful Knowledge. All knew Macvey

Napier of the *Edinburgh Review*; all knew people connected with statistical societies; all had had practical experience with village schools on their estates. None, however, was doctrinaire. Althorp resisted Radical lobbying on the issue of newspaper-tax repeal; Spring Rice was to his right in financial matters.[41] Thus these politicians were able to borrow good ideas from the Radicals without being utterly under their domination.

That Brougham played little part after 1834 has generally been recognised. His only serious contribution was the instigation of the 1833 grant, with Althorp's support, against Radical opposition; he may also have helped clarify Spring Rice's thinking on model schools. His fertile mind continued producing ideas after he lost office, but he inextricably mixed education with reallocation of endowments—a confusion that lost him support. Spring Rice listened to him if he had something to say, but he had no creative influence. In office, however, he had been a useful ally, and Spring Rice used his help when pressing Althorp for aid to model schools in 1834. Similarly, Russell co-operated with the Lord Chancellor in managing the Roebuck Committee. But when the political Ishmael was driven from office, he was pushed as well from the centre of the educational arena.

The place usually assigned to the Whigs must also be reconsidered. It seems clear that the Whigs, even Althorp and Melbourne, were neither hostile nor indifferent to education. Thus they initiated grants-in-aid in 1833 and extended them to Scotland in 1834. In the latter year they wrote the precedent for public support of teacher training, and in 1835 appropriated a sum for that purpose. In 1838 they created the precedent for government inspection. The original grant was conservative, however, in that it made no fundamental change in the structure of British education, but operated through the societies. Althrop had charted, in the debate on the 1833 grant, the direction in which the Whigs were to go, and even Spring Rice, the most creative of the ministerialists, found it difficult to escape his limitations. Although he made the attempt in 1835 with his model-school grant, it was to no avail.

When we reflect on the government's educational policy in the 1830s we certainly see no 'master plan'—some critics, indeed, may entirely deny the appellation 'policy' to what must sometimes look like random responses to daily pressures. But those Whig politicians who wanted to pursue a forward policy had to contend with several hampering factors: the hesitancy of Melbourne and other well disposed if cautious senior colleagues; the need to construct a programme not totally unacceptable to the major interest groups; the danger of charting policy for an issue charged with religious tension; the simple lack of information in an area not served by Royal Commissions. Hence educational policy had to be tentative.

The hypothesis of a ministerial cabal pushing the Whig governments of the early 1830s towards greater involvement in education best explains the origins of the grants. Spring Rice headed the cabal and was its most creative member. For aid he turned to Kerry, to Brougham, and through the Lord Chancellor to Russell and Morpeth. When he became Chancellor of the Exchequer in 1835 he no longer needed the aid of Whigs with more seniority but, as it happened, with less political sense; as a Cabinet Minister with control of the budget he could afford to drop Brougham and, with him, Russell. He worked with Kerry until the latter's death in 1836; thereafter he alone planned Whig educational policy. He was central to the educational history of the 1830s.

Chapter III

THE TREASURY AS SCHOOLMASTER: ADMINISTERING THE GRANTS, 1833–39

After the education grants had passed under uncertain circumstances through the Palace of Westminster they moved on to the even murkier surroundings of the Treasury Chambers, there to be administered by faceless placemen. The administration of these grants, however, was a rather unusual departure from Sir George Harrison's dictum that 'the treasury is a *superintending*, and *directing*, not an *executive* department'.[1] Thus it is worth while to analyse the Treasury's daily dealings with the school societies. Few have studied Treasury administration in the 1830s, and an examination of one facet of its many-sided activities may throw light on its processes and suggest other areas of enquiry. Moreover, recent work in the administration of education has focused on the period after 1839 and an exploration of the earlier period is in order. Most important, since administrative decisions are never made in a vacuum, a probe from this direction may reveal more about both the political background of the Whig grants during the 1830s and the identity of the Ministers behind them.

I SETTING THE RULES

The first request for aid under the building grant of 1833 was made only ten days after the money had been appropriated; the Treasury thus early had to establish rules for its disbursement. The main points of the Treasury minute of 30 August 1833, which established guidelines for the grant, agree with speeches by the Chancellor of the Exchequer, Althorp, on 16 and 17 August. Only new schoolhouses were eligible for government aid, and masters' dwellings were excluded. The minute stipulated that applications had to be backed by the recommendation of either of the two school societies. Enquiries were to be made to see if funds from local endowed charities could be used for education. The minute clearly sought to control the expenditure of funds by providing for an audit and by relying on the societies for certification; the stipulation that local contributions provide half the cost represented an attempt to limit narrowly the extent of State involvement. More important, the minute recognised the special needs of the new towns created by the industrial revolution by singling out these areas to receive most of the funds.[2]

Most of the first applications, however, came from rural schools, and the Treasury reminded the societies in December that the grant was intended for the towns. Three months later it declared its intention of giving preference to those schools offering places for at least 400 pupils, in areas with a population of at least 5,000 souls. Finally, after almost a year of experience, the board required of schools a ratio of two places for every pound requested. Schools that did not meet this test would receive partial grants.[3]

The process of disbursing the grants underlines the Treasury's reliance on the societies. Each society had to submit three documents: a certificate showing the name of the school, the amount of the grant, and the person to whom it was to be paid; another certificate deposing that the local committee had complied with all the Treasury regulations; and a receipt from the local parties showing that their share of the funds had been spent. The Treasury then paid the grant direct to the local management committee.[4] At each stage in the process the Treasury depended upon the societies for honest and efficient adherence to the minute of 30 August.

Important as these precedents were, the sensitive problem of aid to Roman Catholic schools overshadowed them. The Treasury faced this question on 11 December 1833 when it received an application from George Keasley and Thomas Fisher, Roman Catholic pastors at Sheffield. Following its practice with non-Anglican applications, the Treasury referred the letter to the British and Foreign School Society. Replying on 17 January 1834, Henry Dunn, its secretary, declined to recommend the petition on the ground that the school would not be conducted upon non-denominational principles. The Treasury's answer suggests that it did not wish to exclude Roman Catholics: Dunn was told that the board had not asked what the school's principles were, but whether it conformed to the minute of 30 August 1833. Shortly afterwards the Treasury sent on another application to Dunn, from the Roman Catholics of Newcastle upon Tyne and Gateshead, and called his attention to its letter respecting Sheffield. Dunn never answered. By May, however, a policy of delay had apparently been adopted. In that month the London-based Associate Catholic Charities requested aid under the grant. The Treasury replied with a note promising to resume consideration of the application if it conformed to the minute of 30 August. Although this answer might appear conciliatory, as it did not exclude the hope of aid, the applicants, not being Anglican, would have had to get the recommendation of the B.F.S.S. Given Dunn's response to the prior referrals, it would not be surprising if the Associated Catholic Charities received little encouragement. This may explain its failure to press its application.[5]

This policy of delay may have been designed to give Thomas Spring Rice, then the Treasury's Financial Secretary, time to deal with the Sheffield Roman Catholics. When the British Society failed to answer the Treasury's letter of February 1834 he took the matter up personally. Keasley submitted a second request for aid on 31 August 1835. The Treasury acted favourably, but Spring Rice, now Chancellor of the Exchequer, discovered that the school was to be solely for Roman Catholics and that the building bore the inscription 'Roman Catholic School'. He had assumed that the school, although intended primarily for children of that faith,

> would not exclude or give offence to the Protestants . . . . The safest course would be to adopt our Irish plan wh. approved as it has been by Archbishop Murray cannot be by possibility objected to by any Roman Catholics.[6]

He insisted that the 'obnoxious inscription' be removed. Apparently the problem was solved, for Dunn certified in November that the school was to be a British school. In early December Spring Rice informed Keasley that he must submit an official letter before money could be disbursed; the Treasury officially awarded the school a grant on 16 September 1836.[7] We do not know how Spring Rice persuaded Henry Dunn to allow the school to wear the British mantle,[8] but the episode shows that the government was unwilling to allow the school societies to dictate policy. More important, we see that Spring Rice, who pursued a forward educational policy in Parliament, also actively guided administration toward the same ends.

The problem of Scottish Roman Catholics was much more difficult. The industrial revolution introduced steam packets and cheap rates across the North Channel and created a demand for permanent cheap labour that the excess population of the Highlands could not supply. The result was a massive migration of Irish labourers into the area around Glasgow. From there they spread to other large towns, driving down wages and living in the most squalid conditions, rivalled only by their kinsmen in Liverpool. Of all the inhabitants of Scotland, including the Highlanders, they were the worst provided for scholastically.[9]

It was against this background that Andrew Carruthers, Roman Catholic Vicar Apostolic at Edinburgh, applied for a building grant in January 1834. He was informed in March that 'the Appropriation of the Sum voted by Parliament in the last Session has not been extended to North Britain'.[10] Simultaneously Andrew Scott, Vicar Apostolic at Glasgow, approached the Archbishop of Dublin in the hope of tapping the Irish education budget for funds to build schools. The letter found its way to the Treasury in March, and was referred to Spring Rice for a decision; it was he who drafted the memorandum that dashed Scott's hopes. He pointed out that Parliament had limited the Irish grant to Ireland and that the Treasury's administrative decision had confined the 1833 schoolhouse grant to England, but he went on to write a second paragraph, later deleted.

... My Lords will hereafter take the proper steps for appropriating a proportion of any such Grant for Education to Scotland, if it shall be the pleasure of Parliament to extend such grant to Scotland as well as to Ireland.[11]

The episode is of interest, for it shows that, three weeks before the government was criticised in Parliament for not giving money to Scotland, Spring Rice was thinking about such a grant. Moreover, his role in this, as in the other Roman Catholic appeals, reinforces the argument that he was the prime mover behind Whig educational policy. Why, then, did he delete the second paragraph? Conceivably he had not yet been able to convince Althorp that the grant-in-aid principle should be extended to Scotland.

Roman Catholics apparently never officially troubled the

Treasury from May 1834 until January 1838. In the latter month, however, Carruthers applied again for aid. Although an independent Scottish grant by then existed, their Lordships informed him that they could not, without departing from their principles, award funds to a school 'exclusively intended for the Children of one Class of Christians'; they would reconsider the request if the local managers adopted British practices, as had the Sheffield Roman Catholics.[12] Spring Rice's hand is clearly behind this minute.

Scots other than Roman Catholics solicited the Treasury's attention in 1834, and a consideration of the fate of their applications may help to explain government policy. The first Scottish request came from the Education Committee of the General Assembly of the Church of Scotland, created in 1824 as part of a scheme to promote education in the Highlands and Bengal. Its memorial, prepared only two days after the first English application, requested aid to provide schools for the forty-two *quoad sacra* Highland parishes. (Parliament had divided the huge Highland parishes into smaller districts in 1823. These districts were called *quoad sacra*, for they were parishes only for ecclesiastical purposes, the older, larger, parishes retaining civil functions.) The Education Committee argued that local efforts in the Highlands could be relied upon to build the schoolhouses; the major obstacle there to the spread of education was the lack of funds to pay teachers. Spring Rice dealt with the matter, informing the memorialists that as the grant was designed for areas of dense population, their Lordships could not heed their request. The possibility of State aid led other Scottish clergymen to apply. The minister of Cruden parish, Aberdeenshire, applied in November 1833; the Treasury apparently took no action, and the applicant did not press his case. Luckier was the Kirk Session of Dundee. It applied in January 1834, yet the Treasury kept the application active until Parliament had produced a Scottish schoolhouse grant.[13]

Was Scotland excluded to avoid aiding Roman Catholic schools? The sequence of events throws light on the problem. The first two Scottish applications came from Kirk sources; one was rejected because it was not from a great town, the other was never answered. It was only when the third memorial, from the Roman Catholic Carruthers, was received that the Treasury announced that the grant 'had not been extended' to Scotland. Interestingly enough, the same minute that rejected Carruthers also resolved to request Parliament's renewal of the 1833 grant. It seems fair to conclude that the decision to limit the schoolhouse grant to England was taken on this occasion. On the other hand, two weeks later Spring Rice planned to hold out the hope of funds for Scotland to the Glasgow Roman Catholics. We know, moreover, that far from opposing aid to that sect he was later to secure funds, at some effort, for the Sheffield Roman Catholics.

One recalls Lord Althorp's opposition to aid for Scotland in the debate on 14 April 1834 over the English schoolhouse appropriation. After placing it in the context of the Scottish applications, I conclude that the decision to exclude Scotland was taken at Althorp's initiative, not because he disliked Roman Catholics but because he believed that Scotland was so well provided with schools that it did not need state aid. Spring Rice, on the other hand, opposed this decision, and by mid-May had got his way.

Whig ideology, which determined how the English schoolhouse grant would be distributed, emphasised above all the English tradition, local participation by the gentry. Locals were expected to initiate requests and contribute to the costs. Existing institutions such as the school societies were respected. The attitude towards Roman Catholics was also Whig: they might participate in the grant if they renounced their exclusive and obnoxious claims; they were tolerated, not accepted. Whig as well was the Treasury's recognition that the new towns needed special treatment. Whilst Althorp set the basic principle—that of the minute of 30 August 1833—Spring Rice was responsible for its extension and development, and for the formulation of a position on Roman Catholics.

II   THE PROCESS OF ADMINISTRATION

Once the rules had been established the Treasury was prepared to receive applications. These followed a formal pattern. Each application contained two documents, a request from the local school promoters and a supporting certificate from the appropriate school society. The certificate was designed to show that the proposed school was located in a densely populated area undersupplied with other schools, that it commanded adequate and continuing local support, that it would offer daily instruction, and that the school building would be large and of sound construction. Both societies submitted the applications in batches with a covering letter. These applications joined the flow of in-letters to the Treasury Chambers. When the post arrived the correspondence went to the Registry Room. There clerks read each document, docketed it with a précis of its contents, assigned it a number, and directed it to the appropriate official.[14]

Maurice Wright contends that senior Treasury civil servants played a major role in formulating policy and in decision-making. While perhaps the case with other matters, this was not so for the schoolhouse grants. Occasionally the clerks referred items to civil servants, usually J. H. K. Stewart or A. Y. Spearman, successively Assistant Secretary (head of the permanent staff), and to the Junior Clerk, E. T. Crafer, while he was private secretary to F. T. Baring. Most papers, however, went either to Spring Rice or Baring. Both men served as Financial Secretary, the working head of the department. (Spring Rice served from November 1830 to June 1834, and Baring from June to December 1834 and from April 1835 to August 1839.) They performed such routine tasks as ordering applications to be referred to one or the other of the school societies—tasks that one might have expected Junior Clerks to execute.[15]

Baring or Spring Rice presented their recommendations to the Treasury Board, which ostensibly made the final decisions, in the form of a minute.[16] As is well known, however, the Treasury Board by the 1830s was no longer the directing body in the department; the Financial Secretary made the decisions.[17] This may be established by examining the docketing on documents. In one instance the Treasury received a memorial complaining about the administration of the Scottish grant. Baring handled the matter, drafting an answer, the wording of which appeared as a decision of the Treasury Board the next day. In two other instances Baring ordered letters embodying his decision to be sent out without even waiting for the Board's formal approval.[18] Spring Rice and Baring were responsible for the administration of the English schoolhouse grant throughout the 1830s, and the Treasury minutes represent only formal ratification of decisions already taken. Thus the same politicians who defended Whig education policy in Parliament also administered it in the Treasury.

What kinds of decisions were Spring Rice and Baring called upon to make? As far as the English grant was concerned, their decisions involved interpretations of the minute of 30 August 1833; apart from the question of aid to Roman Catholics, they did not touch sensitive political issues. From the beginning, both societies wanted to use the grant to remove debts on schools already built, but the Financial Secretaries interpreted rigidly the minute's stipulation that the grant was reserved for new schools. Similarly, they insisted that schoolrooms must be physically separate from any church or chapel. They were more lenient, however, about the title to the land. Although preferring the local committee to possess the freehold, they allowed long leases at peppercorn rents. They also allowed promoters to change their plans, permitting cheaper building materials to be used, and assenting to the diversion of funds from primary to infant education when the promoters justified their case. Most of the decisions concerned the adjustment of the grant allotted to individual schools. Often the local promoters decided to enlarge their school, and petitioned that their grant be increased. Usually the Treasury approved their requests, increasing their grants by the rule of £1 for every two places.[19]

When Spring Rice became Chancellor of the Exchequer he left the daily administration of the grant to Baring, to whom he passed on all private requests. He also supported his subordinate's unpopular decisions, informing one M.P., brought in by a school to prevent an adverse decision, that 'the decision rests with F. T. Baring, who is guided by very strict rules'.[20] He was not utterly divorced from the process; Baring consulted him about borderline cases and he was always ready to give advice about problem schools. Spring Rice, indeed, was more interested in the grant's daily administration while Chancellor than Althorp had been. Spring Rice and Baring made a harmonious administrative team, at least in respect of the schoolhouse grant. Baring understood his Chancellor's mind; hence their changes in roles after the fall of Peel's first Ministry made no difference to the functioning of the Treasury.[21]

The process of administering the Scottish schoolhouse grant was little different from that for England. F. T. Baring and Lord Althorp were probably responsible for drafting the minute of 21

October 1834, which applied several sections of the minute of 30 August 1833 to Scotland. That is, it limited aid to new schools, excluded masters' dwellings, required half the funds to be subscribed locally, stipulated that all private moneys must be spent before government funds would be disbursed, and bound the recipients to periodic audits and reports. In addition, a new clause announced that the Treasury would deal direct with applications. (The information supplied in England by the school societies was obtained in Scotland from the local authority.)[22]

At first, the same men who administered the English grant also handled the Scottish one. After Melbourne returned to power, however, Robert Steuart, a junior lord from April 1835 to May 1840, shared the Scottish work with Baring. Although the Treasury considered Scottish schools separately from English, its decisions and the rules it applied respecting matters such as aid to existing schools and the size of the grant were similar. In short, the process of administering this grant was indistinguishable from that for the English grant. More successful, however, was the use to which the grant was put. The terms of the first Scottish grant of 1834 stipulated that the great towns were to benefit. Even after 1836, when Spring Rice dropped this restrictive clause, large towns still received the bulk of the money. By the end of 1836 the Treasury had granted a total of £13,738, of which £9273 went to schools in Glasgow, Edinburgh, Paisley, Dundee, and Aberdeen. These towns retained their lead; of the £19,000 actually disbursed by May 1839, they had absorbed £16,000.[23]

The Treasury seemingly possessed an orderly and efficient machine for adminstering the schoolhouse grant, but how effective was its control in reality? The Treasury certainly tried to ensure that its minutes were obeyed. Clerks averaged out the number of square feet per child per schoolhouse, and whenever a school society's report was vague Baring or Spring Rice insisted on clarification before awarding a grant. Nevertheless, the system's great weakness was its use of the school societies as intermediaries. Once, indeed, J. C. Wigram both applied for a grant as a school manager and certified that his application was in order in his capacity as secretary of the National Society. That the Treasury's reliance upon irresponsible bodies for its information resulted in inefficiency and lack of control becomes evident when one considers the schools that were awarded reduced grants because they failed to provide two places for every government pound requested. A common story is that of the National school at Ashton under Lyne, which petitioned in March 1834 for £400, stating that it could raise only half of the total cost of £800. The Treasury offered the promoters a reduced grant because they had not provided enough places; the promoters managed to raise an extra £100 within six weeks. Few schools declined reduced grants, because locals generally subscribed the smallest amount possible, leaving the Treasury to supply the rest.[24]

A second major weakness was that the system encouraged the foundation of schools, in some localities, which were not really needed. Promoters sometimes had sectarian motives and, as a consequence, their schools failed. In 1833, for example, the Dissenters of Great Torrington, Devon, wished to establish a British school because the existing National school required the use of the Catechism. They received a grant of £150. Thirty years later the school was defunct and the building decaying. Another example is the scandal surrounding the National school at Styal, Cheshire. After two Dissenting ministers complained that the vicar was using the building for church services instead, the Treasury discovered that the National Society's own school inspector had been aware of the situation for over a year, and had reported the matter to the Bishop of Chester. The Treasury, therefore, could not ensure that schools were either built where they were needed or maintained once built.[25]

Last, the grant did not serve effectively the large towns and manufacturing areas for which it was intended; 63 per cent of the first grants under the programme were for places of under 3,000 souls. Both societies were guilty of preferring rural areas, but the National Society was the guiltier; 79 per cent of its applications were for places of under 3,000 population, as opposed to the British Society's 63 per cent. The Treasury's tightened requirements of March 1834 failed to solve the problem. In 1835 72 per cent of the National Society's awards and 64 per cent of the B.F.S.S.'s were for places of under 3,000 inhabitants.[26] Subsequent grants up to 1838 repeated this pattern. Nor did the Treasury succeed in aiding large schools, despite its stated intention to favour schools offering places for at least 400 pupils. Most of the schools awarded grants (ranging from 82·5 per cent in 1833 to 93·0 per cent in 1835) had fewer places. Thus existing organs of administration could not increase significantly the means of education for the urban working classes; if the Whigs were to make any advance towards effective administration they would have to move in other areas.

III   SCOTTISH HIGHLAND SCHOOLS

The Whigs moved, but in an unexpected part of the empire. Scotland was reasonably well endowed with schools. Lowland rural parishes had parochial schools; in towns, municipal (burgh) schools and congregational (sessional) schools were common. Parochial schools in the Highlands, however, were few, most schooling being offered by voluntary bodies such as the Society in Scotland for the Propagation of Christian Knowledge, the Education Committee of the General Assembly, and the Gaelic School Society. (The last limited itself to teaching the Highlanders to read the Scriptures in Gaelic.) By the early 1830s these societies' financial situation had become strained. Most of their support came from the pockets of Lowland philanthropists, but Scotland had suffered heavily from bad harvests in the early 1830s; the consequent destitution strained the existing charities. It may well be that donations which would normally have gone for other purposes were diverted to provide food for the hungry; certainly the Scottish school societies' expenditure was exceeding their incomes. It was natural, therefore, that when the Kirk's Education Committee learned of the government's grant in 1833 it should have requested aid. It had decided in that year to ask the government to endow parochial schools in the Highland *quoad sacra* parishes.[27]

The Treasury's negative response to its appeal did not deter the Education Committee; many times between May 1834 and May 1836 it petitioned the Commons and the government, and its supporters spoke privately to Spring Rice, Althorp, and Steuart. The government ignored these approaches, until W. F. Campbell, M.P. for Argyllshire and a heritor (landowner) in the Isle of Islay, who had encouraged the Kirk to dun the government, held 'many meetings' with Ministers and other M.P.s and probably helped arrange the interview between the Education Committee's supporters and Spring Rice in May 1836. On the 13th a large group of Scotsmen, including the Dukes of Sutherland and Argyll,

J. C. Colquhoun, W. F. Campbell, Fox Maule, and J. A. Stewart
Mackenzie, M.P. and chief heritor in the Isle of Lewis, saw the
Chancellor of the Exchequer. They presented three requests.
Besides the endowment of parochial schools in the *quoad sacra*
parishes, advanced intermittently since 1833, they proposed aid to
the committee's own schools and to a Kirk-related normal school.
Spring Rice agreed to the endowment proposal but flatly refused to
aid existing schools. As for the normal school, his comments were
equivocal. While he favoured aid to such a school, he pointed out
that one must first decide who would control it.[28]

Despite its rebuff on normal schools, the committee was
encouraged and began laying plans for elementary schools;
rumours of the impending measure were circulating among
Highland parishes by June. Certainly by the end of June Spring
Rice had begun to prepare a measure. In that month he revised the
Scottish education estimate, dropping the limitations that had
restricted schoolhouse grants to the great towns and model-school
grants to England. These changes were not mere window-dressing;
by allowing public funds to be spent in rural areas they permitted
the government to announce its intention in October of endowing
Highland schools.[29]

But once the Treasury took the decision it turned for advice, not
to the Kirk, but to the commission created to build parliamentary
churches in the *quoad sacra* parishes. The commission was asked to
enquire of local authorities how the Treasury's plans could be
carried out and how many schools would be needed. As the
commission had not met since 1830, some time passed before the
letter reached John Rickman, its secretary. Rickman admitted that
he had lost touch with events in the Highlands, but did not think
the local ministers to be likely sources of accurate information. He
had, however, sent on the Treasury's letter to, ironically, J. A.
Stewart Mackenzie. Mackenzie's response was an awkward
attempt to link State aid with contributions from local heritors;
Baring filed the report and approached the Education Committee
for specific suggestions. Without awaiting an answer, the Treasury
chose to act. By a minute of 31 March 1837 it set aside £6,000 of the
Scottish schoolhouse grant of 1836 for the endowment of Highland
teachers' salaries.[30]

The Kirk's Education Committee submitted its ideas for the
proposed schools in April 1837. The plan's core had to do with

control of the schools. The schools, the committee argued, should remain under the General Assembly's control, with that body appointing the schoolmaster. The committee urged approval in terms that border on a threat: 'its approval will be considered both by the Committee and by the Church as affording evidence of the friendly disposition of the Government'.[31] Neither Baring nor Spring Rice handled the sensitive negotiations with the Kirk, in its last years of pride before the Disruption. Instead the papers were turned over to Steuart, the 'Scotch Lord'.[32] The Treasury saw that the central issue was control of the schools—Baring had marked the relevant passage in his copy of the Assembly's plan, 'This important'—and it may have seemed wise to let a Scot approach his fellows. In late April or early May Steuart produced a long and thoughtful memorandum.

Steuart first discussed the mechanics of endowment. He observed that the Treasury's experience since 1833 was of little use because previous grants had been only for the erection of schoolhouses; this grant proposed permanent endowment. He supported the General Assembly's suggestions, that the government provide the endowment and the locals the building and land (a suggestion that matched both Whig policy and Highland economic realities), and that the endowment generate an income of £22 per annum per school for forty-one schools. Steuart then passed to the question of control. The Education Committee's plan would remove the schools from local control and place them 'morally as well as absolutely under the direction and the control of the General Assemblys [sic] Committee'. This he opposed, believing that the schools should be under the direction of the heritors and kirk session, as the existing parochial schools were. The General Assembly's desire must be thwarted, since it was not consistent with Treasury policy to let irresponsible bodies control public money. The Education Committee should become a body of reference, as the English school societies were.[33]

Spring Rice also turned outside the Treasury for advice, sending papers on the subject to Andrew Rutherford, the Solicitor General for Scotland. Rutherford advised the Chancellor to give the heritors the right of appointing the schoolmaster, subject to the local presbytery's approval. This course would conform to existing law, yet deny the General Assembly too much power. The Chancellor hardly needed the advice to avoid the Kirk's grasping hand, for he had decided that the Highland schools would not depart from the existing pattern.[34] Nevertheless the details remained to be worked out—a task which must have occupied Spring Rice, Baring and Steuart for almost the rest of the year.

In October 1837 the Education Committee, worried, asked 'whether the plan submitted by the Committee has their Lordships' approbation'. In fact the Ministers had had other matters on their minds—an election and a new reign—and they did not take further steps to implement their decision of October 1836 until over a year had passed. In November 1837 Steuart sent the papers to John Richardson, a Scottish parliamentary solicitor, who prepared a Bill that gave the heritors and minister of each parish the right to appoint the schoolmaster. Steuart accepted all Richardson's suggestions save one that would have subjected the appointment of schoolmasters to the approval of either the Treasury or the Home Office. Richardson had expected the Kirk to resent the Treasury's refusal to accede to its demands, but in fact the opposite occurred. When Spring Rice introduced the Schools (Scotland) Bill on 6 February 1838 Colquhoun welcomed it. The real opposition came from the educational left. Joseph Hume opposed the measure on the ground that schools should not be under the control of a particular sect, and demanded that the government should bring in a general measure applicable to both countries. Thomas Wyse also disliked the Bill; it perpetuated the inadequate voluntary system and failed to ensure adequate schooling. Hume and Wyse were joined by William Gillon, an extreme liberal and champion of the Dissenters, to whom any Kirk-connected schools were anathema. The Bill received the royal assent in August, and Spring Rice was now ready to explore yet another uncharted educational wilderness. (And it remained uncharted, for the Select Committee on Scottish Education, created to appease Gillon, held only three meetings and took no oral evidence.)[35]

The Kirk's Education Committee soon attempted to cash in on the government bounty, writing in October 1838 for directions on how to apply. This caught the Treasury unprepared. Spring Rice sent Steuart an outline of Treasury policy at the end of December. The Chancellor suggested that the endowment be a sum double what the school would have been entitled to under the Scottish schoolhouse grant (the total cost of the land and building), and insisted that the money go to new schools in accordance with the

Treasury's consistent policy. There must also be a certificate of fitness for the building. Steuart recognised that the Treasury had to be more generous, and when he drafted the minute of 11 January 1839 he increased the size of the endowment. The Treasury had already set aside £6,000 for Highland schools; now it appropriated £4,000 more. The total sum was to be invested. An endowment under the minute would consist of the interest on a sum equal to double the value of the schoolhose, site, and master's dwelling. The minute required as well that the school must be in the centre of the parish, that the application must be backed by the appraisal of a sworn valuator, and gave preference to new schools.[36]

The endowment of the Highlands was only half of an ambitious plan for Scotland. In July 1835 Stewart Mackenzie had approached Spring Rice for aid to a proposed normal school at Glasgow.[37] The Chancellor agreed at the end of September that Scotland should participate in the model-school grant passed earlier that year, but cautioned that he had not decided upon either a plan or the location of the school. Correspondence between Spring Rice and the promoters of the Glasgow Educational Society continued, with Colquhoun now involved. But the Chancellor was unhelpful: he delayed, not answering letters and referring the matter to Professor Pillans for report.[38]

Simultaneously the Assembly's Education Committee resolved to establish its own training school in Edinburgh. Lacking funds, it proposed to apply to the Treasury.[39] On 13 May 1836, at the same meeting where Highland schools were discussed, the committee's supporters asked for aid for a normal school. Spring Rice refused to co-operate, so Hope Johnstone, a participant, reported.

> Govt. are prepared to propose a vote for this purpose, but Mr. Rice declined to give any pledge as to the nature of the control under which they intend that such Estabts. shall be placed, and indeed He [*sic*] expressly said, that considering such schools a novelty, and not forming part of an existing system, they felt that the question of management was quite open for their consideration.[40]

As his answers to both societies indicate, Spring Rice was not prepared merely to hand over State funds to normal schools closely connected with the Kirk. A few Scots mistrusted the Chancellor's plans. Hope Johnstone feared that the Ministry planned to operate its own schools; Robert Buchanan, an influential member of the Glasgow society, believed that his group had asked for aid to forestall such a move. 'To improve the styles of teaching was one motive to this enterprize, & another was to keep Govt. out of a Department they were anxious to occupy'.[41] Their fears were justified for Spring Rice had resolved to create non-sectarian normal schools.

Writing to Lord Jeffrey in October 1836, Spring Rice mentioned his plans for Highland endowments, but observed that they formed only part of a scheme to reinvigorate Scottish education. The second part offered more difficulties, being politically sensitive. He wanted to build two normal schools, one at Glasgow, the other at Edinburgh. The Chancellor claimed that he would have preferred to have gone through the Education Committee, but the state of feeling was such that, had he done so, the Dissenters would have protested that the schools were only for the Kirk. He therefore proposed a board of managers for each school, selected with an eye to obtaining the confidence of the Dissenters; the schools themselves would be open to pupils of all sects.[42] Nothing ever came of this plan, and Spring Rice sealed its abandonment when he dropped the provision for model schools from the Scottish grant in July 1838. What had thwarted him? The prospect of opposition from the Kirk may have been too forbidding. He might have bartered his normal schools for Kirk support for the Schools (Scotland) Bill.[43] Whatever the reason, Spring Rice's failure meant that Scottish normal schools were fated, as were the English ones, to be sectarian; only a half of his programme limped into existence.

The Treasury continued to endow Highland schools, making annual reports as required by the Act, until 1842. By then it had endowed fourteen schools with an average salary of £30 3s, and the principal, at 4 per cent, was exhausted. The next year the Treasury tacked on to the education estimate an additional £10,000 earmarked for Highland schools. Out of it fifteen more schools were endowed, but the Treasury ceased to report to Parliament. In the end twenty-nine schools received endowments before the final legacy of the Whig dispensation of the 1830s had run its course.[44]

IV   SPRING RICE AND TREASURY POLICY

The Treasury's educational policy for England and Scotland was based on a fundamental principle that the Whigs used to aid

Highland distress in 1836 and which the Russell Ministry was to apply in Ireland a decade later. This principle was that the State should encourage, but not supersede, local efforts to overcome social problems. Because the Whigs stressed localism they insisted that locals provide part, at least, of any funds, and most of the initiative. Thus both Althorp and Spring Rice insisted consistently that a stated portion of the funds for schools must be collected locally, and that the amount of the grant bear some relationship to the degree of local exertion. A co-ordinate principle was respect for existing institutions. This did not mean assent to exclusive claims; Spring Rice always sought to avoid placing excessive power in the hands of the established Churches.

The English grant, however, was ineffective in solving the problems for which it was designed. The reliance upon the societies as conduits was inefficient, and the grant-in-aid formula favoured areas with more affluent and energetic sponsors, which meant country areas. (Anglican parsons and squires were more willing to spend of their substance for the education of their dependants, and had more substance to spend, than Dissenting ministers and entrepreneurs.) An analysis of where and how the grants were spent, although outside the scope of this study, should produce an interesting picture of how squires and parsons allocated their resources.

The ministerial members of the Treasury participated in decision-making and administration to an unusual extent because of the grants' innovatory nature and political sensitivity. The trouble was that their experience was rather limited in nature. Spring Rice and Brougham grasped educational theory, but the others—Althorp, Kerry, Steuart, Russell, Morpeth—could only rely on the rough-and-ready experience of supervising village schools on their estates. None of them, moreover, had any particular links with large towns. Thus the policies they evolved worked better in rural society, well supplied with paternalistic leaders who knew how to take the initiative, than in the more alienated urban world.

Although Spring Rice was aware of these failures, he did not abandon the administrative machinery of the grants. Instead he explored their boundaries in Scotland, experimenting in salary supplementation and toying with the idea of government normal colleges. He was the Minister responsible for the administrative development of the 1830s. He set Whig policy in the Treasury, defended it in Parliament, and obtained the necessary appropriations and legislation. A tolerant Anglo-Irish resident landlord, he obtained aid for at least one English Roman Catholic school. When he left office in 1839 he had come close to exhausting the possibilities of the Treasury grants.

Chapter IV

ALTERNATIVE MEASURES OF STATE INTERVENTION: THE FACTORY AND POOR LAWS IN THE 1830s

The State, of course, was not limited in the 1830s to aiding education through the school societies. Two other realms—the factory and the workhouse—offered space for intervention that the State quickly occupied. Both had the potential for vigorous and comprehensive governmental activity. Provisions for schooling, although ineffectual, had been associated with factory legislation for thirty years, and the schoolmaster was a familiar fixture in the poorhouse. Neither area of State intervention was encumbered by jealous religious pressure groups, careful to defend themselves against government slights, so it might seem that the Whigs could have avoided the traps into which the grant of 1833 led them by creative legislation and administration in these areas. But it was not to be, and the Treasury administration of the schoolhouse grants, feeble though it was, was more successful than were the factory and poor laws in providing basic education for the working classes.

It is useful, however, to examine in some detail the development of legislation and administration in these areas. First, such an enquiry will shed light on both the process of decision-making and the relationships of politicians and bureaucrats. Second, some of the personalities involved were to play prominent roles in the next decade. Last, when the Conservatives attempted to break out of the educational impasse in 1843 they took as their means the legislation and administrative practices of the 1830s.

I FACTORY EDUCATION

Leonard Horner, the factory inspector, when explaining the Factory Act of 1833 to the operatives he was to protect in Scotland, declared that its 'three great objects' were to limit the working hours of children and young persons, to ensure a proper education to the children, and to preserve unchanged the normal working day of adults. But the origin of the specific education clauses in that Act is unclear. Although Maurice Thomas, the historian of factory legislation, attributes them to Edwin Chadwick, the Benthamite civil servant, it is clear that Lord Althorp, Chancellor of the Exchequer, was their most vigorous supporter. He deemed the education clauses one of his Bill's three major principles (the other two were the limitation of children to eight hours of work per day and the inspection system).[1] When, earlier in the session, he had opposed Ashley's ten-hours Bill, which did not provide for education, he declared that

In any legislation upon the present subject there was, it was scarcely necessary for him to observe, one great and paramount object to be kept in view—namely, the promotion of education.[2]

The clauses that he so prized required two hours of schooling per day for all child workers between the ages of nine and twelve years. Employers could deduct one penny per shilling from the children's wages to pay for the schooling; if this charge did not cover the expenses, then the inspector could assess employers *pro rata* by the number of children they employed. The financial sections of the clause were lost in the Lords, however, and the Bill passed into law requiring inspectors to establish schools but denying them the power to finance them.[3]

The government, unwilling to alienate manufacturing interests, influenced the factory inspectors to be lenient in enforcing the law. Thus the inspectors at first confined themselves to matters of detail, rather than attacking basic problems, and it was believed in some quarters that the educational clauses were dead. In 1836, however, Lord John Russell, then Home Secretary, ordered the factory inspectors to enforce the education clauses more strictly. But it proved impossible to enforce adequately the educational provisions of the Act of 1833. The inspectors, uncertain themselves of how to enforce the law, encountered resistance from factory owners. While some manufacturers took an interest in their schools, most failed to comply, complied only formally, discharged their young employees subject to the Act, or forged school-attendance certificates. Why did firms, some of which had long provided schools, dislike the provisions? Underlying their petty complaints—the disruption of time schedules, the paperwork involved, the problem of truancy—was the resentment that, of all employers of children, only they had been made responsible for education. Hence some called for massive State intervention; other wished to shift the burden on to parents by making the ability to read a prerequisite for work.[4]

Although the factory inspectors attempted to cajole employers into compliance, they were too few, had too few powers and too many other responsibilities to be effective in providing schools. They also disagreed among themselves as to the law's requirements and the best way of enforcing those requirements. Leonard Horner and R. J. Saunders advocated the 'relay system'; factory children would divide into three groups, and, at any given time, two would work and one study. T. J. Howell preferred the 'half-time system', which permitted longer school attendance and avoided split shifts. Horner permitted school attendance for two and a half hours on five days a week; the other inspectors insisted on two hours for six days a week. So each inspector was left to do as he thought best in his own particular district.[5]

Where the children were to attend was another problem. If they attended schools exclusively for factory children, perhaps on the premises, they would be treated equally and taught in a manner suited to their special circumstances. But they would be educated in isolation, and on-premises schools opened the door to fraud. If they attended society schools they would get a better education. But the mills were often far from the schools, and the children's unusual schedules made their attendance difficult. Horner and Saunders encouraged factory children in their districts to attend society schools, but only 17 per cent did so; 41 per cent attended factory schools and 42 per cent attended private-venture schools. The Factory Act did not provide funding for education, and parents often preferred cheapness to quality in their children's education. Hence the inspectors were unable to compel attendance at good schools.[6]

The only government financial aid for factory schools came by way of administration, not legislation. It appears to be the case that, from the beginning, the Home Secretary and his junior Minister, the under-secretary, encouraged magistrates to turn over the fines imposed for breaches of the Factory Act to local schools.[7]

(The practice was not sanctioned by law until 1844.) Although we do not know how much money changed hands in this manner, we can assume that such support was certainly irregular and probably meagre.

The factory inspectors, therefore, were limited in their powers. They might tinker with the rules, draw up codes, badger employers, and encourage the government to prosecute violators of the law. These expedients, however, did not touch the fundamental problems blocking the improvement of factory education. Yet the factory inspectors, as a body, were reluctant to submit unsolicited suggestions to the government. Therefore the pressure to amend the factory clauses came from people acting as private citizens, not as civil servants. Horner translated the French Minister of Education Victor Cousin's report on public education in Holland into English in order to bring it to parliamentary notice. More substantial pressure came from Nassau Senior, the famed economist who participated in many of the social enquiries of the 1830s. Concerned to defend mill owners, he argued that the schoolroom compared unfavourably with the factory. The former was 'small, low, close', the latter had 'vast and airy apartments'; the former forced children to sit on uncomfortable forms, while the latter demanded only light work 'which really is not more exercise than a child voluntarily takes'. Senior proposed that the State break with the principle established in the Act of 1833 and shift the responsibility for educating children from the mill owners to the parents. That is, a certain standard of education should be made a prerequisite for employment.[8]

Heeding the mounting evidence, the government moved in 1837 to revise the factory law. Lord John Russell asked the factory inspectors in January to make a comprehensive report of their recommendations for amendment. A year later, when Fox Maule, under-secretary at the Home Office, and thus the inspectors' supervisor, proposed to introduce legislation, he called the inspectors to London to discuss his proposed amendment of the educational clauses. Although we do not have the inspectors' reports, we may guess that Maule and Russell ignored their suggestions, for the Bill they introduced early in 1838 adopted the solution favoured by Nassau Senior and W. E. Hickson, the hand-loom weaver commissioner. It abandoned the requirement of weekly hours of instruction, and instead forbade the employment of children under the age of twelve who could not read a simple book. Young persons aged twelve to eighteen who could not read the New Testament would be limited to forty-eight hours of work per week. The factory inspectors, however, objected to the proposal privately; the government delayed the Bill's second reading, finally allowing it to die.[9]

Meanwhile the factory inspectors undertook a special investigation of the state of factory education. Their reports, presented to Parliament in February 1839, whilst impressionistic, demonstrated that the educational clauses of the Factory Act were, as T. J. Howell put it, 'inoperative'. Thoroughgoing legislation alone, inspector Leonard Horner declared, would improve factory schools.

We can only expect them to be what they ought, when, by a general legislative measure, primary schools of full efficiency for moral and intellectual training shall be widely spread throughout the country, when normal schools are founded for the professional education of teachers, and when, by securing to them a proper provision and respectability of station, persons who have had a good general education may be expected to follow the profession more frequently than is the case at present.[10]

The inspectors recommended that factory children be required to attend school twelve hours per week, Mondays to Fridays, either in schools on the premises, or in district schools created by the co-operation of neighbouring mill owners. Such schools should be eligible for Treasury grants of up to half the cost of building, and for government loans for the rest. The schools' operating expenses should be obtained by deducting up to 3d per week from the pay of each child enrolled. Last, the inspectors requested the power to disallow the attendance certificates issued by incompetent schoolmasters.[11]

A week later, on the 25th, Fox Maule introduced another factory Bill that tightened the regulations of the Act of 1833 in minor, but important, ways. As far as the education clauses were concerned, the measure adopted most of the inspectors' recommendations. Although these clauses were only one part of the measure, they attracted the most attention in debate; the Whig R. A. Slaney proposed that the measure include some provision for the inspection of factory schools, and Charles Langdale, the parliamentary watchdog for Roman Catholic rights, demanded that assurances be given that the factory children would be trained in their own religious beliefs, not in those of their employers. But the government rejected these suggestions: its Bill provided that all factory children were to attend school for twelve hours per week, and that 3*d* per week would be deducted from their salaries for school-pence. Mill owners could combine to establish district schools, and inspectors received the power to declare factory schoolmasters incompetent.[12]

When the measure entered its committee stage on 1 June, education had become an issue of contention and the Ministry had lost control of the House. Hence, while the government saved the inspectors' power to declare teachers unfit from the Tory J. C. Colquhoun's assault, it lost on other points. Lord Ashley succeeded in lowering the amount each child was to contribute by a penny. Sir James Graham, fearing that inspectors might dictate religious training, denied them the authority to prescribe the course of study in district schools; Langdale and Slaney added a proviso that children could only learn the religious creed professed by their parents. The Act of 1833 had not covered silk mills; although the inspectors had pressed for their inclusion, Maule's measure of 1839 also excluded them. Now Ashley carried an amendment to include them against the government. Ashley's second success was the Bill's undoing. In its weak state the government could not hope to erase the amendment; rather than allow the clause to stand, Russell withdrew the entire measure on the 26th.[13]

The factory reformers did not rest; Ashley obtained a select committee on the Factory Act in 1840. Although not dealing specifically with education, it recommended that the employment of children be limited to half the working day. Chadwick, who had long regretted the defeat of the 1833 Factory Act's financial provisions, suggested that Ashley's enquiry could be used to extend the educational clauses. He proposed that the government undertake a comprehensive investigation of factory education either through the Poor Law Commission or by reviving the Factory Commission. But the government merely instructed the factory inspectors Horner and Saunders to prepare two Bills, which Fox Maule of the Home Office introduced in March 1841. One amended the Factory Act; its educational clauses copied those of the measure of 1839. The other, applying to silk mills, adopted the principle of 1838; it would have required children to be able to read as a prerequisite for employment. Maule's two Bills never were debated; they died when Melbourne's government fell.[14]

Horner's comments on these events were pessimistic.

Judging from the Government Bill of [1839], it is not very probable that any material extension of the principles of the present Act will be made, except in the case of silk mills.[15]

The evidence of six years of factory inspection had shown that, in order to provide effective education for child workers, the State must either create a comprehensive system of factory schools or introduce general elementary education. The Whigs, as we have seen, were prepared to do neither.

II   THE NEW POOR LAW

If education was one of the three major principles in the Factory Act of 1833, it played only a minor role in the poor law. Francis Duke, the historian of pauper education, points out that neither the Poor Law Amendment Act of 1834 nor the report of the Royal Commission of 1832–34 treated pauper education in any detail. While the assistant commissioners were instructed to report on the training of pauper children, the report did not lay down specific remedies. Duke believes, however, that implicit in the report were biases in favour of industrial education and separate pauper schools.[16] Yet the royal commissioners' failure to deal systematically with the question is not attributable to lack of evidence.

Reformers had exhibited the parish of Southwell, Notts, as an example of what poor-law administration might be like since 1820, when Sir George Nicholls, one of the overseers of the poor, reformed administration and reduced the rates by applying the doctrine of 'less eligibility'. He refurbished the workhouse and increased its discipline, discontinued parish employment, and cut off outdoor allowances. Having done this, he established a school where the children of labourers on relief might learn to read the Bible and the Catechism. But this example only reinforced the more powerful testimony of the assistant royal commissioners, who went out from London to observe the poor law's practical operation. Scattered throughout their reports appear vignettes of pauper schools all over the country. These showed no pattern. Some children never went to school at all, others studied in the workhouse or in the local National school, and some London parishes packed off the children to establishments in the suburbs—Barnet or Norwood. The assistant royal commissioners' conclusions, however, were unanimous: education was of prime importance in inculcating, as C. P. Villiers put it, 'a spirit of independence' in the working classes.[17] J. W. Cowell argued that

those who were the *best educated*, were likewise the *most orderly*, the *most honest*, the *most industrious*, the *most thrifty*, the *most prosperous*; and that education was one of those remedies for the evils produced by the Poor Laws, to which the Poor Law Commission might properly advert.[18]

Others offered specific remedies. C. H. Maclean recommended that pauper children learn the three Rs and a trade; H. G. Codd and A. Majendie went further to recommend that the learning take place in schools of industry isolated from the workhouse environment.[19] If this were not done, thought R. W. Pilkington, poor-law reform would be worse than useless.

No permanent and real improvement, I feel confident, can be expected in the condition of the poor, but through the improvement in their moral character; their increased comforts must spring from themselves, not from enactments to supply their wants. Instruction may be given, but it is not in schools alone that the great moral battle must be fought; *good* instruction must be afforded, but *bad* instruction, practically administered, through their interests and their passions, must also and above all things be withdrawn.[20]

But when the Royal Commission reported, early in 1834, it said little on the question. It admitted that education was an important means of restoring the rural social fabric, perhaps the chief motive for poor law reform, but it recommended nothing, only observing that the separation and classification of paupers would permit the education of children in isolation. Nor did the Bill presented to Parliament do much. Drafted by Nassau Senior and Sturges Bourne, with the aid of Edwin Chadwick and the solicitor Meadows White, it was rewritten by a Cabinet committee of seven men, four of whom—Lord John Russell, Lord Althorp, Sir James Graham, and Lord Lansdowne—either had or were to have a record of interest in the education question. Yet the only mention of education came in clause 13, which gave the Poor Law Commission the general power to make rules 'for the management of the Poor, for the government of Workhouses, and the education of the Children therein . . .'. Nor did education attract much attention in the debate on the measure. Lord Althorp did not mention it at all; R. A. Slaney praised the classification of paupers because it would facilitate education; George DeLacy Evans and John Halcombe alluded to pauper education in the course of attacks on the Bill.[21]

The related question of religion was of greater interest. Charles Langdale became concerned that Irish Roman Catholic orphans, a growing element in the Lancashire textile towns, might be forcibly converted; to forestall him, Althorp introduced an amendment permitting freedom of choice in religious worship and opening the workhouse to visits by clergymen of any denomination. Unsatisfied, Langdale pressed his own amendment, which would prevent orphans from being raised in any faith to which their godparents objected.[22] Althorp disliked it.

Where children are orphans, placed in the workhouse, and supported at the public expense, it has always appeared to me that they ought to be regarded as the children of the State, and as such they ought to be bred up in the principles of the established religion of the State. I admit, however, that my Honourable Friend has made out a strong case . . . . At the same time, I beg leave to state, that this is a concession which will apply strictly and exclusively to Roman Catholics, because they are the only Dissenters from the Church of England who have godfathers and godmothers.[23]

The conscience clause, with Langdale's amendment, was included in the Bill sent up to the Lords, where it fell under an unusual onslaught. The Archbishop of Canterbury was willing to accept such a clause if the workhouse were placed under the spiritual care of the incumbents of whatever parishes the poor law union encompassed. Lord Wharncliffe, on the other hand, argued that the free entry of Dissenting ministers would disturb workhouse discipline. Lord Brougham, apparently trying to act the peacemaker, proposed that both the original and the archbishop's substitute be dropped. This was done.[24]

When the revised Bill, with the conscience clause omitted, was returned to the Commons, Althorp announced that he would not demand its restoration, for, clause or no clause, he doubted that any Dissenting minister would ever be denied admission to a workhouse. This was not good enough for Langdale, who managed to carry the House with him. Althorp, accepting the sense of the House, restored the clause, and the Lords, following parliamentary convention, accepted the Commons' decision with some grumbling. The result was that the Poor Law Commission had the power to order the education of workhouse children as they wished, so long as they did not force religious training to which the parents, guardians, or godparents of those children objected.[25]

The career of the conscience clause is worth examining because it shows what the political nation really meant by 'education', and what was feared most about the Poor Law Commission's broad power to govern the lives of paupers. Although the historians of the poor law deem the conscience clause unimportant,[26] those actually involved in the events—those M.P.s who debated and voted—thought the issue worth their attention. Indeed, there were only five major changes in the Poor Law Amendment Bill. The Commons limited the law's duration to five years and altered the bastardy clauses; besides dropping the conscience clause, the Lords' only other changes were to require the Poor Law Commission to report to Parliament annually rather than at the Home Secretary's discretion and to restore plural votes to occupiers.[27] The conscience clause clearly should not be dismissed.

Thus when the Poor Law Commission was created in 1834 it had only the broadest of guidelines with respect to education, although these guidelines were still more precise than those for the factory inspectors. But it also had almost unlimited powers to make of pauper education what it would.

III   PAUPER SCHOOLS

The Poor Law Commission, when it went into operation late in 1834, had an administrative structure modelled after the eighteenth-century customs, excise, and other revenue boards. The three bashaws of Somerset House (Sir George Nicholls, Sir Thomas Frankland Lewis, and J. G. Shaw Lefevre), assisted by a permanent secretary (Edwin Chadwick), supervised twenty-one assistant commissioners and corresponded with thousands of local boards of guardians. In turn the bashaws had to submit all their regulations to the Home Secretary for approval and to present an annual report to Parliament. Supervised by a Minister and forbidden to sit in Parliament, yet themselves supervising a chief civil servant, they were neither fish nor fowl, neither politicians nor bureaucrats. In short, the bureaucratic flow of authority and decision-making, so carefully defined later in the century, was haphazard and ill defined.

The Poor Law Commissioners quickly moved to exclude Chadwick, their head bureaucrat, from the centre of power. Chadwick attempted to play the role of a fourth commissioner, but Althorp and the commissioners did not tolerate such an assumption of authority by a doctrinaire Benthamite; they had their own ideas about how the new poor law should be administered. The commissioners exercised a direct and immediate control over the activities of the assistant commissions by dividing the country into three regions, one for each commissioner. Correspondence respecting each region went directly to the commissioner concerned. He made decisions, drafted minutes, and the like. Every afternoon the three met as a board to discuss policy and take important decisions. Chadwick's role was limited to formal attendance on the commissioners.[28]

The Home Secretary, however, did not abdicate his responsibilities, nor did the permanent secretary remain supine. The Home Secretary, although unable to make policy himself, could influence the shape of that policy. The Poor Law Commissioners were required to communicate with other government departments through the Home Secretary, not direct. All their general regulations had to obtain the Home Secretary's approval before being issued. When Lord John Russell wanted to modify the bastardy clauses in 1839, he had J. E. Drinkwater Bethune (the government's parliamentary solicitor) draft the clauses, not the commissioners. But Bethune sent the clauses on his own initiative to Chadwick for comment. Hence the permanent secretary could covertly influence policy. For example, in 1837 the commissioners proposed to issue a general order permitting labourers to send to the workhouse those of their children whom they could not support. Chadwick, who opposed this policy, convinced Russell that each family should have to enter the workhouse as a unit, or not at all; the Home Secretary refused to approve the order. Chadwick was also eager to write articles for the *Edinburgh Review*, based on the unpublished data at Somerset House, to propagate his views.[29] But Lord John Russell, the Home Secretary throughout the commission's early period, although interested in education, seems not to have made it his special concern with respect to the poor law. And Chadwick, not all that interested in the question, did not take it up until he saw that it could be used against the bashaws.

As for the bashaws themselves, they were concerned in the early days with erecting the machinery for uniting parishes into unions, ridding workhouses of abuses, ending both outdoor and monetary relief, reforming medical relief, and generally establishing precedents for the housing and treatment of paupers and the governance of local unions. Nevertheless they included in their general regulations for workhouses provisions requiring pauper children to have at least three hours' per day instruction in reading, writing, religion, 'and such other instructions . . . as are calculated to train them to habits of usefulness, industry, and virtue', and permitting the board of guardians to appoint a master and mistress for each workhouse. Other regulations allowed licensed ministers of religion to enter the workhouse for religious instruction, excused Dissenters from Church on Sundays, and required the schoolmaster and schoolmistress to aid the workhouse supervisor to keep order and 'due subordination'.[30]

Early in their work the Poor Law Commissioners made an important policy decision that influenced the development of pauper education. Benthamite efficiency as preached by Nassau Senior and Edwin Chadwick required a separate workhouse for each category of pauper, but there simply were not enough paupers in the southern rural unions to warrant the construction of separate accommodation. Hence the commissioners adjusted dogma to fit reality by choosing classification within a single mixed union workhouse. Similarly, the assistant commissioners had to create new programmes to meet the unexpected. At first they encouraged local unions to establish schools, appoint good teachers, and improve teaching methods. They found, however, especially in rural districts, that the number of eligible children was small and the guardians' unwillingness to spend money was great. Thus a second and better solution was worked out: to combine unions into districts for the provision of education.[31]

Some historians have suggested that the man most responsible for the evolution of pauper education was the assistant commissioner James Phillips Kay, who later became the first permanent secretary of the Education Department. Francis Duke argues convincingly, however, that his role has been overrated.[32] Duke points out that Kay was not at first interested in pauper education at all. It was the custom to allow assistant commissioners to make one or two reports a year on subjects of their own choosing. Kay, in his first year and a half, chose to write on labour migration and medical clubs. It was not until 1836, when Chadwick asked him to report on the apprenticeship system, that Kay had to consider education in a systematic manner. Thereafter his reports take more notice of workhouse schools. Kay was further encouraged in this direction by a friend he had made among the civil servants—the assistant commissioner E. Carlton Tufnell. Tufnell had studied industrial training and workhouse schools earlier than had Kay, and of his own volition. By late 1837 and early 1838 Kay was praising the district school scheme in his reports and before the select committee on the poor laws, while Tufnell was quietly attempting to persuade unions to form district schools.

Duke suggests that the district school scheme was 'in the air'. At the administrative level, there were already asylum and audit districts, not to mention the poor law unions themselves. The idea of district schools was clearly suited to solving the practical problems of workhouse education; a number of assistant commissioners took up the idea simultaneously during the winter of 1837–38. On the educational level, however, Kay and Tufnell (both influenced by W. E. Hickson) were probably responsible for the elements of industrial education and teachers trained in Scottish methods. The Poor Law Commission's educational policy before 1839 had been vague—although it did not apply the principle of 'less eligibility' to education, it did believe that children should be sent out to work as soon as they had learned the rudiments. Tufnell and Kay, however, returned full of ideas from David Stow's Scottish model school in September 1837, and the Poor Law Commission allowed them to collaborate with Charles Mott, the assistant commissioner for London, on improving Aubin's contract school at Norwood, which contained over a thousand pauper children from metropolitan parishes.

Kay once defined education as 'sound religious instruction, correct moral training, and a suffent extent of secular knowledge suited to [the child's] station in life'.[33] His view had been conditioned by his experiences with a particular kind of working-class child—the pauper child. He believed that the first task of education should be to eradicate the influences of the home and neighbourhoods characterised by drunkenness, filth, crime,

instability, and irresponsibility. Thus he insisted that it was not
enough to teach pauper children the three Rs, or to indoctrinate
them with religious dogma. They must first break the poverty cycle
by learning to be clean, to save, to be humble, and to avoid friendly
societies operated by publicans. This moral background would
then allow them to make good use of the trades they would learn in
the poorhouse. Religion played a significant part in Kay's ideas.
Each workhouse was to have an Anglican chaplain who selected the
books used for doctrinal training and taught the Catechism.
Dissenters could absent themselves from the Catechism and
Scripture; their ministers had access to the workhouse to give
sectarian training. In practice this meant regimentation and
vocational training. At the Norwood model school children
marched to and fro and obeyed commands and whistles. Yet they
also prepared for a productive life, learning the practical trades of
seaman, blacksmith, tailor, cobbler, tinker, and carpenter.[34]

   The Poor Law Commission ultimately adopted their ideas as the
appropriate curriculum for the district schools.[35] There were,
however, serious problems that ultimately proved the undoing of
the district school scheme. First, government and commissioners,
believing that there were too many assistant commissioners,
stopped filling vacancies. Thus the overburdened assistant
commissioners would soon have even more work, and could ill
afford the time needed to form district schools. Second, the Poor
Law Commission did not have the legal authority to compel the
building of workhouses (and hence schoolhouses) or the hiring of
proper teachers (even if such were available), or to dissolve by fiat
Gilbert or local Act incorporations. Consequently the commission
had to proceed unofficially by cajoling the local guardians. Third, a
proposal of W. E. Hickson's clouded the issue and threatened
hostility for the entire concept of district schools. Hickson proposed
that the poor law form the basis for a national system of education
by establishing central common schools for all working-class
children. Although he wanted to avoid the stigma of poor law
schools, his proposal was unlikely to reconcile working-class
families to the schools.[36]

   Cajoling the guardians was perhaps the most difficult
impediment of all. Local research has shown that the supposedly
Benthamite doctrinaire centralisation of Somerset House does not
adequately reflect local realities. To begin with, there tended to be

a continuity of personnel between the less efficient old poor law and the new. Moreover styles of administration, degrees of resistance to central bullying and of willingness to spend money, the influence of local gentry, and the power of the assistant commissioner on the spot, all varied from union to union throughout the country. At some workhouses a pauper taught the children; at others the governor or a member of his family gave what instruction they could. And if there were no workhouses, as was the case in parts of Lancashire, how could there be schools?[37] For all these reasons the Poor Law Commissioners did not give the district school scheme high priority. In later years Chadwick claimed that the commissioners actively opposed the scheme as part of their conspiracy against him, but this testimony is the product of a bitter and biased partisan. Rather, it appears from the commissioners' correspondence that they encouraged those who advocated pauper education and district schools; in their public reports of 1838, 1839, and 1840 they requested legislation authorising them to create the district schools. True, their public comments thereafter were muted, but the explanation lies not in any hostility to education. Rather, they were fighting for their lives, as Parliament began an inconclusive debate on whether the commission itself should be renewed.[38]

The authority of the Poor Law Commission expired in 1839, and it was necessary in that session to renew the commissioners' powers. But circumstances seemed to be working against the bashaws. The new poor law had been unpopular from the beginning; it was unfortunate that the financial and industrial depression of 1837 followed immediately upon its introduction into the manufacturing north. Opposition to the bastilles grew in the country and re-emerged in Parliament. And doubly unfortunate was it that the need to renew the commission came in 1839, when the supine Melbourne Ministry retained office, if not power, only because the Queen declined to give her confidence to Sir Robert Peel. It was a dramatic scene on 29 July when Russell lost control of the House to his enemies, who promptly restored the allowance system to the Poor Law Amendment Bill. (So much confusion was there that one Member who wanted to vote against outdoor relief somehow found himself a teller in its favour.) Seeing how things were going, Russell withdrew the measure, renewed the commission for a year, and waited.[39]

But the rot continued to sap Whig parliamentary strength. Russell by 1839 had agreed to the Poor Law Commissioners' request for authority to create district schools. His amendment Bill of 1840 gave them the power to compel unions and parishes to form districts, but he had to substitute for it a one-year continuance Act in order to preserve the very commission itself. He tried again in 1841, but his enemies succeeded in emasculating the measure by requiring the approval of the majority on each board of guardians to the creation of the school district and by forbidding the expenditure of any funds if as many as one-fifth of the boards of guardians opposed a rate. This was not the only defeat the government suffered in 1841; it again gave up the measure, this time to fight a general election. It lost, of course, and the fate of the poor law and pauper education now passed into Tory hands.[40]

IV CULS-DE-SAC

What could the government do to educate the people? If it wished to do so through the factory or poor law, it would have had to be much more creative in its legislative initiatives than it was. If all had gone as planned, the Poor Law Commission would have been responsible for the care of between 45,000 and 55,000 pauper children under sixteen years of age. Russell recognised the need to educate these children in his abortive Bills of 1840 and 1841; just before the Melbourne Ministry fell, he had proposed to open the district schools to non-pauper children as space permitted. But the popular hostility to the new poor law combined with his party's weakness to prevent any legislative growth in that direction. Factory schools might have served perhaps 30,000 children, but even greater legislative initiatives were required here. The lack of financial provision in the Act of 1833 meant that the vast majority of working children attended sub-standard factory or private-venture schools; the inspectors did not have the authority to disallow attendance certificates issued by obviously incompetent schoolmasters or to raise funds to pay qualified teachers. The Melbourne Ministry was prepared to grant them authority to do at least the first, but again the government only moved when it was too weak to enact its legislative programme.[41]

The failure of the factory and workhouse solutions was a pity, for they avoided the sensitive religious issue that bedevilled general education as administered by the Treasury. Paupers, save perhaps Irish, simply did not care about religion.

The idea that the religious prejudices of such persons can ever be shocked by attendance on our Church service, seems to me to proceed from a total misconception as to the habits & feelings of the poor on this subject. They never concern themselves with those points of difference which divide Protestants. Their religious impressions are confined to a knowledge of those fundamental principles of Christianity, on which all parties, Churchmen & Trinitarian Dissenters, are alike agreed. ... But as for questions of predestination and free-will, whether instrumental music in a sacred edifice be an abomination or otherwise, whether the Church may be best governed with bishops or without bishops; about these and such like points they never trouble themselves.[42]

The religious convictions of factory children are less clear, but one may be forgiven for supposing that they were no more rigorous.

The same politicians who administered the education grant also contributed to policy formulation for the factory and poor laws; civil servants played a limited role. Recent research makes clear that it is incorrect to see the new poor law as exclusively a Benthamite creation. The instructions to the assistant poor law commissioners in 1834 indicate non-Benthamite as well as Benthamite concerns, and the politicians who drafted the new poor law were concerned to strengthen, not supplant, the rural social hierarchy.[43] The civil servants who went out into the field to administer the factory and poor laws were limited in what they could do, and the Westminster politicians by no means swallowed their recommendations whole. In short, administration in these areas parallels administrations at the Treasury.

If factory and pauper district schools could not answer the question, then what would? Clearly the political nation had the answer, for despite the blandishments of these 'special-interest' schools, it had never lost sight of the optimum solution: locally governed rate-aided schools supervised by a central authority. And the experience of factory and pauper schools made it clear, that that was the only direction in which the government could go.

Chapter V
MOVING TOWARDS A BOARD, 1836–38

The schoolhouse grants had failed either to provide all the schools needed or to satisfy most educational interest groups. At first both school societies had welcomed the grants, but soon the unequal distribution between them soured the British Society. Expecting the first grant to be divided equally, it submitted only enough applications to cover its share. More aggressive, the National Society asked for the full £20,000. The British Society fastened upon the Treasury minute of 11 July 1834, which required the ratio of 10s per place, as the cause of its small portion; as year succeeded year its complaints grew more shrill. The National Society, awarded the lion's share, remained complacent until shaken by the winds of Oxford churchmanship.[1] Nor were educational politicians satisfied. The Radicals used the grant's meagreness and lopsided distribution as debating points; they really wanted a general Bill on Continental principles. Any half measure—any Whig measure—was not enough. Other M.P.s and educational reformers also pressed for a general measure, but one based on Ireland rather than on Europe. The educational centre—Brougham and the Whigs—looked for politically practicable alternatives to grants-in-aid. Spring Rice had probed for the administrative boundaries of the grants, thought seriously of State normal schools, and even considered adding a borough rate for elementary education to the Municipal Corporations Bill.[2]

This general dissatisfaction increased after 1836 as it became clear that factory and pauper schools were not realistic alternatives to a national educational system. More pamphlets and petitions appeared and Parliament expended more time on the education question. The voices were legion and the answers many, but no one prophet had received the call to lead the nation from its educational wilderness. Yet this debate, inconclusive as it was, formed the prelude to the coming State intervention.

I   THE YOUNG GENTLEMEN

Oxford churchmanship shattered the National Society's complacency, turned it into an innovative educational organisation, and frightened Whigs, Radicals, and Dissent into action; the young William Ewart Gladstone introduced that churchmanship into the society. His family's long connection with the West Indies led Gladstone to interest himself in the slavery question, and his maiden speech was on the emancipation Bill. One clause in the measure promised the freedmen education on liberal and comprehensive principles. Gladstone opposed this, demanding that the former slaves be educated at Church-controlled schools. His interests moved to education in general, stimulated by his service on the Roebuck Committee (which he called 'a Radical-Education-General-Religion Committee'). By the end of 1834 he was corresponding with the Rev. Benjamin Harrison, a clerical friend, about threats to religious education. He was new to the question, however. Harrison suggested articles for him to read and promised to have Thomas Dyke Acland, Gladstone's Christ Church contemporary, then touring Europe, give him information about Prussian schools.[3]

Then, in January 1835, Gladstone became under-secretary for the colonies. He discovered that Thomas Spring Rice, who had headed that department in the last months of the Whig Ministry, had set afoot extensive plans to educate the ex-slaves. To train masters, Spring Rice proposed to establish a non-sectarian normal school headed by a master from the British Society's Borough Road School. Gladstone was not in office long enough to undo Spring Rice's work, but he prepared a memorandum on the subject that reasserted the Church's rights within the limits stipulated by the abolition Act.[4] (This also almost brought him to his first resignation crisis, for Lord Aberdeen, the Colonial Secretary, 'was not prepared to stand upon those conditions which [Gladstone] regarded as essentially necessary'.[5])

Gladstone's experience had brought home forcefully the need to snap the National Society out of its complacency and to strike back at those who would use public funds to support non-sectarian, or, worse, secular education. He sent his West Indian memorandum to Bishop Blomfield for comment and began to think systematically about the nature of education. In the next two years his interest grew and his circle of correspondents widened. He learned about the Irish educational system from a representative of the Kildare Place Society, read up on pedagogical theory, and visited the Borough Road School. He also discussed the matter with Joshua Watson, Lord Lincoln, Harrison, Acland, Henry Goulburn the younger—indeed, with almost any religiously inclined friend or visitor.[6]

The catalyst that converted this group of young Tories, of which Gladstone was but one member, into an effective pressure group was provided by G. F. Mathison, an office-holder at the Mint and a devout churchman. Sometime in late 1837 or early 1838, Mathison approached Acland and the two began to discuss concrete proposals to found diocesan boards of education, middle-class schools, and training colleges, all connected with the National Society. The two held informal discussions with the Bishop of London and Lord Ashley, and with a group of bright young men: Lord Sandon, Gladstone, S. F. Wood, Winthrop Mackworth Praed, Philip Pusey, and Thomas Tancred, among others. When Mathison's health broke down in mid-March 1838, eight of the young Tories formed a committee to carry on, and expanded their correspondents to include W. F. Hook, Mathison's cousin, and Henry Goulburn the younger.[7]

Their discussions culminated on 14 April 1838 when Acland, Wood, Gladstone, and Sir Walter Farquhar (who, although an Evangelical, supported their work) had a long talk with the Archbishop of Canterbury. The young Tories presented a memorandum, drafted by Acland and Wood, containing several points for discussion. They contemplated expanding the curriculum and improving the teaching in National schools. They would modify the National Society's textbook policy to admit books other than those published by the S.P.C.K., thereby enabling secular subjects to be taught. They proposed that the society improve the quality of rural schools and enter the field of middle-class education. A network of diocesan training colleges should be established, supported by diocesan boards of education and linked with cathedral chapters. Thus they hoped to improve teacher training and methodology. Last, they would improve the status and emoluments of their schoolmasters. Howley approved these subjects for enquiry.[8]

Three days before, the National Society, no doubt encouraged by

Blomfield, Watson, and Wigram, had established a subcommittee
to examine its operations. During the following month the 'Young
Gentlemen', as the older National Society members called
Gladstone and his friends, urged their programme upon the
subcommittee. Their negotiations succeeded; on 12 May the
society established a 'Committee of Inquiry and Correspondence'
to consider how to improve the state of education under its aegis.
Half the committee's sixteen members were old hands in the
society; half were Young Gentlemen. More important, the working
papers that both the subcommittee and the Committee of Inquiry
and Correspondence used were identical with the original paper
that had received Howley's approbation. Negotiations continued
throughout the summer as the reluctance of older members to
change was worn down. Here Gladstone played a central role.
When the Committee of Inquiry resolved itself into four
subcommittees on 19 May to examine the proposals more closely,
Gladstone drafted suggestions for all four. Ultimately the
committee reported recommendation of most of the plans; by
September Acland was already writing to at least one diocese to set
in train plans to form diocesan and archidiaconal boards of
education, a key part of his ginger group's programme.[9]

On 28 May 1839 the National Society sponsored a public
meeting at Willis's Rooms to unveil the newly energised society.
Resolutions declared that education should be religious in nature
and clerically controlled, that diocesan boards should be
established, and that the society's normal school should be
improved. In less than two years the National Society had ceased to
be a complacent recipient of government funds and had launched
an ambitious programme of parochial schools, training colleges,
and commercial schools for the middle classes. In short, it proposed
to create on its own a truly national system of education on the
principles of the Established Church.[10]

This revitalisation of the Church party on education came as a
result of its infusion with the new blood of High Church politicians.
Acland, Gladstone, Mathison, and their circle of young M.P.s and
clerics had responded to the call to arms from Oxford. Unlike the
older High Churchmen Inglis and Phillpotts, the newer based their
defence of the Church on its sacred character as the Church by God
established, not simply on its political character as the Church by
law established. The two groups had close connections and co-

operated on such issues as education, university reform, and the Church Commission, but differed in fundamental outlook. Gladstone and the Young Gentlemen were neither Tractarians nor Puseyites, if by the former we mean those who helped write the *Tracts*, and if by the latter we mean those who listened entranced to Pusey's sermons. Rather, they were practical politicians whose need to deal with reality helped them to occupy a moderate position. They were sacramentalists who believed that the Church, the chief dispenser of God's grace, transcended human institutions.[11] Thus the Church replied to its critics on a broad front. Aggressive Dissent called forth defenders, and the education question forms as well a chapter in the history of the Oxford Movement.[12]

II SLANEY'S COMMITTEE

The educational centre, in the person of R. A. Slaney, also raised the question early in the parliamentary session of 1837–38. On 30 November 1837 Slaney moved for a select committee to examine the problems of urban working-class education. Using blue-book statistics, he claimed that, despite general improvements during the past thirty years, the working classes still lacked access to an effective system of working-class education under State auspices. But since Slaney saw no chance of agreement on a common system between the Church and Dissent, he concluded that the State's only choice, if it wanted improvement, was to strengthen, not supplant, the school societies. He then sketched such a plan. He would authorise the levying of a rate in each parish of over 5,000 inhabitants, to which the government would add a quarter; the whole would be divided between the societies. He also proposed a board, or a Minister, of education to exercise central supervision. Lord John Russell, then Home Secretary, had no objection to a select committee, but any educational measure should either originate with the government or else have its detailed and preconcerted support. He continued by urging caution. The religious feelings of the country must be consulted; one should not imitate foreign countries; parliamentary time was limited. When he said that the government should involve itself in education he meant no commitment to any specific plan.[13]

Slaney weighted his committee heavily with Whigs. Poulett
Thompson, Poulett Scrope, Sir George Strickland, Thomas Wyse,
and Benjamin Hawes were among the ten Whigs and Radicals to
receive seats; from the Tory side, only Peel, Sandon, Ashley, Sir
Stratford Canning, and T. G. B. Estcourt were invited. This led
Henry Goulburn twelve days later to complain. After denouncing
Whig partiality, he proposed adding Philip Pusey, W. E.
Gladstone, and T. D. Acland. In a compromise, Pusey and
Gladstone replaced Thompson and Hawes; Acland and William
Clay, a left-wing Whig, were added later.[14] But if party balance was
thus restored, actual attendance threw the committee into Tory
hands. Of the thirteen members who had an opportunity to attend
all ten sessions where witnesses were questioned, eight attended six
or more times, and five of the eight were Tories. Only Slaney
attended all ten sessions, but Pusey met nine and Gladstone eight.
On the other hand, Wyse attended but five.

The Tories, five of them Young Gentlemen, seemed interested in
obtaining facts rather than opinions, and tendentious questions
were far fewer than in the committee of 1834. They questioned J. P.
Kay, the assistant poor law commissioner for East Anglia, about
reports of the Manchester Statistical Society. Dunn and Wigram,
secretaries of, respectively, the British and National Societies, were
examined on technical matters such as the supply and demand for
schools, the relationship of local promoters to the parent societies,
and the cost of education per pupil. Lesser witnesses such as J. R.
Wood of the Manchester Statistical Society and Henry Althans, the
British Society's school inspector, were similarly questioned. The
secretaries of the two school societies recognised the deficiencies of
the Treasury grants. Wigram, examined by Slaney, admitted that
the principle adopted by the Treasury in distributing grants was
unfair to the towns. Both Wigram and Dunn agreed that it was
difficult for the societies to ensure that schools were not alienated to
other purposes. Although both societies had inspectors, each
depended upon correspondence, inadequate though it was, to keep
abreast of its schools in the provinces. Wyse then asked Wigram
whether the State should employ inspectors to safeguard public
funds. Wigram agreed that this would be a good thing, provided
that the inspectors were answerable to the societies, and not to the
government.[15]

The religious question arose out of even the most factual matters.

Kay, questioned about workhouse schools in his district, mentioned that the children learned the Catechism unless their parents or guardians objected. This led Gladstone to ask whether many objected. Kay said that few did, but added that there were few Dissenters in his district, save in the towns. Gladstone then asked whether it were not the case that townspeople entered rural workhouses, and pressed Kay again about the extent of objections to the Catechism. He wanted to extract an admission that Dissenters did not mind Anglican training. Gladstone also asked Dunn whether he would object to State grants for schools where the Bible was not read. Dunn's reply was rather confused. He would require Bible reading, with Roman Catholics and Jews exempted; in the same breath he contended that to make Scripture-reading the price of education was not beneficial. Dunn also underwent close questioning from G. W. Wood, Scrope, Ashley, and Canning on how non-denominational Scripture-reading worked in practice. Dunn had to admit that in the nature of things the schoolmaster's own position coloured his presentation of the Bible.[16]

Slaney, of course, had his own solution to the religious problem, and attempted on several occasions to extract support for it. He asked Kay if a rate of sixpence in the pound were enough to provide the necessary schools. Kay agreed, but only this fish took the bait. Wigram maintained that jealousies between the two societies would make a rate unpopular, and would not even agree that 'some great exertion' was needed to improve education; he thought that the parliamentary grant should be increased. Slaney could not have expected to land Wigram; his great disappointment came when Dunn slipped away. Slaney asked Dunn whether the plan to divide a parochial rate between the two societies would be acceptable; Dunn thought not. Slaney then suggested a board of education empowered to inspect schools and to divide the rate between the two societies according to the number of children attending each. Dunn replied that the plan might work if the board had the confidence of Dissent as well as of the Establishment. But then he had second thoughts, observing that the Quakers might add a school rate agitation to their Church rate fight. A better solution would be a national grant. Slaney recast his proposal, but Dunn refused to admit that it would work, taking a harder line the more Slaney pressed him.[17]

The Young Gentlemen also played Slaney's game, pushing their ideas when they found an opening. Occasionally they were blunt, as when Pusey asked of Wigram a question that spelled out their teacher-training programme.

> With a view to improve the conditions of your schoolmasters, should you approve of such a plan as the following: that probationers should enter at the age of eighteen into a normal school in London; that they should remain two years; that after two years they should undergo an examination as to character and acquirements, and if they went through it creditably, receive a certificate, and be appointed as an assistant schoolmaster in the first instance; that after three years they should undergo a second examination; that having passed through that, they should receive a second certificate, which should entitle them to promotion under the society; that if they acquitted themselves well in their situations as schoolmasters, at the end of a certain number of years, say every ten years, they should be entitled either to a small increase of salary, or to promotion to some higher school; and that when they were in a state which required them to be superannuated, they should be entitled to a retiring pension from the Consolidate Fund?[18]

Usually they were more subtle. After Slaney had asked Dunn about qualifications for teachers, Sandon intervened to have Dunn agree that the knowledge of teaching methods was not enough, that a master had to be 'imbued with religious principles'. When the subject arose again, he asked Dunn whether attendance at a Sunday school had good moral effects on a prospective teacher.[19]

Slaney was well aware of the religious problem and may have attempted to approach the Young Gentlemen through Acland's father. On 10 July 1838, when the committee's investigative work was over, he presented seven resolutions to form the basis of a report. Three were crucial to his plan. He proposed that State aid to the two societies be expanded, that Roman Catholic schools be eligible for aid if the Scriptures were read, and that a board of education be established. (He had dropped his suggestion for a parochial rate, perhaps because he knew it to be hopeless.) Only nine members of the committee, five of whom were associated with the Young Gentlemen, attended that day. When the committee considered the proposal to increase aid to the societies, Sandon moved substitute wording that endorsed the Treasury's principle of 10s per place. The vote was four to four, with the Young Tories evenly split, but Slaney gave the casting vote to Sandon. If he were trying to buy support for this plan he failed, for the committee also negatived aid for Roman Catholics and a national board. Thomas

Wyse's absence is striking, for he was intensely interested in the question. He surfaced two days later, tried to reopen the proceedings to evidence, and then moved that the problem of education could be solved by 'the well-directed efforts of the Executive Government, under the sanction of the legislature'. He was soundly defeated. Wyse's solution to the religious problem differed from Slaney's, and he had attended only half the evidence-gathering sessions. He had apparently abandoned the committee, reappearing only to make a point.[20]

Slaney, then, lost his battle to have the committee adopt his plans. This was to be expected, for he represented no influential pressure group. Advanced Liberals, who wanted a national system under State control, disliked his plan to make the societies the channel of government funds. W. E. Hickson, a prominent member of the secularist Central Society of Education, who later edited the *Westminster Review*, put this attitude well.

I am sorry Mr. Slaney has got a Comm'ee. It will waste time. He proposes to give all the money rais'd to the two great School Societies. I would rather stand still for ten years.[21]

Nor did the right expect positive results from his committee; Gladstone saw its investigations only as a way of suspending discussion on national education, thereby giving the Young Gentlemen 'a safe and precious interval' to mobilise the Church.[22] And, of course, the British Society, which might have benefited from Slaney's proposals, had rejected them. Given this lack of backing for Slaney's ideas, it is not surprising that the committee came to the useless conclusion that it could not recommend any improvement on the existing grants.

III WYSE'S MOTION

One reason for Wyse's inactivity on the Slaney Committee may have been his own ambitious plans. On 21 August 1836 a group of Radicals, political and educational, had met at the Thatched House Tavern, St James's. They decided to form a study group under the name 'Central Society of Education', but ultimately to seek membership of the British Association for the Advancement of Science. A committee including Thomas Wyse, James Simpson, and William Rathbone arranged to meet at Liverpool in September 1837, at the same time as the British Association. The ginger group failed of adoption by the British Association, probably from the latter's fear of entrapment in political and sectarian controversy, and set up on its own. Its steering committee, which included Augustus De Morgan, B. F. Duppa, W. E. Hickson, William Ewart, George Grote, Benjamin Hawes, Sir William Molesworth, and C. P. Villiers (names familiar to students of Unitarianism and middle-class radicalism), elected Wyse as chairman.[23]

The society attracted a wide range of supporters. Lansdowne, Russell, Slaney, and Robert Steuart of the Treasury were life members. Among the annual subscribers were Leonard Horner, the factory inspector, Seymour Tremenheere, soon to be a school inspector, E. Carlton Tufnell, the poor law assistant commissioner, Lady Noel Byron and Maria Edgeworth, both educational reformers, William Rathbone, leader of the Irish-system party at Liverpool, Harriet Martineau, the political economist, Joseph Hume and Richard Potter, Radical politicians, and Denis Le Marchant, Brougham's former private secretary. Thomas Spring Rice, a subscriber, became a life member in 1839. Among those who dropped out after the first year, having discovered that secular education was not for them, were William Allen of the British Society, and Nicholas Wiseman, later to be transmogrified into the first Cardinal Archbishop of Westminster.[24]

Its enemies claimed that the Central Society of Education was in fact Wyse and Duppa (its secretary), the rest of the names being window-dressing. This probably was the case, for its ideas parallel those in *Education Reform*. The society was a lobbying body, its main function being to publish papers on current ideas in teaching methods and child psychology, and on foreign educational systems. It attacked the standards of instruction in society schools and urged the abandonment of the monitorial method. The C.S.E. believed that schools could be improved only through government intervention. The religious problem could be solved by separating religious from secular training on the Irish model.[25] The form of government intervention should also follow Ireland.

A Board of Education for England, another for Scotland, a third for Ireland, all acting under the minister of Public Instruction here, with large powers over new and old endowments, and with adequate funds, composed fairly, and acting under constant Parliamentary and

Government inspection; . . . this, I conceive, to be the first preliminary to all real reform of a general nature in our national education . . .²⁶

The C.S.E soon earned the enmity of the British and Foreign School Society, or at least of its secretary, Henry Dunn. It produced a tract, *Strictures on the Publications of the Central Society of Education*, in 1837, which bitterly attacked the C.S.E.'s criticism of the Borough Road School. Dunn also engaged in a battle of letters in September and October 1837 in the pages of the *Morning Chronicle*. He castigated 'certain parties who have but recently appeared' on the issue, who 'atone for past indifference' by attacking all existing means of education, and reminded his readers that Wyse, as a Roman Catholic, was suspect.²⁷

Wyse toured a number of industrial and commercial centres, including Liverpool, Sheffield, Manchester, and Leeds, in mid-1837, to promote the Irish solution. In Parliament, he had intended to ask for a select committee but, forestalled by Slaney, he moved an address to the Queen, praying that she would appoint a board of education to administer the English schoolhouse grant. His motion was debated on 14 June. J. C. Colquhoun, the Scottish Tory, charged that Wyse threatened a system that was functioning well and played down the insuperable religious difficulty. He then quoted Brougham to the Lords of 16 April 1834 to show that one could not create a system to which all religious groups would agree. Nor was secular education a solution to the problem. Colquhoun also warned of the latent powers of Wyse's board. It would have more power than the Poor Law Commissioners and would control all the charities, levy rates, and dictate to trustees and masters. Local committees would be powerless before these bashaws. Colquhoun's speech provoked attacks from several Whigs and Radicals. Benjamin Hawes, Edward Baines, Sr., William Clay, and R. A. Slaney charged him with misrepresenting Wyse's proposals. All Wyse wanted was an administrative body to do well what the Treasury did poorly. He had proposed neither a general system nor secular education. Colquhoun seemed to object more to Brougham's ideas than to Wyse's. Wyse's proposal was moderate and necessary, and ought to be adopted.²⁸

The Treasury Bench also rejected Wyse's proposal. Lord John Russell defended Treasury administration of the grant and contended that the interests of education were best served by giving more money to the society that raised more, rather than by dividing

the grant equally between them. He agreed with Wyse, however,
that not enough children received education; although the present
system was as efficient as it could be, it could not satisfy all the
educational needs of the country. The State, Russell maintained,
had not exhausted its role in education, but he professed himself
unable to say what that role might be. In view of the many
disagreements among supporters of education it would be better to
wait until there was greater unanimity of opinion on the question
before agreeing to Wyse's proposals. Spring Rice echoed Russell,
declaring that the best course was to call the problem to
Parliament's attention rather than to press the motion to a
division.[29]

Wyse's motion failed. It was a party vote: Radicals and Irish
supported the motion; Whigs and Tories opposed. Although Wyse
himself was identified with the Irish educational system, his motion
merely proposed a national board of education. The Radicals had
pressed for such a body since 1833; their support was therefore to
be expected. The Irish, in their turn, probably voted against the
government in this instance out of support for the Irish system, not
from a desire to topple Melbourne.[30] The failure of Wyse's
resolution spelled the end of his society, which published its last
collection of papers in 1839. Although never officially disbanded, it
was effectively defunct. Its activities represent the high-water mark
of Radical pressure for a general measure of national education.
Radicals, increasingly isolated after 1838, were never again to
mount so formidable a challenge.

IV   BROUGHAM'S BILL

The most important legislative move towards a central board of
education, both in time expended and in results, came from the
House of Lords. In 1830 Henry Brougham had exchanged power
for position by accepting the woolsack. That decision isolated him
from his source of political strength, extra-parliamentary public
opinion. As the Grey–Melbourne Ministry faltered to an end,
Brougham discovered his fatal weakness; hoping to save himself, he
abandoned the Whigs and, almost frantically, sought political
alliances with both Peel and the Radicals. When the Whigs
returned to power, Brougham asked for his old job. Melbourne

wanted a tractable Cabinet, however, and would have nothing to do with him; Brougham learned from his morning newspaper that the Prime Minister had given the Great Seal to Lord Cottenham. This final insult drove Brougham from London; he retired from politics for a year, spending his time between Brougham Hall and Cannes.[31] When he returned to the Lords early in 1837 he took up the education question.

On 2 February Brougham introduced his Education and Charities Bill, an expanded version of his Bill of 1835. He proposed a board of education to consist of three Ministers (the Lord President, Lord Privy Seal, and Home Secretary), the Speaker of the House, and three permanent legal commissioners. The board would have been empowered to administer the parliamentary education funds, inspect schools under the Charity Commission or in receipt of State aid, and dismiss or pension schoolmasters; it also would have had wide powers over educational endowments. In addition, a clause would have authorised a municipal education rate. Brougham did not further the Bill's progress and dropped it on 29 June, stating then that he had introduced the measure in the first place to provide a subject for discussion. Certainly he seems to have been more concerned with producing an article on education for the *Edinburgh Review* than advancing his Bill. Yet the Bill was for him a serious measure, for less than a month after its discharge he began redrafting it.[32]

The British and Foreign School Society, meanwhile, had become increasingly dissatisfied with the existing arrangements for distributing State funds, but could get no satisfaction from Spring Rice. William Allen of that society wrote to Brougham in May, complaining that the Chancellor of the Exchequer had to do 'something more for the *Liberal Plan*'. By August the correspondence became regular. Allen grew increasingly hostile towards the Church, declaring that if the Tories 'got the upper hand' the British Society should turn to extra-parliamentary pressure. He apparently approved of Brougham's Bill, lending his name to the pamphlet version of Brougham's speech on the issue after the B.F.S.S. refused. If Allen liked the Bill, Dunn, the British Society's secretary, did not. He had torn it apart in a memorandum of February. His basic objection was to Brougham's having linked education with the reform of charities. To pass an education Bill was difficult enough; adding charity reform would only create enemies. Dunn also criticised specific clauses, opposing both the requirement that the permanent commissioners be lawyers and the retroactive inspection of schools. This memorandum may have circulated among the members of the British Society's general committee, and may have led to its refusal to approve of Brougham's plans.[33]

In late August Allen asked Dunn to draw up a statement on how the government should aid education for Brougham's guidance in preparing legislation. Dunn in essence wanted the State to adopt the British system. Thus he insisted that any board of education must include either representatives from each society or one able to hold their trust. The board should establish unsectarian schools with religious instruction confined to the Bible, a proposal that would effectively deny aid to the Church. In what is clearly a reference to secular educationists, Dunn remarked that a board of education should not

discourage *Scriptural* Instruction to make room for 'Phrenology' or 'the cultivation of flowers' or some other transcendental trash which may happen to lay hold on their imaginations . . .[34]

Allen had attempted to throw his society behind Brougham's measure, but was thwarted by Dunn, who wished to see the British system adopted by the State. In October the British Society sent a delegation to explain its views on the Bill to Brougham. The interview was apparently unsatisfactory, for the committee, in Allen's absence, passed resolutions insisting upon the reading of the Scriptures in the schools.[35]

Meanwhile the Ministry, in the person of Lord John Russell, was preparing to take up the education question. Although an over-optimistic hint had appeared in the July number of the *Edinburgh Review*, the first move did not happen until August. Brougham then wrote to Russell in alarm at the possibility of the education question being made a party issue. Having devoted his life to it, despite the sneers of those who called it his 'hobby', he resented the newcomers who had taken up the question. Unimpressed, Russell complained to Melbourne that Brougham was 'like the dog in the manger' about the question, and declared that the government must take it out of his hands. Having obtained Melbourne's permission, Russell replied to Brougham on the 15th in a letter that initiated a regular correspondence. Russell liked Brougham's Bill of 1837, calling it 'a very sound, & safe plan for education'. By October Russell professed himself satisfied with a redrafted Bill. The board of education remained substantially the same as in the Bill of 1837, but Russell wanted the poor law guardians rather than municipal corporations to levy local education rates. The big problem, he thought, was whether the measure could avoid the disputes among those who wanted non-sectarian religious training, those who wanted sectarian training, and those who would divorce religious from secular instruction. Brougham, however, would have nothing to do with the poor law unions lest education share in their unpopularity.[36]

Russell seemed sanguine of the Bill's chances. He admitted that it must weather 'a pitiless storm both from the Church and the Voluntary Quarter', but he considered the fears of Lord Lansdowne, the President of the Council, on this point excessive. Indeed, Russell's having shown the papers to Lansdowne in mid-September suggests that he not only thought the Bill had a chance but was even thinking of making it a government measure. (W. E. Hickson later claimed that Lansdowne had intimated as much to him.) But then, some time in October or November, Brougham came up with the idea of linking parochial education boards with an extension of the franchise. Russell thought such a move unwise, but Brougham persisted. The Bill he introduced on 1 December followed Dunn's advice to withdraw charities from the national board's purview, empowered municipal corporations to levy a school rate, and included a conscience clause. From then on, Brougham's proposals ranged from the bizarre to the lunatic. Parochial boards of education were to be elected by voters qualifying for a host of 'fancy franchises' and those who forged certificates of eligibility were to be subject to transportation. Only the eccentric Earl of Winchilsea answered direct Brougham's long and rather rambling introductory speech; Bishop Blomfield and Lord Lansdowne, both of whom also spoke, were more concerned with exploring the role of the Central Society of Education. Should we not then assume that few took Brougham or his Bill seriously? The measure, like the one the session before, never received a second reading.[37] Brougham had failed to obtain government support; while he reintroduced it in 1839 it remained a stillborn project.[38]

Melbourne was cynical about Brougham's efforts: 'Brougham

evidently wants to keep hold of the education question & for aught
I care he may do so.[39] The Prime Minister directed his cynicism
not at Brougham's object but at his motives; Melbourne believed
that Brougham was currying favour with the Radicals. Slaney also
thought this was the case. Other former friends such as Lord
Holland, Macvey Napier, Russell, and Spring Rice found it hard to
explain the former Chancellor's actions.[40] His only road back to
power was that of Radicalism, and he attempted to tread it once
again. (Brougham admitted to his friend Napier of the *Edinburgh
Review* that he had been writing to Radicals of various shades for
most of 1837; he denied, however, that he had either made or been
made any offers.[41]) Thus when he returned to the education
question in 1837 and 1838 he muddled it hopelessly with charity
reform and franchise extension. The Radicals did not trust him, for
he had abandoned them once before; his undependability drove
away the Whigs.

Both the British and Foreign School Society and Lord John
Russell had opposed Slaney's and Wyse's schemes; both shrank
horrified from the Young Gentlemen. Yet both had taken
Brougham's education Bills seriously. Then Brougham's fertile
mind devised his outlandish franchise proposals—and in the
twinkling of an eye he had lost his credibility. Brougham did not
understand what he had done. He maintained that his proposals
were no more unusual than the enfranchising of £10 householders,
and only ensured that the electors would be responsible. Odder was
his optimism. He was convinced as late as 29 December that he and
Russell 'had come to a perfect understanding', that the government
'are entirely agreed', and that Russell's objections to the franchise
were only 'prudential' in nature.[42] '*All* reformers are come over to it
everywhere.'[43] The grand and confident tone of these statements is
made more piquant by their utter lack of substance. Brougham was
a man of many crotchets who had a remarkable capacity for self-
delusion; he had become what he would later call Lansdowne, 'a
superannuated viper, having the venom, but wanting the tooth'.[44]

V   GOVERNMENT POLICY EMERGES

By 1838, then, the political nation had admitted the need for
educational reforms. In the parliamentary debates, in the

periodical literature, in the tracts, one fails to find a voice raised against the need for working-class education, or against the need for some sort of reform. William Cobbett, the last great opponent of education, was dead. Even the cynical Melbourne, whose cynicism on most matters was a pose, did not oppose educational reform from principle.[45] But, in the nineteenth as in any other century, it was not enough to be for reform. Wyse's confident belief was terribly wrong: 'In a Reforming age, with the instruments of correction so numerous and so well adapted in our own hands, to *state* an abuse ought to be to *correct* it.'[46] It is easy to drive one devil out; it is not so easy to prevent seven worse from taking its place.

The political nation, therefore, whilst agreed on the need for reform, disagreed on specific remedies. Most wanted greater State interference in the form of a central body to govern the expenditure of State funds. Yet even here there was disagreement. Was the State to run its own schools on the Irish system as the Central Society of Education wished? Was the State to fund the school societies as Slaney proposed? Was it to follow Dunn and adopt the British system? Was there to be a mixed system as Brougham suggested? The Church—or at least the National Society—rejected these solutions in favour of a free hand. Yet it, too, looked for reform. While the British Society retained the monitorial system, the Young Gentlemen urged the expansion of the curriculum, the extension of working- and middle-class schools, and the improvement of teacher training. They wanted their own school system—aided, perhaps, by the State, but Anglican in nature.

Before education could be reformed the religious problem had to be solved. Most politicians of education agreed that religion was an essential, if not the essential, part of education, but to say that begs the question, for there were three ways of providing religious education. The first simply stipulated that it must be under the auspices of the Church. The second was the latitudinarian pan-Protestantism of the B.F.S.S., which taught only those beliefs held in common by most Protestants. The third was the Irish solution, providing for the common reading of Bible extracts purged of tendentious passages and separate denominational training. Each of these solutions had its adherents, and Norman Gash conflates them when he writes that 'a powerful movement led by Brougham, Wyse, Slaney, and Roebuck, supported by political Radicals in general, pressed for a national system of State-directed lay education'.[47] These men did indeed press for a national system, but each in his own way. They co-operated at times, voting for each other's resolutions, supporting each other's Bills, and subscribing to each other's societies, but their solutions to the religious problem differed.

The government did indeed come under pressure, but the pressure was from several directions, and the government's first move was early, in August 1837, before the pressure reached its height in the 1837–38 parliamentary session. Lord John Russell, who had until then deferred to Spring Rice, suddenly emerged as the Ministry's spokesman on education. Spring Rice's great ambition was to be Speaker of the House. He had thought of standing in 1835, but was dissuaded by Melbourne, who wanted him on the Treasury Bench. By the end of 1837 he was thinking again of his goal, for there were rumours of Speaker Abercromby's retirement.[48] Men tend, moreover, to wed themselves to their work; as Chancellor, Spring Rice had tied himself to grants-in-aid. And as his colleague Duncannon put it, the 'drawback' in his character was 'that he takes no grand view of questions, but unfortunately looks too much to the minute'.[49] Hence he found it hard to abandon the experience of five years for a new approach.

The Whigs in general needed, but could not find, new approaches to the problems of British society. The programme they had advanced in 1830—the reform of Irish and ecclesiastical abuses, the extension of civil and religious freedom—had lost its lustre by 1837; the inconclusive election of that year enhanced the Radical position in Parliament. Hence the Whigs needed to advance 'practical domestic improvements, . . . fresh content and a change of emphasis . . .'.[50] So Russell, although quiet since 1834, took up the education question. A long-time supporter and president of the B.F.S.S., he was identified with 'liberal' principles. By August 1837 he had concluded that Treasury grants-in-aid did not answer the problems of education and that Spring Rice was not likely to produce an adequate answer within that framework. But unable to produce his own programme, he re-entered the education question in the context of Brougham's solution. This fact coloured Russell's ambitious programme of 1839, to which we now turn.

Chapter VI

THE CREATION OF THE COMMITTEE OF COUNCIL, 1838–39

Under Lord John Russell's aegis the government at last made the positive effort that educational innovators had demanded in the preceding parliamentary session. Yet the pattern for State intervention, traced and cut by so many hands, produced but a skimpy garment with which to cover the educational nakedness of a nation's children. If the Church and Tories, as is well known, wielded the shears that trimmed Russell's scheme, whose hands drew it? His liberal biographer gives all the credit to him,[1] but the responsibility for the government's scheme of 1839 was shared. Spring Rice and Lansdowne, the educational politicians of the 1830s, were as responsible as Russell for the Whig programme.

I   THE EVOLUTION OF RUSSELL'S SCHEME

After his decision to drop Brougham's Bill in December 1837 Russell played a negative role in the House, striking a note of caution in the debates on Slaney's and Wyse's resolutions, declining to commit the Ministry to anything. Nevertheless, William Allen of the British Society had not despaired of obtaining favourable action from the Home Secretary. In mid-April 1838 he sent Russell a memorandum (inspired, it would seem, by a paper sent him by Slaney, entitled 'Suggestions for the Advancement of Education'[2]) presenting his society's position on State intervention. He recommended first the creation of a national board of education having the confidence of all religious sects, dealing directly with local school committees, and regulating only secular instruction. Second, this board should encourage normal schools, but not operate its own. Third, there should be mandatory Bible study for all children save Jews and Roman Catholics, with a conscience clause exempting Dissenters from the Catechism. This temporary measure must lead ultimately to a general scheme on comprehensive and Bible-based principles. On 11 August a B.F.S.S. delegation visited both Russell and Spring Rice to ask for a measure. Stung to action, Russell informed Allen two days later that he had submitted the latter's memorial of April to the government, which endorsed the points on Scripture-reading and the conscience clause and proposed to make them obligatory in all State-aided schools save those of Roman Catholics and Jews.[3]

Russell sent a copy of his letter to Spring Rice, who replied at length and with horror. To make Allen's Scripture rule the price of State aid, Spring Rice warned, was to ask the National Society, without negotiation, to abandon its basic rule for that of its rival. Worse, while Russell would deny aid to exclusively Anglican schools, he proposed to fund schools exclusively Roman Catholic. Was he prepared to meet the storm that such a rule would raise, one in which the Church of Scotland would join? Russell, however, played down these fears. He grudgingly agreed to discuss the plan with the Bishop of London (although he doubted the Church's willingness to co-operate), but he would not compromise on the Scripture rule, 'and I should not be afraid of meeting the Church upon it'. Although Spring Rice repeatedly urged Russell to negotiate with the Church, the Home Secretary had written it off as implacable. If Spring Rice thought that the Church could be brought round, said Russell, 'pray write to the B. of London'; for his part, he now believed that it was time to abolish the schoolhouse grant rather than allow the Church, 'the richest portion of the community', to collect the bulk of it. Spring Rice sent a worried report to Melbourne, but the Prime Minister dismissed his fears of defeat.[4]

Russell was determined to move. Late in August he issued unrealistic orders to the Poor Law Commission to produce, in twelve weeks, a count of church-sittings, students, and illiterates in England and Wales.[5] After a trip to Ireland in September he developed a scheme which was submitted, late in October, to Lord Chancellor Cottenham (who had so far taken little interest in the matter) and Spring Rice. He proposed a Bill authorising poor law guardians to levy a rate to support schools wherein the Scriptures would be read; if the Catechism were to be taught, it would not be compulsory for the Dissenters. Further, he projected a Royal

Commission to examine endowments. He opposed, however, a board of education.

> I doubt very much about a Central Board. Wyse would be inevitable & fatal. The plan of excluding religion I hold to be bad in itself, & impossible if it were good.[6]

Rather, he thought that either the Lord President or the Home Secretary might be charged with inspecting schools, distributing grants, and supporting model schools out of the parliamentary grant. (He had, apparently, changed his mind about abolishing the schoolhouse grants.) As for the National Society, Russell suggested that it receive a sop from the surplus of the church lease fund. 'Would not the Church be gratified by such an aid?'[7]

Spring Rice observed that Russell's plan not only ignored important administrative and religious questions but was politically unsound. What provision would be made for religious training? Who would appoint the schoolmasters, run the schools, select the textbooks, and set the curriculum? Would fees be charged? What would happen to the existing schoolhouse grants? What about teacher training schools? '[A]ll these are points which may & ought to be considered.' As for giving surplus lease funds to National schools, 'that would never do'. Since the Church objected to using such funds to repair church fabric, it hardly would welcome their use for education. In any case, Russell's Bill might well be lost in the Lords. Undeterred by this advice, Russell submitted written proposals, now lost, to the Cabinet at the end of November. Probably the proposals were substantially those of the month before. A Bill was involved, for Russell sent an outline to J. E. Drinkwater Bethune, counsel to the Home Office, to draft in early December.[8]

The government, meanwhile, had suffered steady Church and Tory pressure since January 1838, when the Rev. Francis Close, Vicar of Cheltenham, published five letters attacking the Irish system and the Central Society of Education, Wyse's pressure group. In early August the 'Lay Union for the Defence of the Established Church' linked the Central Society's programmes with Whig education policy since 1833. The *Times* seized the issue, denouncing

well-meaning enthusiasts, the tendency of whose projects is to betray the education of the country into the hands of a set of democratic empyrics and atheistical boards . . .[9]

Two leaders attacked the C.S.E., warning that it planned a *coup d'école* in the forthcoming parliamentary session. In mid-August the newspaper discovered the British Society's memorandum of April; early in October the newspaper obtained and printed a copy of Russell's letter to the Poor Law Commissioners of August. At the end of the month Close, who had attacked Wyse when the latter had visited Cheltenham in 1837 to promote the Central Society of Education, held up Russell's survey as the sign of a Whig plot.[10]

The Church and the Tories therefore knew that something was afoot; both were prepared to resist any Whig assault on their position. Sir Thomas F. Fremantle, one of Peel's lieutenants, had obtained a copy of Russell's letter to the Poor Law Commissioners, and may have passed it on to the *Times*. Deducing that the Whigs planned something, he reported direct to Peel in October.[11] For his part, Peel recognised that the Whigs, defeated on church rates and the appropriation of Church revenue, had now to turn to education. That question, he thought, offered the best ground on which to fight.

. . . there is no ground on which the members of the Church, if united . . . can so confidently and successfully defy agitation. They have it in their power to act independently of Sovereign, Ministers, and Parliaments; . . .
    It won't suffice to abuse the Government plan.
    There must be a cordial concert between the clergy and the laity, and a determination to undertake a duty which probably can only be well performed by voluntary exertions, unaided by Government . . .[12]

William Allen doubted Russell's ability to withstand the pressure. He wrote to Brougham of 'such a crisis in our great cause as we have never experienced before'; he declared that Russell 'well knows' that the British Society would never accept Anglican demands.[13]

This pressure reached its height on 22 January 1839, when the prelates Blomfield and Howley called on Russell to assert, as Blomfield put it, 'the claims of the Church to conduct the education of the people'. These claims were that the master of any State-aided school be a churchman, that the incumbent be its chief manager, and that the Catechism be compulsory. Blomfield and Howley, involved with the Young Gentlemen's regeneration of the National Society, advanced these claims in an uncompromising manner when they saw Russell on the 22nd. And Russell, at last realising the degree and power of his opposition, capitulated by withdrawing his scheme to substitute a much more modest one. Spring Rice lamented the 'victory . . . of the Church against the Dissenters', and the slapdash plan that saw the light of day differed considerably from Russell's earlier ideas.[14]

II THE TORY ATTACK IN PARLIAMENT

The plan Russell presented to Parliament on 12 February not only reversed his former position; it seemed as well to have been a stopgap measure.[15] His original scheme stressed local rate-aided schools; intervention from the central government would have been confined to a school inspector responsible to a Cabinet officer. Now, however, he abandoned the local element entirely, to propose a board with powers not confined to mere inspection. He proposed a five-man committee of the Privy Council—the Lord President, the Lord Privy Seal, the Chancellor of the Exchequer, the Home Secretary, and the Master of the Mint—to administer 'all matters affecting the Education of the People'. Specifically, the board would control the parliamentary grant for England and Wales (Scotland was not mentioned) and operate a normal school. Russell hoped that 'a temperate attention to the fair claims of the Established Church, and the religious freedom sanctioned by law' would produce a course of religious training acceptable to all groups, and pointed to the work of the Poor Law Commission, especially in London, as an example of what could be done. He also raised the possibility of payments to schoolmasters and grants to society-connected normal schools.[16]

But his speech introducing the scheme was vacillating. Although he now intended to appoint the Committee of Council by royal fiat, he hoped later to introduce legislation for rate-aided schools on the parochial level. He admitted that the existence of the school societies prevented any major government programme; the State could neither suddenly supplant their schools nor compel them to agree on common religious instruction. Hence the government had taken certain limited steps—the board and normal school—as an experiment.[17] Russell could, however, assure the House that the building-grant system was at an end.

. . . it certainly was not the intention of Government to propose another grant of £20,000 for the erection of school-houses. It would be a matter of consideration whether there should this year be any grant for that purpose or not.[18] But, at all events, supposing a grant to be made, it will not be for so large a sum as £20,000.[19]

Parliamentary reaction was mild. Lord Ashley declared that the plan was 'well calculated to excite alarm in the friends of religious education', but Sir Robert Inglis observed that it could have been worse—at least the government had abandoned the Irish system as a model for England. Tory politicians, however, disliked the plan's vagueness. Goulburn, Dungannon, Sandon, Peel, and Gladstone all wanted to know the board's policy. Russell professed not to know; once the board was appointed, he said, it would deliberate rules.[20]

The appointment of the Education Committee of the Privy Council on 10 April confirms the plan's slapdash nature. The Master of the Mint was dropped, leaving a four-member committee with a narrowed field of endeavour. Although, in February, it was to consider 'all matters' related to popular education, in April it was limited to the superintendance of 'any Sums voted by parliament'.[21]

The Committee of Council soon issued its rules in the Education Minute of 13 April 1839. The committee announced plans to operate a normal school and an annexed model school of about 500 children aged three to fourteen years. Religious training in both schools was to follow the practice in workhouses. Bible-reading was compulsory for all, but Roman Catholics might read their own version. A full-time Anglican chaplain was to superintend religious instruction, but provision was made for visits by Dissenting ministers. The committee also threatened to reduce State aid to denominational schools. Although the minute reaffirmed the building grants, it limited them to £10,000 per annum. It also relaxed the Treasury regulations by making independent schools eligible for them and by removing the link between the size of the grant and the amount of local contributions. A sop went to the societies: a grant of £2,500 once for all to each for its normal school. In addition the committee reserved the right to grant 'gratuities' to deserving schoolmasters. Finally, the minute provided for the appointment of a secretary and two school inspectors. Having made its plans, the Committee of Council at once set about looking for both a site and staff for the normal school.[22]

But the minute of April transformed Conservative attitudes from tepid annoyance to active hatred. On 30 April Lord Stanley complained because the House was unable to vote on the measure, and the Bishop of London denounced it on 3 May. In the country, the Church and the Tories mounted a campaign against it that by 31 May had generated 242 petitions, bearing 26,603 signatures, protesting against any educational programme 'not based on the Established Church'. Nor was opposition confined to the Church. The Wesleyan Methodists attacked the measure in May for permitting Roman Catholic teachers and 'the corrupted Romish translations' of the Scriptures into the schools. The Bedchamber Crisis, added to the religious opposition, was too great, and the Cabinet decided to abandon the normal school. A new minute of 1 June limited the Committee of Council to doling out building grants of £20,000 per annum and inspecting State schools. And the £10,000 model-school grant of 1835, which had been earmarked for the abortive government scheme, was at last divided equally between the two societies.[23]

The government's capitulation did not, however, put an end to the affair. Rather, the Tories decided to bring down the entire edifice. They welcomed conflict on such a question, for as Graham put it to Wharncliffe at the beginning of the year 1839 power was within their grasp, despite the crisis of government.

I know not how the present government is to stand; and it is not our business to prop it. But the Country itself, I fear, is almost ungovernable, and the Crown in alliance with Democracy on the slippery verge of Rebellion would seem doomed to fall. The Conservatives, however, in Talent, growing Numbers, and might of Property, are a mighty Body; and if we remain firmly united, true to our Leaders, and if the life of the Duke of Wellington be spared, great as the dangers and difficulties may be, I cannot dispair [sic].[24]

The Bedchamber Crisis had shown that the Whigs could no longer control the House. The government's majority dropped on several issues—free trade, Ireland, Jamaica—yet Tories saw office denied them because of the Queen's intervention. Thus the divisions on the education question, although coming after the crisis, still formed part of the Tories' major attack upon Whig policy. Peel's problem was to find an appropriate vehicle for the attack, to support the Church's educational claims without giving the impression that education was subservient to party. Hence he wanted to co-operate with Whig bishops, and he focused his party's opposition on the Whig education scheme, not on the building grant. The Tory leadership met on 10 June to plan strategy. They selected the tactic of moving a resolution, when the House went into supply on education, that the Queen revoke her Order in Council appointing the Committee of Council; Stanley received the task of drafting it. The final version, moved on the 14th, was an amalgam of Stanley's, Peel's, and Lord Mahon's ideas. Lansdowne, ever skittish where education was concerned, smelled defeat; Russell asked the Queen not to detain M.P.s at a palace function that evening, lest the government lose the division.[25]

Debate raged for a fortnight. The House debated Stanley's resolution on 14, 19, and 20 June, finally rejecting it by a vote of 280 to 275. On the 24th the House in Committee of Supply debated and approved the education estimate by the even narrower vote of 275 to 273. (The narrowness of these divisions is remarkable. J. W. Croker, long a Tory political observer, had expected the government to keep its 'usual majority of from twenty to thirty'; the Duke of Newcastle expected a Whig majority of twelve.)[26] If one compares these division lists with those for Ireland in April and Jamaica in May, one finds that M.P.s voted along party lines. Indeed, fewer defected on education than on other questions. Only four M.P.s who voted with the government on Ireland and Jamaica defected on education,[27] but eight who had voted with them on Ireland and education defected over Jamaica.[28] It would be mistaken, therefore, to think that the division was one between educational progressives and reactionaries, or that the government's slim majorities reflected deep-seated opposition to schools.

Thus the education estimate, on which the Committee of Council depended, barely survived the Tory onslaught. But one last act remained to be played. The Tories determined to attack the government in the House of Lords, where they had an assured majority. After a series of meetings with other party chiefs at Apsley House during the last week in June, Peel and Ellenborough drafted a set of resolutions, which the Archbishop of Canterbury presented to the Lords on 5 July. The resolutions decried the granting of wide powers to the executive without legislation and proposed an address to the Queen requesting her to abolish the Committee of Council. Tory strength in the Lords told, and the resolutions were passed by a vote of 229 to 118.[29]

On 11 July the Lords presented their address to the Queen. As Lady Howick recorded in her and her husband's joint diary, they received short shrift.

This was the day the address of the Lords went to the Queen (as Lady Flora's body was removed in the night to be embarked on one of the Scotch steamers) and the peers assembled in considerable numbers. The ministers of course went and as H[enry] left home late he got to the tail of the string and after the Chancellor's carriage. They were hooted by the mob near the Palace and this mob was evidently led on by Messrs. H. Baring C. Forrester etc [sic] who were on horseback in the midst and telling the people who to cheer and who to hiss. The Queen read her very sharp answer with the most perfect composure.[30]

The Tory attack had succeeded in further shearing an amputated programme and had given notice to the government that in the field of education it ventured at its own peril.

III THE SCHEME'S SOURCES

If Lord John Russell was not solely, or even chiefly, responsible for creating the Whig education programme of 1839, then with whom did he share the task? There are two schools of thought on this question. One looks to Ireland for the roots of the scheme, while the other looks to the new poor law.

James Murphy believes that the Irish example in general and the Liverpool Corporation schools in particular stimulated Russell to activity and moulded the form that that activity was to take. In January 1836 the newly reformed Liverpool council, instigated by William Rathbone, a Unitarian who later helped Wyse found the Central Society of Education, proposed to open the corporation schools, then exclusively Anglican, to children of all religious persuasions on the Irish pattern. The school day would begin with a hymn taken from the selections of the Irish Education Commission; textbooks would be drawn from the same source; denominational training would occur in the final hour of the school day. The proposal generated considerable public controversy, which reached the national press. Liverpool Tories defeated the Radical M.P. William Ewart in 1837, but the municipal elections later in the year produced a Liberal victory and a dramatic muting of the campaign against the corporation schools. 'It seems safe,'

Murphy adds, 'to assume that the success of the Liverpool liberals
in the municipal election . . . did not go unnoticed in government
circles.' But he sees a closer link between the Liverpool schools and
the Whig scheme of 1839. Lord John Russell had visited Liverpool
on 2–3 October 1838, on his way back from Dublin, as the guest of
William Rathbone, then mayor. He visited one corporation school
and praised them at a dinner in the town hall. It was more than
coincidental that only a few weeks later Russell prepared his
education scheme.[31]

We know that, of the members of the Committee of Council, Russell and
Lansdowne, at least, were well aware of what had been happening in
Liverpool, and had every reason to believe that the Liverpool Education
Committee had succeeded in that task. It seems reasonable to suggest that
the Committee of Council, when it decided to adopt a policy so similar to
that pursued in the Corporation Schools, might well have been
encouraged, if not inspired, to do so by the success which appeared to
have attended the Liverpool experiment.[32]

So Murphy concludes that the influence of the Liverpool example
upon the government scheme 'seems certain'.[33]

Some contemporaries certainly thought the government had had
the Irish system in mind. J. C. Colquhoun and C. J. Blomfield
attacked its proposals as the spawn of the Central Society of
Education, as the *Times* did; it was a common Tory charge. The
Whigs, however, denied it at the time. Lord Lansdowne strongly
rejected such an interpretation, and James Kay, the Committee of
Council's secretary, published by authority an open letter in the
newspapers denying any connection between the two systems.[34]
There were, moreover, several crucial differences between the Irish
system and the Whig scheme. First, the Irish ·education
commissioners had few official ministerial connections,
maintaining considerable independence from the Treasury, the
Cabinet, and the Lord Lieutenant. Russell, however, had at first
rejected any central commission at all; when he adopted it, he
included only members of the Cabinet. Second, while the Irish
system excluded religious formularies and allowed the reading only
of selected Scriptural passages, Russell's schemes would have
provided for the Catechism and full Bible, and, in the normal
school, an Anglican chaplain.

Far from deriving encouragement from the Irish example,
Russell was on record, both in Parliament and in private

correspondence, as against its importation into England. He preferred the solution of the British and Foreign Society. His presence in Liverpool in October 1838 must be fitted into the context of the discussions and planning that went on before and after his visit. It is difficult to see how the Liverpool example could have influenced the programme Russell envisioned later in the month. It seems most unlikely, therefore, that the Whig scheme of 1839 can be ascribed to the influence of the Irish system, or of Thomas Wyse, its main adherent in England.

Richard Johnson offers another solution to the problem of the influence on Lord John Russell. He believes that Russell received advice from three quarters: Thomas Spring Rice, who reminded him of political realities, Lord Lansdowne, who urged him to give any board of education the minimum of power, and, acting in co-operation, J. P. Kay and R. A. Slaney.[35] The last two men, he thinks, were of greatest influence. There are, however, several problems.

The degree of co-operation between Kay and Slaney is questionable. Johnson sees continuing contact between Kay and Slaney from December 1837. His source is a letter of Kay's to one of the Poor Law Commissioners of that month, which he thinks refers to Kay's testimony before Slaney's select committee on education of 1838. But the document probably does not refer to that committee at all. In it Kay mentions that he is arranging his papers to testify before an unnamed select committee about pauper education in East Anglia. When Kay appeared before Slaney's committee on 26 February 1838, however, he complained that, since he had been 'suddenly called upon' to testify, he had no documents to substantiate his remarks. It is more likely that Kay's letter refers to his appearance before the select committee on the poor law, where he was questioned about pauper education in East Anglia, and to which he submitted papers.[36] Their relations remained tenuous, even after Kay had testified before the Slaney Committee. When Slaney asked to see Kay's report on the training of pauper children, he asked not the author but his superiors. Kay's reaction, moreover, was cool.

I return Mr. Slaney's note thanking you for your kindness in forwarding it to me for my opinion.

I cannot see any objection to Mr. Slaney's having the Report to *read*.

When he has read it, the question of its publication may be discussed, and will be in no respect prejudiced by Mr. Slaney's perusal of the M.S.[37]

Neither Kay's surviving papers nor Slaney's journal indicate any co-operation; indeed, Kay's name never appears in the latter before 1839. Hence it is difficult to accept the hypothesis that the two men co-operated in any meaningful sense.

Kay's and Slaney's individual roles are as dubious as their conjoint role. In later life Kay liked to see himself as the main instigator of the Committee of Council's normal-school plan. Writing in 1877, he claimed that Lord Lansdowne had summoned him early in 1839 to tell him that the government was planning to create the Committee of Council. When Lansdowne asked him what should be the committee's first step, Kay suggested that it establish a normal school. Lansdowne replied that he and Russell 'were well inclined to such an enterprise.'[38] It seems highly unlikely that after a year and a half of planning the Whig leaders would have turned to an assistant poor law commissioner to ask what they should do.

Then what influence did he have? Kay probably drafted the Education Minute of 13 April; the distinction it makes between 'general' and 'special' religious training and its stipulations respecting the duties of the chaplain are similar to those in Kay's memorandum for the Poor Law Commission on the duties of the workhouse chaplain.[39] But on two other occasions Russell ignored his advice on government policy. Kay had proposed the establishment of a government normal school in London in October 1838; the plans Russell showed the Cabinet in November did not include such a school. Kay suggested that the government support a Church normal school in addition to its own in May 1839; Russell did not adopt this method of defusing Anglican hostility.[40] Clearly Kay was called upon to supply educational expertise but he was not allowed to initiate policy.

Slaney had even less influence. He had offered to serve as an unpaid education commissioner in October 1838, at a time when Russell had no plans to create such a commission; he apparently knew nothing of the government's plans until Russell, Spring Rice, and Sir John Hobhouse briefed him in January 1839. Slaney wrote to Spring Rice on the 16th, presumably in response. Spring Rice's reply suggests that Slaney had little to contribute; the Chancellor of the Exchequer explained that it would not do to include representation of the Church or Dissent on a central board. Slaney wrote again, but Spring Rice did not answer. Slaney interpreted Russell's scheme of February 1839 as an adoption of his proposals to the education committee of the year before, but such a conclusion hardly fits the facts. Slaney had never made clear who should serve on a board; his offer to serve suggests that he probably envisioned a non-political board including representatives of the sects on the Irish model. He had stressed consistently the societies' roles in education—roles that Russell's hardly emphasised—and looked to non-political boards to supervise activities in other areas of government concern. (He offered to supervise sanitary legislation without pay in 1844.) But Russell never considered such an approach to the educational problem. It is difficult to see Slaney's hand in the affair.[41]

Johnson claims that Slaney influenced the government's policy on inspection in 1839, just as he had been responsible for introducing inspection into the Treasury grant in 1838. Johnson advances three grounds for this contention. Slaney kept in close contact with the Whigs. He, Kay, and Edward Baines, Sr., saw Russell on the same day that the Committee of Council approved its inspection minute. When Slaney defended the June programme in Parliament he stressed inspection and aid to destitute areas—elements that Johnson ascribes to his influence. This seems unconvincing. First, there is no evidence in Slaney's, Russell's, or Spring Rice's papers that Slaney was in close contact with the Whigs. Second, Slaney's interview might have been about many other topics besides inspection. (Does the fact that Lord Morpeth and Thomas Wyse had an interview with Russell on 12 February prove that they influenced the education scheme that the Home Secretary unveiled that evening?) Unless one has corroborating testimony such evidence is useless. Third, since aid to destitute areas had been a government concern since 1833, and since the government had certainly adopted inspection in 1838 of its own accord, Slaney's speech can mean no more than that he supported the Whig programme. It therefore seems unlikely that Russell was influenced from this quarter.[42]

Finally, Johnson, following Canon Burgess, the historian of the National Society, believes that the activities of the Young Gentlemen acted as a 'catalyst', forcing Russell's hand. The evidence is a circular from the Committee of Inquiry in the Russell papers; Russell had marked a passage stressing the need for the Church to act before the State pre-empted the field. Further evidence is in Russell's attack on the Young Gentlemen in his Commons speech of 12 February. This also seems unlikely. Russell sent the circular to Spring Rice for comment on 27 October 1838, and he had probably received it only shortly before. If so, its receipt in September or October could not have been a catalyst, since he began planning in August. Nor could the threat offered by the Young Gentlemen have caused him to take up the question in the first place, for he had done so in August 1837, long before they formed a group. (Spring Rice did not think too much of the 'threat'.)[43] Their activities undoubtedly strengthened Russell's resolve to persevere, and may perhaps account in part for his hostility to the Church, but they had no other significance.[44]

The hypotheses offered by Murphy and Johnson leave one dissatisfied, for neither comes to grips with all of Russell's ideas, and both concentrate on the scheme finally presented to Parliament. If it is correct to believe that any explanation of Russell's programme must take into account his plans prior to January 1839, then it seems fair to conclude that neither scholar's account is fully satisfactory. After tracing the evolution of Russell's ideas, one concludes that the influences upon him in the 1839 affair came from quarters closer to the government.

What happened was this. Russell had left the education question to Spring Rice after 1834, but the need to inject new ideas into the faltering government convinced him that the time was right for legislative action; hence he approached Brougham in August of 1837. This came to nothing because Brougham, hoping to recapture his old radical constituency, hopelessly muddled the education question with franchise extension, and Russell backed off in December. Pressed by Allen and Dunn of the B.F.S.S., Russell revived the question in August of 1838. Once he had developed his ideas, he turned to Spring Rice for comment in October 1838. Spring Rice, however, believed them to be politically unrealistic and to beg several important administrative questions. Russell dismissed these warnings, with what consequences we are aware. Committed as he was to action, he produced a stop-gap measure, drawn in part from his earlier schemes, in part from the poor law. He abandoned the local element entirely and proposed a board with powers not confined to mere inspection. His programme was born of desperation: had he turned to Kay for succour? Certainly Kay had recommended such a normal school in October 1838.

Lansdowne was more important. When shown Brougham's and Russell's working papers in 1837, he opposed their ideas for local rate-aided schools. Influenced by the educational writing of W. E. Hickson, he recommended an increased grant and the creation of a board, by royal fiat, authorised to inspect schools and run a normal school. His contribution to Russell's plans of October 1838 is unknown. Russell had planned then to make either himself or Lansdowne the responsible Minister for education; it seems logical that the two would have discussed the matter. Lansdowne did not move to the centre of the stage until after Russell's confrontation with Howley and Blomfield in late January 1839. It is significant that Russell presented his plan to Parliament in the form of an exchange of letters between himself and Lansdowne. More significantly, the plan's priorities were those Lansdowne had advanced in 1837. Once involved, Lansdowne strongly supported Russell, canvassing the Whig bishops. It was due to Lansdowne that Russell had a programme to announce on 12 February.[45]

Why was Russell's original programme so incredibly stupid politically, and his final scheme a stopgap? How could one of the greatest Whig politicians of the nineteenth century, who had successfully piloted the Great Reform Bill of 1832, have spawned it? Russell was proud of his family's great heritage, and the events of the seventeenth century were as real to him as those of the nineteenth. He was convinced that 'the spirit of priestcraft . . . has been continually engaged in extending the spiritual, and restricting the temporal, power'. He feared particularly that spirit's attempt to subvert the minds of children into 'servile obedience [to] the syllogisms of Aristotle and the abuses of the Roman Church'.[46] His anti-clericalism encompassed the Church of England, particularly High Churchmen and Tractarians; hence he refused to make the slightest effort for accommodation. As A. J. P. Taylor puts it, he 'was a Protestant in the sense of being hostile to the Church of Rome, but not a Christian'.[47] He was also a man who avoided consultation. His colleague Howick was struck by 'his habitually uncommunicative temper & his love of doing everything himself & entirely his own way'.[48] This potent combination led him to rash acts—the Stroud address, the Hampden appointment, the Durham letter. In 1839 it led him to ignore political and religious realities. He did not consult Spring Rice, the Minister who had been responsible for Whig education policy since 1835, until late in his planning, and then he ignored the advice. Nor had he spoken with Edward Maltby, the Bishop of Durham, to whom he later turned when Prime Minister for advice on matters of patronage. Only after the Church had forced him to face reality did he turn to others.

It would have been difficult at any time for the government to have produced a plan acceptable to both Church and Dissent: in the year of the Bedchamber Crisis, Church and opposition were even less disposed to conciliation. To this equation one must add the way that Russell produced the programme—a way dictated by his anti-clerical and secretive personality. The result could only have been confrontation, and the government could be thankful that it had salvaged as much as it had.

Chapter VII

THE COMMITTEE SEEKS A ROLE, 1839–42

The education question rarely occupied Hansard during the three years after the Committee of Council's creation. The Radical William Ewart moved for a responsible Minister of Education in April 1841; he withdrew his motion after a twelve-column debate. In May R. A. Slaney proposed a Bill authorising a school rate for rural parishes, but no discussion followed and he dropped the matter. The question did appear in the debate on Peel's motion of no confidence in June. Dr Lushington, the Whig, gave it eleven lines, and J. C. Colquhoun, the Scottish Tory, one sentence; Slaney allowed it an independent clause.[1] These muted debates do not reflect indifference to the problem, for the real debate raged elsewhere. Britain had, now, a central board of education, but what was its role to be? Bowing to opposition from the Church and Conservatives, the government had limited the Committee of Council's sphere of action to inspection and the administration of those funds appropriated for education. Yet what might the power of the purse not do? Upon this point battles were fought, both within and without Whitehall; their results were that the Committee of Council found itself even more circumscribed than before.

I STAFFING THE DEPARTMENT

Before the Committee of Council could function, it had to find civil servants to do its work. Clerks and copyists were transferred from the Privy Council establishment, but those officials most concerned with the committee's educational role, the school inspectors and the permanent secretary, were brought in from outside. There was no lack of candidates, for educationists had always seen State intervention as a source of employment. Thus, whenever it appeared that the State might act, Brougham was deluged with letters begging for jobs. When the day came, the Committee of Council received at least half a dozen unsolicited applications, but the places were filled by the exercise of traditional patronage. The committee decided on 15 August to appoint two part-time inspectors, one for National and the other for British schools. (The government requested the Bishop of Chichester to nominate the inspector of Anglican schools, hoping thereby to appease the Church.) It was not until November, however, that it selected John Allen and Hugh Seymour Tremenheere for the posts.[2] In both cases Lansdowne, the president of the council, made the choice.

Allen, a priest, was examining chaplain to William Otter, Bishop of Chichester, and Chaplain to King's College, London. It is not surprising, then, that Otter nominated him to Lansdowne. Lansdowne interviewed Allen on 23 November. The Lord President assured hm that he would inspect only Church schools, and that his government job would not require him 'to put off the character of a Christian clergyman'. After consulting Bishop Blomfield, who advised him that, as the Committee of Council was there to stay, the Church's interests would be best served by placing sympathetic personnel on its staff, Allen accepted. Tremenheere, the inspector for British schools, also received his job through patronage. B. F. Duppa of the Central Society of Education suggested that he apply for the post; he had as well the support of E. W. Pendarves and Sir Charles Lemon, M.P.s for Cornwall, and William Erle, his fellow revising barrister on the western circuit. This influence no doubt obtained his interview with Lansdowne, Duppa's friend, in November. As for Lemon, Russell wanted to make him the Lord Lieutenant of Cornwall because his father 'always stood by Fox'.[3]

Although both men had tenuous associations with education, it seems likely that Lansdowne had selected them mainly for religious reasons. Both men's credentials were such as not to alienate either the Church or Dissent. Allen's connection with King's ensured his orthodox churchmanship; that Otter was his patron seemed to show that he was no narrow High Churchman. Tremenheere also was a churchman, but as a Whig he was not likely to alienate Nonconformists. He had made a name fo himself by contributing to the *Edinburgh Review*; his membership of the Central Society of

Education demonstrates his interest in education. Both were young and able, and both seemed safe religiously.

The selection of James Phillips Kay to be the Assistant Secretary[4] of the committee of Council was perhaps a more purely 'educational' appointment. Kay, born in 1804 into an Independent family from Rochdale, seemed destined for a career in business. Yet at some point in the early 1820s he must have decided to break out of his own Lancashire Nonconformist milieu. Kay's route was the high road to Edinburgh, where he took the M.D. degree in 1827. He set up practice in Manchester. There he flirted briefly with Radicalism, helping to form the Manchester Statistical Society and quoting *Mask of Anarchy* to the crowd in 1832. His desire for advancement led him to seek government employment; he asked Brougham in 1833 to make him a commissioner in lunacy. His statistical work was more fruitful, for he was able to meet the influential Nassau Senior and Lord Kerry. Senior may well have got Kay his first job in the civil service; Kerry almost certainly brought Kay to the attention of his father, Lord Lansdowne. Kay became an assistant poor law commissioner in July 1835; as we have seen, he had emerged by 1839 as one of the foremost experts on working-class education. Hence his appointment was logical.[5]

Unfortunately, Kay had a number of weaknesses that interfered with his administrative work. Although he had conformed to the Church of England at some point in the 1830s, he still bore the Nonconformist stigma; churchmen, already suspicious of government intentions, saw his appointment as a direct challenge to Anglican claims. More seriously, Kay soon gained the reputation of being cold, devious, and managing. He alienated the school inspectors, and his dealings with both the National Society and the B.F.S.S. were never cordial.[6]

If the Committee of Council therefore had for its chief civil servant a man singularly unfitted to win the Church's trust, whose personality interfered in his relationships with the inspectors, it was more fortunate that in its formative years it had two able adminstrators at its head. These were the two Lords President of the Privy Council, Lord Lansdowne (1839–41) and Lord Wharncliffe (1841–45). After Wharncliffe's death the Duke of Buccleuch became Lord President for the short remainder of the Peel Ministry; Lansdowne returned to office in 1846.

Lansdowne was almost a stereotypical Whig grandee—civilised,

cultivated, tolerant, with broad acres. Although an effective
parliamentarian, he was unambitious and did not pay close
attention to the details of administration. Brougham, as energetic
as Gladstone but less disciplined, complained that Lansdowne
neglected the judicial work of the Privy Council, the bulk of his
responsibilities before 1839. Wharncliffe, passionately interested in
horses, was equally interested in West Riding politics and railways;
very much a Peelite, he paid attention to his Cabinet duties.
Norman Gash thinks that 'he matched his large property with fair
talents'.[7] Before 1843, moreover, both Lansdowne and Wharncliffe
had two great advantages over Kay: age and experience. Kay was
aged only thirty-five when he became the Education Department's
secretary, and all his administrative experience had been gained at
the local level. Lansdowne and Wharncliffe, however, were at the
height of their careers, with years of experience in Whitehall behind
them. These two men, not Kay, guided affairs during the three
crucial years when the religious question brought the work of the
Education Department to a standstill just as it was preparing to
commence activities.

II THE INSPECTION CONTROVERSY

Despite their failure to bring down the government in June 1839,
the Church and the National Society carried on the battle. The
National Society broke lances with the Committee of Council in
July, when it applied for its share of the £10,000 model-school
grant, asking to know the conditions upon which the government
was prepared to grant the funds. The Committee of Council's reply
was conciliatory, assuring the National Society that although
inspection was a *sine qua non* for State aid, the State would interfere
with neither religious training nor the management of the schools.
The committee professed itself pleased with the National Society's
plans for the normal college; it offered to follow the
recommendation of the Bishop of Chichester in appointing the
inspector as 'a guarantee to the National Society of the friendly
intentions of the Committee'. (But, determined to act impartially,
it sent a similar offer of aid to the B.F.S.S.) In October it inserted in
the daily press promises that inspectors would be appointed
specifically for Anglican schools, that they would be churchmen,

and that, other things being equal, the committee would give preference to clergymen. The National Society, however, refused to admit into its schools any inspectors unconnected with the Church.[8]

No concession short of utter abdication would have satisfied the National Society. Although the society allowed the correspondence to drag on until the end of November, it had decided to refuse all co-operation with the government. It ceased submitting cases for aid to the Committee of Council and promised to match the government building grant that would have been awarded to schools unwilling to accept State aid. (The society had the wherewithal for this act of defiance, for one of the fruits of the great meeting of 28 May 1839 was the formation of an aggressive subscriptions committee.) The stage was thus set for a war of attrition. The society hoped that if it waited long enough the State would capitulate; the government believed that if it gave way on minor points while remaining firm on the inspection issue the society would withdraw its demands.[9]

Simultaneously the society's General Committee decided to enforce its rules more stringently. Schools wishing to join the society had to bind themselves to teach the Catechism, take the children to church, hire only churchmen as teachers, report annually to the society, make the parish priest a trustee, and abide by the decision of the Diocesan in case of dispute between the clergyman and the school managers. This meant that the children of Dissenters had to conform to the Church, so the Rev. James Gratrix, Rector of Halifax, asked on behalf of the factory inspector Leonard Horner, Lord Ashley, and the Bishop of London for the Catechism to be made optional in factory schools, where attendance was compulsory. The General Committee was at first lenient, allowing managers of factory schools to excuse children from Catechism if parents so requested, but later it reversed its position, declaring that no sufficient reason had been shown to excuse children from Catechism. The central body's rigidity was paralleled at the local level. When district National schools were planned for the diocese of Lincoln it was at first decided that children of Dissenters would be excused from both church and Catechism. The archidiaconal board, however, reversed this decision, resolving that all schools under its jurisdiction must adhere to the National Society's stipulations.[10]

The Church's resolve remained firm, even under the blandishments of taxpayers' money. By the end of January 1840 the Committee of Council had received 228 applications for aid from National schools, and had awarded them £19,895, but 126 of them refused grants totalling £12,504. To be sure, the Committee of Council instituted an *ad hoc* category, that of 'Church Schools', to attract Anglican schools not connected with the National Society, but only nineteen took the bait. The National Society also waged its war in a positive manner by appointing its own inspectors. At the national level, the Revs. James Hill and Henry Hopwood were hired to inspect; on the local level, the dioceses of Salisbury and London hired inspectors.[11]

The *Times* helped to stoke the fires of controversy by damning Lord Brougham and the Committee of Council in its leading articles, printing correspondence from managers of National schools, and reporting public meetings attacking the inspection plan. In Parliament, Sir Robert Peel and Sir J. Y. Buller, Tory M.P. for Devon, denounced the government scheme when they moved no confidence in the Ministry in January 1840. The government tried to fight back. Kay wrote a semi-official pamphlet, *Recent Measures for the Promotion of Education in England*, in defence of the Committee of Council; that body distributed copies to editors and other moulders of public opinion. But the Church-and-Tory voice would not be stilled.[12]

The dispute with the largest educator of children in England thus threatened to bring to a halt the Whig education scheme. As if this were not enough, however, it appeared that the Committee of Council was to become involved over the same issue with yet another Established Church—the Church of Scotland. After the committee went into operation, the Kirk's Education Committee had written to the Treasury to object; in reply, the Treasury agreed to remove the Schools (Scotland) Act from the Privy Council's hands. This failed to mollify the Kirk, however; in August the Education Committee resolved to petition the Queen in protest against the Committee of Council's inspection requirements. The government had Kay write to Thomas Chalmers, in the hope of obtaining his support; Kay sent a copy of his pamphlet, *Recent Measures*, and flattered Chalmers by claiming to be his disciple. The Kirk remained hostile, however; its Education Committee wrote in December to demand a clarification of the inspectors' role and suggested that the Committee of Council consult it before appointing any.[13]

Meanwhile it was necessary to make some attempt to begin work, and Lord Lansdowne prepared guidelines for Kay's drafting of the instructions to inspectors. Kay produced a circular and a set of instructions that the Committee of Council approved, with what revisions we do not know, on 4 January 1840. These charged the inspectors with spreading educational improvements as well as with seeing that schoolhouses were in good shape. They were carefully reminded, however, that their position was purely advisory. They should at all times co-operate with the local management committee, announce their presence to the local clergyman or to the secretary of the school committee, and examine the school in their presence. Above all, they must never interfere in a school's internal policy, but rather always uphold the authority of committee over teacher, and that of teacher over pupil.[14]

On the same day the Committee of Council decided to enlist the Kirk's support. The committee sent a copy of its instructions for inspectors to the Education Committee of the General Assembly, and offered to submit the name of its proposed Scottish school inspector to the Education Committee for comment. And the man it chose for the post was the Education Committee's own secretary, John Gordon.[15] That religion, not professional expertise, was the main factor in the selection is evident from Monteagle's comments on the affair.

. . . we have a meeting of the Committee of Council on Education this morning which I must attend. I am charmed to think that on this subject we are likely to have the full confidence and co-operation of the Committee of the General Assembly.

Do you know Mr. Gordon, Secretary to the University of Edinburgh, what sort of man is he as we are about to name him Inspector for Scotland?[16]

Although Gordon declined the job to remain at Edinburgh, the government's second choice, John Gibson of the Madras College grammar school, St Andrews, was equally acceptable to the Kirk.

The agreement with the Church of Scotland made it difficult for both the Committee of Council and the National Society to maintain their rigid stances. Indeed, they arrived at a compromise by July. We are indebted to Nancy Ball for our understanding of this compromise; one may add a gloss here and there, but her work remains unshaken.[17]

Ball believes that the break in the deadlock between Church and State came when Bishop Blomfield decided to co-operate. She rightly points out that his interview with John Allen in November 1839 shows that he believed the correct policy for the Church to be to see its own men appointed as inspectors. He opposed, moreover, the hard-liners who resisted any government grant under any circumstances.[18] He approached Russell and Lansdowne in the spring of 1840. Lansdowne arranged a conference with Howley and three other prelates, memoranda were exchanged, and other meetings followed. Howley proposed that the archbishops should have the power annually to appoint an inspector, subject to the Committee of Council's concurrence. The inspector would report directly to the Diocesan, not to the Committee of Council; his instructions would be the joint production of the prelates and the committee. In short, Howley would have reduced the committee to the status of paymaster.

Lansdowne watered down this heady brew. He proposed that the government appoint the inspector with the concurrence of the Archbishop of Canterbury; that he report directly to the committee; that his appointment be permanent unless revoked by either side; and that, besides his instructions from the committee, he receive special instructions from the Archbishop of Canterbury. Howley disliked it, calling it 'a repetition of [Lansdowne's] former offer in a less simple, and less convenient form'; he was inclined to reject it.[19] Why he did not is a matter of speculation. Thirty-five years later John Sinclair, the National Society's secretary, claimed that he had convinced Howley to reconsider; his recollections, however, are of dubious worth.[20] In any event, Howley continued negotiating and ultimately accepted the principle that the State, not the Church, should have the right to name the inspector in the first instance. Although Howley had not obtained all that he wanted, he had obtained all that he thought he could safely get.

I found that the Committee of Council would not give up the nomination, and as they have conceded all other points—I do not think that the public would have gone with us, had we come to a rupture on this.[21]

The final agreement, known as the 'Concordat', was embodied in the Education Minute of 15 July 1840. It provided that before any inspector for National or Anglican schools was appointed, each archbishop would be consulted with respect to his province; both might suggest names, and no person would be appointed without their concurrence. The appointments would be during the pleasure of either the Primates or the Privy Council. The inspector's instructions with regard to religion would be framed by the archbishops and would form part of his general instructions. The general instructions would be sent to the archbishops before being issued. Although the inspector would report directly to the Committee of Council, copies would be sent to the archbishops and to the Diocesans involved. Last it was agreed that the Committee of Council would award grants to schools only in proportion to the number of children to be educated and to the amount of money raised locally, save in special cases.[22] This document defined the relationship between the Church and the Committee of Council until 1870.[23]

Had the State surrendered to the Church? The Concordat was in fact a compromise. The National Society had objected to State inspection fundamentally because the power and authority of the inspectors emanated not from it but from a secular body. After the dust had settled, that secular body still remained the source from which their authority proceeded. In its turn, the Church had obtained most of what it wanted. It had, first, a voice in the selection of the inspector. Second, by securing from the State the concessions that the inspector would look into both secular and religious instruction and that his religious instructions form an integral part of his full schedule, the Church obtained a repudiation of the position of the Central Society of Education, that sectarian training could be compartmentalised into the last hour of the school day. Last, it preserved its advantage as the wealthiest of the denominations by obtaining the provision that only in special cases would the State favour schools in areas where subscriptions were low. These were, of course, manufacturing areas where the industrial, Dissenting classes were less willing than the landed, Anglican classes to contribute to the betterment of their dependents.

III   THE WORK OF THE COMMITTEE

Once the staff were found and the inspection controversy settled, the Committee of Council was able to enter into operation. It is important to look at its work during the first few years of its life, for it then set the precedents for most of the future developments in educational policy. It is therefore worth while to discover its decisions and those responsible for them.

The basic document that governed the Committee of Council's policy was the Education Minute of 24 September 1839. Its drafting began in late July or early August when Kay, acting on Lansdowne's instructions, obtained copies of the Treasury minutes of 30 August 1833 and 21 October 1834, and studied the Treasury procedure for awarding grants. His task was to adapt Treasury policy to the needs of the Committee of Council, as expressed in the Education Minute of 1 June 1839.[24]

Kay's approach was purposely misleading. For public consumption he emphasised the Committee of Council's limited sphere.

. . . the functions of the Committee are limited to 'superintend the application of any sums voted by Parliament for . . . public Education.' These functions are therefore precisely similar to those which were exercised by the Treasury in the years 1835, 6, 7, and 8.[25]

In private, however, he contended that the committee's terms of reference were broader than those of the Treasury. Hence he envisioned greater freedom on the part of the former in the expenditure of its funds—its financial acitivity would not be limited to the building of schools.

Kay therefore recommended that the purchase of the school site be included in the grant, not realising that such had been the Treasury practice. The committee should also use its funds to provide gratuities for schoolmasters, to purchase books and teaching apparatus, and to repair and enlarge schools. He further contended that the committee should exercise its power to award aid to 'poor and populous places' where subscriptions were low. At the same time, he believed that the Committee of Council had the opportunity to shake off the influence of the societies. Because the State employed inspectors and envisaged aid to schools not connected with either society, the Treasury's stipulation requiring referrals to them must be dropped. Last, he emphasised the role of the inspector in securing conformity and improvement at the local level.[26]

Lansdowne circulated Kay's proposals to Lord Monteagle (as Spring Rice had become), F. T. Baring, Monteagle's successor at the Exchequer, and Lord John Russell. Monteagle opposed any major deviations from Treasury policy (and Baring followed in his wake) on the grounds that the Committee of Council had neither staff nor funds to provide services beyond the building of schoolhouses. Only in rare cases would he approve of aid to schools in depressed areas or unconnected with the societies, and then the government should encourage them to affiliate with the appropriate society. He further maintained that school inspectors should only gather and publish facts, and let public opinion exact improvements from the local school committees. Always concerned with the government's precarious parliamentary position, Monteagle believed that if the Committee of Council deviated from the 10s rule for Dissenters' schools the Church's wrath would fall upon its head. For public consumption he stressed the precedents for freedom of action in the Scottish and model-school grants; in private he proved unwilling to hold to those precedents. For all his creative ideas, Monteagle hated telling people what they did not wish to hear; his dread of the price of confrontation led him to take the easy path.[27]

Kay accompanied Tufnell on a six-week Continental tour shortly after producing his memorandum; before his return, the Committee of Council issued the minute of 24 September. This minute was a compromise between Monteagle's and Kay's positions; Russell and Landsdowne were probably the mediators. Its adoption in Kay's absence should not be seen as some sort of devious plot, although he had been led to believe that the Committee of Council would not meet while he was gone.[28] His function had been merely to prepare a working paper for discussion, and the decision rested with the Committee of Council. His presence in London would probably have made little difference to the outcome.

The minute adopted the Treasury requirement of six square feet per pupil, the 10s rule, and the stipulations that promoters expend all local funds before requesting payment of the grant and bind themselves to audits and reports. It required certain assurances similar to those demanded by the Treasury before aid would be awarded. Thus the Committee of Council would obtain, from either its own inspector or the appropriate school society (an evident compromise between Kay's and Monteagle's positions), proof that the case was worthy, that no local charity could provide aid, and that annual support was likely. In Scotland, the committee would turn to 'some competent authority there'. Lastly, the minute provided that if an applicant for aid did not plan to affiliate with either school society 'the Committee will not entertain the case, unless some special circumstances be exhibited to enduce their Lordships to treat the case as special'. 'Special cases' were of three kinds: schools in poor and populated areas, existing schools in need of aid, and schools in England and Wales not affiliated with either society.[29]

Kay returned to London a fortnight after the Committee of Council had promulgated the minute; he drafted a long report for Russell that included an impracticable scheme for schools financed by local taxation and governed by a conscience clause—in essence what Brougham and Russell had considered in 1837. That Kay could advance such a scheme five months after the Bedchamber Crisis, four months after the government had squeezed the education budget through the Commons with a two-vote majority, suggests that he had little understanding of political realities. It seems clear that the Church would never have accepted such a programme.[30] Instead, the Committee of Council increased its influence quietly.

The State could do little to improve teaching beyond granting aid to the societies' normal schools. The committee's printed minutes for 1840–41 included essays by Kay on techniques of teaching reading, writing, and vocal music, in the hope that schoolmasters might improve their teaching skills. The Committee of Council could do more to improve the physical surroundings of learning. It required applicants for building grants to describe the location of the school site, any near-by marshes or bogs, how the building was to be drained, and whether 'any vitriol works, tanneries, size manufactories, slaughter-houses or other noxious trades' adjoined the school. The promoters were expected to obtain the aid of an architect to prepare plans of the building; they had to provide sufficient heat, ventilation, and exercise space. In short, the Committee of Council wanted security of tenure, regular maintenance, and healthy surroundings for the children.[31]

The Committee of Council also attempted to influence education in more subtle ways. It reprinted its annual reports, from the *Parliamentary Papers*, in an octavo edition for the general public. By a policy lasting until 1855, each State-aided school received a free octavo copy annually. The committee used this publication to disseminate Kay's ideas on pedagogy and school management, and to exhibit specifications and cost estimates for school buildings of various sizes in order to save local promoters the expense of drawing up their own plans, to indicate the expected standards of heat, lighting, and ventilation, and to show the correct way to arrange classroom furniture. School committees that adopted these plans were eligible for extra funds to help build masters' dwellings. The committee's subtlety at times approached the devious. The first volume of annual minutes included an appendix of sample legal forms: conveyances of school sites for various categories of schools and indentures for apprentice schoolteachers. The introductory paragraph in the version presented to Parliament explains that the forms are not obligatory, but have been included only to help school managers avoid legal fees. In the octavo version that explanation is deleted, thus leaving the impression that the documents were required. (The Committee of Council made the forms mandatory in December 1840 after the octavo had already appeared.) Either Kay, who was responsible for editing the minutes for publication, or the committee wished to encourage local school trustees to use standard legal forms.[32]

The direction of the State's concern shifted from the material to the religious where special cases were concerned. The committee produced a separate minute and application questionnaire for these in December 1839. It required applicants to explain their objections to affiliation with any society, to describe the nature of the religious training to be offered in the schools, to state whether children would be excused from indoctrination to which their parents might object, and to guarantee that the Bible would be read daily. If any school was to affiliate with a particular congregation, the committee wanted to know the number of people in the area to be served who belonged to that denomination. These facts being shown, the Committee of Council would then limit aid to cases where State aid was indispensible to provide competent working-class education, and where the Scriptures would be read daily. It declared its intention of giving preference to schools that provided religious instruction similar to that offered in society schools, and that did not require a catechism or attendance at a particular church for its pupils.[33]

From the beginning, the Committee of Council charted a conservative path in its handling of special cases. The committee departed from the Treasury's rigid rules, to accommodate schools that would not have qualified for aid before 1839, in only a handful of cases, and its policy reinforced the fundamental principle on which State aid was based—grants in aid of local contributions. The committee reserved only £4,000 out of its first annual grant for such cases. It declined to aid the payment of a teacher's salary at Forfar; although willing to help pay for repairs to two other schools, it refused to grant funds for debt reduction. Yet it offered the Stirling Infant School £133 to help finance a school under a church—something the Treasury would never have countenanced. Equally cautious was its aid to independent schools. It refused aid to promoters at Lincoln who had planned to affiliate with a local Independent chapel unless they joined the British Society. On the other hand, it awarded grants to a Wesleyan school near Leeds, and to a school controlled by the local clergyman at Allenheads, Northumberland. Between January 1840 and February 1841 the committee awarded seven grants totalling £913 7s to schools unconnected with either school society in England and Wales; in 1841–42, after the Concordat, it awarded only £38 to one school.[34]

The Committee of Council's cautious policies may be attributed as much to internal divisions among its members as to the external hostility and suspicion of the Church. Six men sat on the committee that approved the Education Minute of 24 September 1839. Of them, only Russell supported a significant increase in the level of State intervention; Monteagle and Baring were cautious, and Lansdowne fell somewhere between. (The positions of Henry Labouchere and Lord Duncannon are not known.) Sir George Grey, added in time to help approve the minute of 3 December, would probably have leaned towards Russell's position. As for Lord Clarendon, who joined in January 1840, we do not know. It seems, then, that cautious, conservative views predominated on the committee.[35]

The Whigs had thus created precedents for by-passing the societies and expanding the availability of grants. Besides the minutes of September and December, which in theory freed their hands, they actually awarded aid to a few independent schools. But they hardly used these precedents at all, perhaps because they encountered opposition from previously friendly quarters.

IV THE NORMAL-SCHOOL CONTROVERSY

Writing to Russell in 1843, Kay-Shuttleworth (as he was now known) declared that the religious issue lay at the heart of the education question.

> When your lordship and Lord Lansdowne in 1839 appointed me Secretary of the Committee of Council on Education, I understood the design of your Government to be to prevent the successful assertion on the part of the purely ecclesiastical system of education . . . .
>
> I, however, understood your lordship's Government to determine in 1839 to assert the claims of the civil power to the control of the education of the country . . . .[36]

Tremenheere put it more succinctly; he referred to 'our opponents the High Churchmen & the Newmanites'.[37] This is more accurate as well, for to fend off High Church ecclesiastical claims the Committee of Council made major concessions to the Protestants.

As with inspection, so with aid to normal schools, Scotland provided the occasion for compromise. It will be recalled that a deputation from the Glasgow Educational Society had approached Monteagle in 1836 to ask for aid for its normal school. Although Monteagle declined then to give any definite answer, the Glasgow society raised £2,000 on its own and launched impressive plans to build four schools for a thousand children. Besides subventions from both the Treasury and the Committee of Council, the society relied on loans to maintain its over-ambitious building programme, for local subscriptions were scanty. Its buildings and debts increased, and it requested £5,000 in February 1840 to finish the last wing. It received £2,500. But costs and debts continued to mount, and the Glasgow educators were back for more in fifteen months.[38] The Committee of Council responded by ordering John Gibson, its inspector of Scottish schools, to study the situation. He reported unfavourably in July 1841.

> . . . although the Course of Instruction to which [the students'] Attention is directed . . . embraces many important and interesting Branches of

Knowledge, . . . yet it seems to me to have a Tendency to render their Instruction as Teachers superficial and desultory . . . .[39]

Meanwhile David Dickson and John Gordon of the Kirk's Education Committee proposed that the Committee of Council guarantee financial support to enable the General Assembly to take over the Glasgow normal school and to build another at Edinburgh. In return the Kirk would provide £500 per annum for each school. The Committee of Council, now Tory-controlled, offered a settlement that would have placed the schools under effective State control. In return for grants of £5,000 each for normal schools at Glasgow and Edinburgh and annual maintenance grants of £500 per school, it claimed the rights to concur in the appointment of the school's rectors, to fire them at will, and to end the maintenance grants at any time. After objections from the General Assembly, the Committee of Council withdrew its stipulation respecting the rectors, trusting to the power of the purse to exert sufficient control over the schools.[40]

One should not exaggerate the degree to which the Glasgow Educational Society was independent of the Kirk. Nevertheless it seems clear that, in practice, the Committee of Council was unable to assert the civil control of education in Scotland. Certainly the Tories tried, when they proposed that the committee approve the rector. But what else could be done? It was clear from the inspector Gibson's reports that the Glasgow Educational Society had not the resources to operate the normal school; what other organisation was there in Scotland to run it but the Kirk?

If the Kirk was satisfied with its position *vis-à-vis* the Committee of Council, other groups were not with theirs. The Committee of Council rejected the request of the Presbyterian Church of England to have the same privileges as those of the Church of Scotland. The British Society, however, was also restless. Henry Dunn, the society's secretary, feared that the government would sell out non-denominationalism in order to placate the Church. As early as April 1839 he had joined Sir Culling Eardley Smith, Edward Baines, Sr., Joseph Pease (the first an Evangelical churchman, the latter two Yorkshire Dissenters), and several members of the B.F.S.S.'s General Committee in a deputation to the Committee of Council. The deputation opposed government-operated schools, and contended that the State should inspect secular training only, leaving religious instruction to voluntary subscribers, and deny aid to schools that required compulsory catechisms. The government realised the need to conciliate the British Society; Russell recommended in July 1839 that the Queen, who had earlier donated £100 to the National Society, give a like sum to its rival. The British Society was prepared initially to co-operate with the government. It accepted the Committee of Council's inspection requirement, its General Committee resolving that 'such inspection will be cheerfully allowed'. The government's agreements with the Churches of Scotland and England, however, changed this attitude.[41]

The British Society complained in January 1841 that the Committee of Council's agreements with the two Established Churches put it in an inferior position. Hence it demanded that the inspector of British schools be required to submit duplicates of his reports to it, and to encourage local schools to use the parent body's books and to send their master to the Borough Road School for training. The Committee of Council readily compromised, agreeing to send the British Society copies of its inspector's reports, but declining to permit him to recommend lessons or books. When the Tory committee assumed office late in 1841 Lord Wharncliffe, the new Lord President, confirmed the agreement. A new problem arose, however, over the precise terms by which the government would award annual maintenance grants to the Borough Road School. Correspondence and interviews dragged on between March 1841 and June 1842. In the latter month Seymour Tremenheere, the inspector of British schools, reported that the society's schools in London left much to be desired, and his judgements were unrelieved by kindness. Concerned, Wharncliffe induced him to coat the bitter pill by adding comments about the spirit of improvement that he had found among the masters, but the British Society was not appeased. It denounced the 'spirit and tendency' of Tremenheere's report, calling it 'an elaborate attempt to show that the entire system of instruction pursued by the society is essentially defective'.[42]

Wishing to avoid a confrontation, Wharncliffe ordered Kay-Shuttleworth to approach the British Society, and enlisted the aid of Dr Stephen Lushington, a co-founder of the Society for the Diffusion of Useful Knowledge and Whig M.P. for Tower Hamlets, who had friends on its General Committee. The more extreme

Dissenters had so committed themselves, however, that the moderates on the committee could not persuade them to back down. The dispute became public in November 1842, when the *Eclectic Review* castigated the government. Repeating arguments advanced earlier by the British Society, the anonymous article complained that while the inspectors of National and Scottish normal schools were servants of their respective sects, the Borough Road School was inspected by one over whose appointment the B.F.S.S. had no control. Worse, the government planned to create a centralised system on Tractarian-tainted Church principles, but under the State's control, and to that end was undermining the British Society by introducing uniform teaching methods. Inspection was 'an unfair, partial, and mischievous visitation' because Tremenheere, the inspector, was an 'avowed foe' of the monitorial method. Wharncliffe feared that this article was the sign of a new and serious battle.[43]

The British Society had written to Wharncliffe on the eve of the controversy, demanding that the Committee of Council's inspection of the Borough Road School be made contingent upon the continuance of maintenance grants, and complaining about its lack of any voice in the selection of inspectors. Wharncliffe attempted to compromise. Although the government was bound to insist upon inspection in perpetuity, it offered to select inspectors who possessed the society's confidence and to receive suggestions about any aspect of inspection.[44] It remained to be seen, however, whether Wharncliffe's move might form the basis for a stable relationsip, or whether the British Society, unsatisfied with this concession, would demand more.

V   THE COMMITTEE'S FIRST THREE YEARS

The main task of the Committee of Council during its first three years was to discover its limits of action; it had to arrive at acceptable compromises with the school societies. The Whigs managed to compromise with the two Established Churches; the Tories tried with the B.F.S.S. But the Conservative accession to power in 1841 did not mean that the Church could now control education policy. The fact of a Conservative government certainly eased the Education Department's relations with the National

Society. Gladstone arranged a face-to-face meeting in November between John Sinclair of that society and James Kay-Shuttleworth which mollified suspicion on both sides. (The *Times*, however, continued its attacks on the Education Department and denounced Kay-Shuttleworth's theories of education as 'quackery' and 'practical infidelity'.) A month later Lord Wharncliffe underlined the government's mild line by telling the Ripon Diocesan Board of Education that, although the Ministry supported Anglican education, it could not confine financial aid to the Church. Monteagle's claim, that the Peel Ministry's stance was 'a wholesale adoption' of Whig measures, exaggerated the reality, but there was certainly no immediate or marked shift in policy.[45]

Throughout this period, governments, both Whig and Tory, had pursued a similar policy. Although both preserved the authority of the Committee of Council whenever they could, neither used to the fullest the options for by-passing the societies given them in the Education Minute of 3 December 1839. The Committee of Council, then, had not solved the problem debated in the 1830s: how could the State increase the means of working-class education without offending powerful and mutually opposed religious interests? When Peel came to power in 1841 his government took up the problem, and proposed to circumvent central administration entirely.

Chapter VIII

THE FACTORY BILL OF 1843: A TORY ALTERNATIVE

It is the duty of the opposition to oppose; it is equally the duty of the government to govern. The Conservatives inherited in 1841 a government agency limited in scope and involved in a dispute with the British and Foreign School Society. Yet despite their opposition to the Committee of Council out of power in 1839, the Conservatives in power in 1841–42 had attempted to preserve, if not expand, that department's authority. They faced, however, the jealousy and suspicion of the school societies towards each other, and towards the State. Their major adventure into the field of educational legislation, the Factory Bill of 1843, was an attempt to circumvent these obstacles. Althorp's Factory Act of 1833 and Russell's Committee of Council of 1839 were only beginnings in their respective spheres; the former had not stilled the voices of industrial reform, nor the latter the voices of educational reform. The Conservatives in 1843 proposed to combine the two and lay the foundation for a national system of education through factory schools.

I DRAFTING THE BILL

The Hungry Forties made factory reform urgent. Four bad harvests in succession had increased the price of food; over-speculation and crash caused wages to decline. Those who could read the factory inspectors' reports, or the bankruptcy columns in the *Times*, did not dispute this; nor did Sir Robert Peel, Sir James Graham, and their supporters from manufacturing areas—the M.P.s J. Stuart Wortley (Wharncliffe's heir) and Beckett Denison of the West Riding and William Beckett of Leeds, the manufacturers Rand and Walker of Bradford. Their moderate policies, however, satisfied no interest group. Their factory and poor-law policies alienated short-timers and Chartists; their new corn law satisfied neither the Anti-Corn Law League nor their own agricultural wing; Whigs disliked the income tax. Peel's moderation extended to religious matters; he wanted to do what he could for the Church without alienating Dissent. Graham, the new Home Secretary, also was a moderate who believed that society, although needing improvement, was basically sound. His friends in the 1830s had been moderate administrative reformers; he distinguished himself in office then as a reforming First Lord of the Admiralty; he and Peel were in accord as to the problems of the day. He was also a moderate churchman who resigned from the Grey Ministry in 1834 because, although ready to reform ecclesiastical abuses, he opposed any measure that might injure the Established Church.[1]

Graham's thoughts turned to education after Henry Brougham urged him in October 1841 to consider a 'general parish plan' of State-supported education and followed up with two memoranda in January 1842, which Graham thought enough of to pass on to Peel. The Home Secretary, however, decided to revive the Factory Bill that the Whigs had advanced in 1839 and 1841; late in September he circularised the factory inspectors for their opinions on how the law should be changed. The inspectors who contributed most were those who had prepared the earlier Bills, Leonard Horner and R. J. Saunders. Graham selected them for their religious connections as much as for their expertise: Horner had influence with the Dissenters and Saunders with the Bishop of London. Although Horner has had the better press, Saunders was the more aware of the need for a thoroughgoing reform of factory education.[2]

Horner believed that the Factory Act's education clauses, although not perfect, were reasonably successful, and his ideas for improvement were vague. He pointed to the Poor Law Commission as a model to follow, but avoided specifics. He advocated common schools for all save Roman Catholics and Jews, who should have their own schools. As for the relationship between Church and Dissent, he suggested only that the former should have its rights and the latter its freedom of conscience. Before legislating, he believed, the government should create a commission to investigate the problem. Saunders's refrain, on the other hand, was 'the schools are not much improved'. Factory education appeared more often in his reports than in Horner's, and he had concrete plans, which Horner had not. Testifying before Lord Ashley's select committee on factories in 1840, he proposed Treasury building grants for factory schools. These schools, although governed by lay boards elected by the local subscribers, should have daily Scripture and Catechism classes, with episcopal approval required for both the teachers and the books used for religious training; the local clergymen could enter the schools at all times. His position had not changed by 1842, when, in a special report on factory schools, he recommended that schoolmasters should be churchmen and that the schools be used on Sundays for Anglican worship. He helped build National schools at Leeds and Bradford for factory children, and urged the society to support four experimental factory schools in his district. It is not surprising that the version of the Factory Bill produced under Graham's supervision had a strong Anglican tinge.[3]

Drafting of the measure began in January 1842. Kay-Shuttleworth claimed that Graham had accepted a plan that he had shown the Home Secretary. In fact he was only one member of a team that consulted Bishop Blomfield, prepared the clauses, and submitted them to Graham and Wharncliffe, the Lord President, for revision. The result was two Bills, one for factory children, the other for pauper children. The education clauses in the proposed Factory Bill would have created schools governed by elected local boards of managers who would have the right to choose the schoolmaster. Blomfield, however, disliked the clauses because they did not concede enough to the Church, and Graham dropped them.[4]

Then in the summer months of 1842 burst the strikes and riots in Lancashire and the Midlands. Graham in particular was deeply disturbed, since he believed that 'a manufacturing people is not so happy a people as a rural population, and this is the foretaste of becoming "the workshop of the world" '.[5] As pragmatic as Peel, Graham believed that

cheap bread, plenty of potatoes, low-priced American bacon, a little more Dutch cheese and butter, will have a more pacifying effect than all the mental culture which any government can supply.[6]

But Kay-Shuttleworth, 'tremulously sensitive to alarms', took a more apocalyptic view of affairs and urged Graham in August to tame the working classes with education. The Home Secretary thought that Kay-Shuttleworth's schemes were a 'nostrum' unlikely to correct immediate evils.[7] Nonetheless, given both the existing pressures for factory reform and Graham's own reforming personality, it seems likely that he would have returned to the Factory Bill even if the strikes had never occurred.[8] The unrest may have influenced the form which that legislation was to take. The National Society made a point of showing that Anglican workers had not participated in the riots; might this have led Graham to embrace Saunders's Anglican solution?[9]

The work of revising the Bill began quite late in the year, when Graham issued well-nigh impossible instructions to Saunders, Horner, and Kay-Shuttleworth, on 10 December, to

meet the views of the Bishop of London as far as you can, without . . . a rupture with the British and Foreign Society, whose perverseness at this juncture may defeat the last chance for the diffusion of education which has presented itself in our time.[10]

The clauses were complete by the 27th and received the sanction of the Archbishop of Canterbury and the Bishop of London a few days later. Graham's Bill, the most radical educational legislation yet sponsored by the government, proposed district schools open to all children in the area. An eight-man board of trustees, comprising the incumbent and churchwardens *ex officio*, two ratepayers and two millowners appointed by the justices of the peace for annual terms, and the donor of the schoolsite, were empowered to levy a school rate and appoint the master and his assistants, subject to the Diocesan's approval. The Bill required the master to lead the children in daily prayer and Sunday church attendance and the incumbent to catechise the children each day; Dissenters and Roman Catholics were permitted to study secular subjects in lieu of the Catechism. Existing schools that taught factory children and used the Anglican liturgy might come under the Bill's provisions, a clause applicable only to National schools. Finally, the Bill permitted employers to accept attendance certificates from other schools if school inspectors judged them 'efficiently conducted'.[11]

Although one cannot follow in detail the drafting of the Bill, it appears in broad outline that Saunders contributed the most. The congruity of his ideas with the Bill's provisions has led A. H. Robson, the historian of factory education, to attribute the pro-Anglican clauses to his influence. It has been alleged, however, that

Kay-Shuttleworth was responsible for the conscience clause. He told Russell, four months later, that in preparing the Bill he had done all he could 'to prevent the growth of any system which would interfere with a comprehensive scheme of combined education'; Saunders, who wanted the measure to require schoolmasters to be churchmen, complained to him of that omission. As Saunders had advocated a conscience clause since at least 1840, it is unlikely that he had to be convinced by Kay-Shuttleworth to include one in this Bill. No doubt Kay-Shuttleworth, an ardent anti-clericalist, did his best to defeat Saunders's ideas. He was unsuccessful.[12]

II   THE BILL'S CAREER

As the session of 1843 approached, Graham searched out support for his Bill. He approached the Bishop of Chester, through Wharncliffe the Bishop of Ripon, and even dropped a hint to Lansdowne.[13] He proposed, moreover, to use Lord Ashley, who had tabled a motion on education for late February. It has been supposed that Ashley's motion was a government blind, for Graham unveiled his measure during the debate.[14] But Ashley learned that that government would support his motion only three hours before he rose to speak, and in any case his pathological hatred of the Tory leadership would have prevented any co-operation with the Home Secretary.[15] Ashley's powerful speech on the occasion, which called the political nation to stave off revolution and immorality by providing sound education, is one of the better-known Victorian orations. For our purposes, however, it merely provided the perfect opportunity for Graham to announce his Bill. He declared that his measure sought to avoid both party and religious differences and to compromise without offending any scruples. Thus Roman Catholics could operate their own schools, the Church could veto the schoolmaster and had a representative on the board of trustees, and Dissent had a conscience clause.[16]

The reaction to Graham's proposal brought out objections that were to be the Bill's undoing. Lord John Russell declined to commit himself, observing only that the question ought not to be one of party or sect, and that on the basis of Graham's explanation the Bill seemed good. Other speakers were not so friendly. Lord Sandon, a former Young Gentleman, seconded by Augustus

Stafford O'Brien, a Whig, complained that Roman Catholic interests were unprotected and that Dissenters, although taxpayers, had no voice in selecting schoolmasters. Charles Buller and Sir R. H. Inglis raised objections from the left and from the right, but Benjamin Hawes, Radical M.P. for Lambeth, raised the most serious stumbling-block. Although public education was necessary to counteract 'certain periodicals' circulating in mill towns, he viewed the Bill with severe reservations. Hawes believed that the trusts' composition gave too much power to the Established Church. Since Dissenters would oppose such a scheme, he urged the Ministry to modify the clause.[17]

By the time the Bill received a second reading on 24 March the opposition had established itself both within and without the House, and what unanimity had existed a month before was lost. Criticism focused on six points: the method of choosing the schoolmaster, which effectively barred Nonconformists from the job; the difficulty the Bill presented for Roman Catholics, who would not read the Authorised Version; the constitution of the board of trustees, which gave the Church too much power; the Bill's poor economics, which would divert child labour from textiles to other areas; and, for backbench Tories, the measure's failure to give to the Church the final authority over the schools. A host of prominent M.P.s, including Sir George Grey, Thomas Milner Gibson, Benjamin Hawes, F. T. Baring, Joseph Hume, Thomas Dyke Acland, and Richard Cobden, joined in the attack. The Bill's formal approval on second reading fooled no one, and the Cabinet postponed further consideration until after Easter. Peel and Graham hoped that the month's respite would calm the Dissenting opposition and allow the Anglicans time to reorganise.[18]

The delay served only to give Dissent time to organise mass meetings in the provinces. The meetings, usually chaired by Dissenting ministers, passed resolutions condemning the Bill because it gave clerical control to the schools, offered Dissenters a 'degrading' alternative to Anglican catechising, interfered with the freedom of parents to choose their own schools and of mill owners to hire whom they pleased, and gave rate-levying powers to an irresponsible body. Roman Catholics also objected to their children being exposed to Protestant prayers and Bible-reading, and other groups—the Protestant Dissenting Deputies, the synod of the English Presbyterian Church, the Catholic Institute, the British and Foreign School Society—condemned the Bill.[19] The Methodists held their peace until mid-April. Graham had negotiated with them, but regretfully reported to Peel that they opposed concessions to either Anglicans or Roman Catholics in an unexpectedly hostile tone. The Home Secretary concluded that they had gone

the whole length of the bitterest dissent, and the sole reservation opposed to perfect equality of sects is against the Roman Catholics alone. It is quite clear that the Pusey tendencies of the Established Church have operated powerfuly on the Wesleyans, and are converting them rapidly into enemies.[20]

Ashley also attempted to conciliate the Wesleyans, interviewing Jabez Bunting, their leader, on the 26th. Bunting confirmed that hostility to the Puseyites had motivated the attacks. Although Bunting wanted to co-operate with the Established Church and the Conservative Party, he had lost control of his followers. 'The language in which we are vilified by [the Puseyites],' he told Ashley, 'so exasperates our people that we cannot restrain them.'[21]

If Dissent actively opposed the measure, working-class and Anglican opinion was indifferent. Chartists, who generally viewed the Churches as instruments of oppression, were hostile to the school societies and to any government measure that might strengthen them. The mass of workers held no strong religious feelings, attending church in rural districts where it was customary, but staying at home in towns. Against such indifferentism the religious appeals of the Bill's opponents and supporters would have had little impact. Some Chartists made the Bill an issue at the local level. At Halifax and Leeds, Chartists attempted to pack anti-Bill protest meetings in order to praise the shortening of the hours of child labour and to demand that the trustees be popularly elected, but this activity was designed to advance their own interests, not to further the Bill. Graham, indeed, could take comfort only from the *Times*'s left-handed support. Although withholding total approval of the measure, it declared that 'the main principle upon which it is based is, on the whole, not an unsound one'. A few Anglican organisations such as the Deanery of Manchester and the Huntingdonshire Education Board supported the Bill, and the Tory *Sheffield Mercury* urged supporters 'to make up with energy for past delay'. Such was the extent of popular pressure for the Bill.[22]

Its opponents mounted massive drives to petition Parliament

against the measure. Members presented the first petition, that of the Roman Catholic clergy of Manchester, on 21 March. Between then and 7 April, shortly before Graham announced his intention of modifying the Bill's educational clauses, a total of one petition for and 656 against the measure (the latter with 42,998 signatures) appeared in the Commons. Pressed by his party to do something, Lord John Russell introduced concrete proposals to modify the Bill on 10 April. His resolutions, designed to allay Nonconformist opposition, would have introduced elected trustees to the local education boards, allowed Roman Catholics to read the Douay Bible, and withdrawn religious training from the schoolmaster's hands. Graham drew the sting from the resolutions by announcing his intention to revise the measure along similar lines. The pressures remained, however. Between 10 and 28 April seven petitions supporting the measure, far overshadowed by the 6,299 opposing addresses, appeared on the table of the House.[23]

Graham and Kay-Shuttleworth revised the Bill, announcing the modifications to the House on 1 May. As a sop to prejudice, the Committee of Council could forbid Protestant children's attendance at schools maintained by Roman Catholic mill owners. Other changes sought to conciliate religious scruples and to open the school boards to candidates elected by the ratepayers. The revised Bill failed to please its opponents. Russell now joined other M.P.s in attacking the measure. Provincial assemblies continued to meet, pass resolutions against the Bill, and flood Parliament with petitions. Between 1 May and 17 June the House received 145 petitions supporting the measure as against 15,873 (with 2,602,010 signatures) in opposition. The *Times*'s lukewarm support cooled further. It now found the Bill's principles to be 'unworkable' because of the insuperable religious divisions.[24] Graham's tactic had thus failed.

It was clear that the Factory Bill was dead. Graham wanted to bring it to a vote, but the government decided to drop it in a sharply divided Cabinet on 15 June. Although Peel feared that the success of extra-parliamentary pressure in this case would put a 'premium on future agitation', [25] those who wished to drop the Bill saw the strong probability that the measure, if carried, would be unenforcible and would add resistance to the collection of rates to the existing tithe agitation. Wharncliffe, moreover, argued that good could be done by increasing the existing grant. Peel found the

Cabinet evenly divided: Stanley, Wellington, Buccleuch, Lyndhurst, Haddington, and Aberdeen voted to proceed; Graham, Ripon, Wharncliffe, Hardinge, Knatchbull, and Gladstone voted to drop the clauses. Peel settled the issue by choosing withdrawal.[26]

III   THE BILL'S ENEMIES

The opponents of the Factory Bill of 1843 did not reject working-class education *per se*. Why, then, did the Bill arouse such bitter disapproval? Graham's measure struck at almost everything that Nonconformists and middling-class manufacturers held dear: religious equality, fear of popery, jealousy of the landed interest, abhorrence of governmental intervention and bureaucracy. No measure could have been better designed to arouse these interest groups, awakening as they were from their eighteenth-century torpor to discover that they were masters in the workshop of the world.

Most opposition to the measure took the form of a cry for religious liberty. Opponents deemed the proposal bigoted because it was a direct attack on Nonconformists and Roman Catholics. The measure would have created Anglican-dominated schools and the conscience clauses would not have provided sufficient safeguards. But deeper religious fears underlay this opposition, for the Bill was deemed 'unscriptural', 'delusive', and 'conducive to the propagation of error'.[27] The Church of England was

a system of spurious christianity, with its baptismal regeneration, its apostolical succession, its confirmation and absolution, its creeds and formularies, scarcely less opposed to the revealed will of God.[28]

The problem was that the appearance of Tract XC in 1841 had blown away the precarious balance within the Church between High and Low schools, and seemed a sign to Dissent that the Establishment was drifting up the Tiber. Graham's Bill, which benefited this semi-papist Church, declared Edward Baines, Jr., editor of the *Leeds Mercury*, had been produced by R. J. Saunders, that 'very zealous and bigoted High Churchman'. Dissenters could not allow their children to be placed under the supervision of clergymen tending to Rome.[29]

Dissenters also feared that the Bill would perpetuate landed, aristocratic values by entrusting children's plastic minds to men subservient to upper-class Anglican monarchical ideals. Children inculcated with the spirit of Toryism would lose 'the free spirit and brave thoughts which constitute the noblest heritage of man'. Thus Dissenters took the Bill's limitation to industrial areas as a calculated insult, for aristocratic reformers always painted in darkest colours the condition of the industrial districts and never admitted that mill towns were 'the seats of industry, intelligence, virtue, and religion'. Aristocratic Westminster, moreover, had more brothels than anywhere else in England; the Dean and Chapter of Westminster permitted such stews to exist, yet forbade Protestant worship on their property. Thus the Bill attacked Dissent rather than vice.[30]

Finally, opposition to the measure reflected at least three issues related to the *laissez-faire* economic doctrines prevailing in middling-class and Radical circles. First, the Bill offended those interested in governmental retrenchment, for it would require an expanded civil service and inspectorate, interfere in the parental right to choose schools, and open up endless areas for the State to extend its powers. The second issue involved the belief that the laws of the market place should govern the schoolroom. Opponents of the measure feared unfair competition from the district schools; with assured funding from local taxation, they might become so much better than existing schools that the latter would lose their pupils. The Bill would have regulated silk mills excluded from the Act of 1833 and reduced the hours of child labour from eight to six and a half per day. Ever opposed to the limitation of labour, the Baineses of Leeds seized upon these changes. This last debating point hardly attracted the attention that others did; it was but a tinkle in the cacaphony emanating from the West Riding.[31]

Adherents of the Church of England played a passive role in the Bill's downfall. The bulk of the Establishment, lukewarm to begin with, cooled further after Graham bowed to the opposition and were indifferent to the plan's demise. Many bishops were suspicious, disliking its concessions to Dissent; some Evangelicals feared that the measure favoured the Puseyite wing of the Church; High Churchmen protested the Bill's latitudinarianism, finding in the scheme 'a colouring of Church principles, but it is only skin deep', for it granted the sects equal privileges with 'the one true faith'. Even Ashley and Gladstone, predisposed towards the measure, strained at Graham's assurances that the schoolmaster would not teach doctrine or proselytise.[32] The National Society and the Church, which had accepted the Concordat of 1840 reluctantly because it admitted State supervision and aid to the sects, observed that Graham's measure, although giving the Church preferential treatment, still conceded a conscience clause to Dissenters and maintained the principle of State control. Determined to exercise its canonical and prescriptive right to be the educator of the nation, it opposed any concessions to Dissent.[33]

How could Graham's Factory Bill, designed to do all it could for the Church without alienating Dissent, have safely weathered the passage between the Scylla of Anglican prerogative and the Charybdis of Nonconformist discontent?

IV   THE BILL'S SIGNIFICANCE

What greater significance has this episode; how important really was the demise of the Factory Bill, 1843? To be sure, even counting the others eligible to attend the district schools, it is unlikely that many more than 30,000 children would have benefited in 1843, and the Bill would have affected significantly only Lancashire and the West Riding, where most of the factory children were to be found. Hence only a tiny portion of the population lost when Graham withdrew his measure.[34]

Rather, its importance lies in part in its might-have-beens. Factory district schools were free from the stigma attached to pauper district schools, and Graham envisaged their growing to encompass the entire country. 'If I succeed in large cities and the manufacturing districts,' he wrote, 'my plan is easily capable of extension.'[35] The Factory Bill of 1843 was an attempt to lay the foundation for a national system of education: rate-aided schools, governed by local boards of education, open to children of all sects, and subject to the supervision of the Committee of Council. The Bill's failure had profound effects upon the supporters of combined education. Slaney, Ashley, Howick, and Kay-Shuttleworth all concluded from the episode that a public education scheme ought never to be raised again.[36] It was certainly the case that the Peel Ministry drew back; the Factory Bill of 1844 made no provision for schools.

If this episode represents a signal defeat for the forces for combined education, it also saw the first great triumph for that Nonconformist propaganda machine operated so well by the Anti-Corn Law League. The agitation of 1843 was carefully orchestrated, with speakers, petitions, resolution, movers, and seconders prepared in advance. The discipline is evident when one examines the petitions presented to the House of Commons. Petitioning against the Factory Bill began on 21 March; after seven weeks 13,369 memorials bearing 2,068,059 signatures had been tabled. Then petitions of this nature ceased to arrive; not a single petition 'that the bill might not be passed into law' arrived after 9 May. Instead, on 12 May, petitions 'against the amended clauses' began arriving; by 17 July the House had been swamped by 12,150 memorials bearing 1,972,946 signatures. These petitions, far from being a spontaneous expression of public sentiment, were designed to maximise the number of documents deluging the House. On 4 April, for instance, William Aldam, Whig M.P. for Leeds, presented 234 petitions. Their signers, however, totalled only 450 names. Hence most of the petitions must have been signed by only one or two people. Clearly, someone in the provinces could turn petitions on or off like tap water.[37] So 'political Dissent' had scored its first triumph; after 1843 it pursued greater quarry.

The religious history of the 1840s is dominated by militant Nonconformity, both Roman Catholic and Protestant, and the Church, itself split over Tractarianism, was caught between. If the Papal Aggression of 1850 symbolises the challenge to Protestantism inherent in Roman Catholicism's 'second spring', then the defeat of the Factory Bill reflects Dissent's ability to deny the Church the privileges of establishment in the name of religious equality. As Norman Gash puts it,

> The lesson of the crisis was clear . . . . The Church of England, as a State establishment, could no longer in practice call upon the State either for wider pastoral privileges or even for peculiar financial assistance. This in itself marked a fundamental change in Church-State relationships which no amount of Anglican activity or confidence could undo.[38]

Yet 'political Dissent' had secured its victory in 1843 at the expense of a measure that might have provided England with the basis of a State school system thirty years before Forster's Act. It was not to be, and the State now had to decide what was to be done.

Chapter IX

THE ROLE ESTABLISHED, 1843–48

The defeat of Graham's Factory Bill forced the Committee of Council to expand its influence through administration. Lord Lansdowne had thought it a virtue that the schoolhouse grant was 'of a temporary nature, that it can be modified at pleasure, that it can be revised at any moment, and that it can be enlarged on any future occasion . . .'.[1] The Conservatives agreed, preferring 'the cautious and gradual extension of the power and the pecuniary means' of the Committee of Council to any legislation, especially after the failure of the Factory Bill.[2] This quiet growth occurred: by 1848, the State offered grants-in-aid for teacher training, dwellings, salaries, books, supplies, and playgrounds. That these new grants existed is well known, but a study of their implications is enlightening. What were the sources of the grants? Did Conservative and Whig policies differ? How did educational pressure groups react to the extension of the State's role?

I TORY POLICY: SETTING THE COURSE

First, the Conservatives had to complete the unfinished business of 1843. The Factory Act of 1844 permitted schoolmasters to deduct fees from each child's wages and gave factory inspectors the powers to disallow school certificates and to allocate to education the fines collected for breaches of the law. In addition, the Poor Law Amendment Act of 1844 finally authorised the creation of pauper district schools in London and a few other conurbations. The State thus abandoned a decade of experimentation to segregate pauper and working children in their own special-interest schools. The main thrust of Conservative activity, however, was in the realm of administration. Meeting in Cabinet shortly after the Factory Bill had been withdrawn, Peel, Graham, Lord Stanley, Henry Goulburn and W. E. Gladstone vetoed Wharncliffe's proposal to extend aid to Roman Catholic and Wesleyan schools. But Peel suggested that the scope of the grant be enlarged by using public funds to build masters' dwellings.[3] After consulting with the National Society, Wharncliffe instituted the new regime in November. He began by settling the long festering dispute with the British Society over inspection. Tremenheere was transferred to the Home Office and Wharncliffe acceded to the British Society's demand for a concordat, agreeing to submit his nominee for inspector of British schools to that society for approval. The precedent of 1840 was thus confirmed; school inspectors, appointed along denominational lines, must be acceptable to the sect whose schools they inspected.[4]

In the same month the Committee of Council promulgated the Education Minute of 22 November, which offered grants for building masters' dwellings and for the purchase of teaching apparatus and furniture. The school inspectors, especially John Allen, had alluded in their reports to the need for adequate books, slates, maps, and playgrounds, and the minute only regularised prior practice. In 1841–42, for instance, the Committee of Council awarded three grants to build masters' residences and one each for 'fittings' and a playground. More important, Sandon and Sinclair of the National Society had urged Wharncliffe on to expand the grant. The committee also brought into operation the long-neglected minute of 3 December 1839, for special cases. The Disruption of the Church of Scotland made this necessary, for the newly created Free Church had to build an entire school system from scratch. But the precedent for aid to Scottish schools unconnected with the Kirk had been set earlier; by 1844 the Committee of Council had already aided in Scotland one Roman Catholic, two Episcopal, four non-denominational schools, and one connected with the Infant School Society. By 1848 the State had aided thirty Free Church schools.[5]

In a related move, Wharncliffe secured legislation in 1844 to enable endowed schools to obtain aid from the Committee of Council. The trustees of small endowed schools were unable to meet the Committee of Council's inspection requirement, for their trust deeds (modifiable only in Chancery—which is to say, not modifiable at all) usually stipulated who the visitors were to be.

(The perceptive John Allen had brought this problem to Wharncliffe's attention.) His measure, the 'Education of the Poor Act' (7 and 8 Vict., cap. 37), which passed through Parliament in May and June 1844, provided that, the terms of any charitable endowment notwithstanding, it would be lawful for school inspectors to examine such schools.[6]

An increased grant was one weapon in Wharncliffe's armoury; another was an expanded inspectorate. The Lord President instructed inspectors in August 1843 to pay closer attention to each school's financial condition than had hitherto been the case, and in December 1844 to inspect the schools that had received aid from the Treasury before 1839. (The Whigs continued this trend by assuming the inspection of pauper schools in December 1846.) Further, Wharncliffe had Kay-Shuttleworth prepare plans for systematic visitations of schools in industrial and mining areas. The added grants and increased tasks demanded more labour from the inspectors and generated more correspondence for the overburdened clerks, so Wharncliffe appointed five new school inspectors in 1844 and enlarged the Education Department's establishment in 1845. More important, he asked the Cabinet in 1845 to increase the education estimate from £40,000 to £150,000. Here he lost to the objections of Henry Goulburn, Chancellor of the Exchequer, who feared that such a rise would annoy Roman Catholics, Congregationalists, and Wesleyans, who did not participate in the State's largesse. (And, of course, Peel's fiscal policy pledged budget surpluses to cover the abolition of customs duties.) Wharncliffe had to rest content with an increase to £75,000.[7]

Goulburn's concern was justified, for having been defeated in open combat the government was charting a delicate and circuitous course between right and left. Hence the Peel Ministry's spokesmen in Parliament did not advertise their policy. When Thomas Wyse asked Graham in February 1844 whether the government planned, 'by increased pecuniary grants, or new regulations, to give greater efficiency and extension' to the Committee of Council, the Home Secretary evaded the issue. The next year, J. C. Colquhoun asked Goulburn whether the committee planned to change its regulations, there being 'some little uneasiness on the subject in the public mind'. The Chancellor of the Exchequer denied that such was the government's plan. Such glib responses annoyed the educational left; William Ewart, the Radical, countered with an annual motion demanding a detailed oral explanation of the education vote to match those for the military, naval, and ordnance estimates. Although Peel and, later, Charles Wood, Russell's Chancellor of the Exchequer, agreed to the proposal's expediency in 1846, the first such statement was not made until 1851.[8]

Lord Wharncliffe died on 19 December 1845; his successor as Lord President, the Duke of Buccleuch, did not join the Committee of Council until the end of January of the following year. By then the potato blight and the corn law crisis had put an end to further Tory educational programmes. Wharncliffe, however, had shown how the State might avoid the religious question yet still play an active role in education. By extending the grant to cover purposes other than the building of schoolhouses his minute of November 1843 initiated a process that led to State support for teachers' stipends, capitation grants, and payment by results. Greville's assessment of Wharncliffe's career seems fair:

. . . he addressed himself to the Education Department with great zeal and labour. He conducted it very fairly and liberally, too liberally for the High Churchmen, who regarded him with distrust and dislike, and who were deeply offended at the plainspoken way in which he rebuked them for their obstinate and illiberal counteraction of the beneficent intentions of the Government. He had not weight enough, however, in the Cabinet to obtain as great an extension of the system as he would have desired.[9]

II WHIG POLICY: THE MINUTES OF 1846

The Whigs put education on the agenda of reforms when they returned to power in 1846, but their programmes, in their essence, were logical extensions of Conservative policy. This was true of the Whigs' first and most dramatic policy: government subsidies for the training of teachers.

The Whig Committee of Council, on 25 August 1846, produced a curious directive to Lord Lansdowne, the Lord President. Heeding the numerous memorials that it had received from local boards of education, school inspectors, clergy, and gentry (all of which recommended that bright children be apprenticed to assist schoomasters), the committee instructed Lansdowne to draft such a programme, and to consider pensions and gratuities for schoolmasters. Four months later appeared the Education Minute of 21 December 1846, which created a comprehensive system of State-supported apprenticeship and teacher training. Managers of schools approved by the inspectors could nominate good students, at least thirteen years old, to five-year apprenticeships as 'pupil-teachers' under the master. (For schools where the master could not provide the required extra instruction the inferior position of 'stipendiary monitor' was created.) Pupil-teachers and stipendiary monitors received salaries of £10 and £5 respectively at the end of their first year; success in annual examinations brought increments of £2 10s. The minute further created 'Queen's Scholarships' of £20–£25 to enable pupil-teachers to attend normal schools. The normal schools themselves would receive grants of up to £30 per scholar for each of the three years of the course. Schoolmasters who had attended normal school or who supervised pupil-teachers were eligible for annual stipends from the government in addition to their regular salaries; they could apply, after at least fifteen years of service, for retiring pensions of no more than two-thirds of their annual salaries.[10]

The minutes of 1846, a watershed in the history of British education, dictated the internal organisation of elementary schools and introduced payment by results, a Victorian panacea to ensure a well trained administrative class. Whence did the idea come? Kay-Shuttleworth claimed sixteen years later that he had devised the idea for pupil-teachers in 1837, and that after he moved to the London district he created a model school at Norwood to put the idea into effect. This is a myth, for he was indebted to foreign sources. He based his ideas, he told the Slaney Committee in 1838, on visits to Holland, to the Edinburgh and Glasgow normal schools, and to Lady Bryon's school at Ealing. Kay-Shuttleworth and E. C. Tufnell, his colleague on the Poor Law Commission, expanded the experiment in 1840 when they founded the Battersea Training School for apprenticed students. The apprentices studied at Battersea for three years and served as pupil-teachers in the Battersea Village school for two. At the end of this five-year period they would, if passing an examination, become salaried 'assistant teachers' in selected pauper schools for the last two years of their indenture.[11]

Kay-Shuttleworth's visits in the late 1830s broke no new ground, for others could visit the Continent, or Scotland (where the General

Assembly's Education Committee was in the process of regularising the position of assistant teachers), or else read translations of Victor Cousin's reports on the Dutch and Prussian school systems. (By 1845 factory and school inspectors recommended aid to assistant teachers and apprentices as a matter of fact.) Two such tours occurred in 1834, when Philip Pusey and Thomas Dyke Acland visited Prussia and Switzerland. Thus Continental practices entered the discussions of the Young Gentlemen and influenced the plans of 1838. Their effect on the National Society is evident. Between 1836 and 1840 the society substituted for monitorialism the use of apprenticed pupil-teachers at the local level in York, Salisbury, and Ripon, and at the Central School, Westminster. By 1845 the Diocese of London possessed a well articulated system of teacher-training in which children served as assistant teachers for three or four years, followed by two years at a training college. To the National Society, 'assistant teacher' was much more than old monitor writ large. In contrast, the British Society, under the conservative hand of its secretary, Henry Dunn, clung to monitorialism until 1847, and only ten of the seventy-five students at the Borough Road School in 1852 were pursuing as much as a full year's course. The explanation of the difference between the two societies lies in the influence of the Young Gentlemen. Through their stimulus the National Society devised a pupil-teacher system independently of Kay-Shuttleworth.[12]

Conservative policy, furthermore, was directly responsible for the State's adoption of the pupil-teacher system, as Buccleuch's response to the minutes of 1846 suggests: 'I believe that upon nearly every one of the points we have upon previous occasions had discussions . . .'[13]

After the government's normal-school proposal of 1839 had been defeated, the Committee of Council instituted annual maintenance grants to the two Scottish normal schools, and to those of the National and British Societies. And there the matter rested, until the Conservatives reassessed their educational policy in 1843. The Education Minute of November 1843 abolished for the future the annual maintenance grant for normal schools, allowing only these grants already awarded to be paid out. This move freed Wharncliffe to draft a plan of apprenticeship that would have offered normal schools grants of £20–£25 for each student who, after a year's attendance, was certified by the inspector to be competent. He dropped the plan, however, perhaps because it did not answer the special problems of teacher-training, and announced in January 1844 a stop-gap building grant of £50 per student place for new normal schools.[14] That bought him time to refine his ideas. He ordered Kay-Shuttleworth in November to draft a plan providing for

A system of apprenticeship of the most promising scholars who would receive an annual stipend from the government.

A system of rewarding the masters of the elementary schools.

A system whereby the apprentices would assist the master in conducting his school.[15]

Kay-Shuttleworth's proposal was a more sophisticated version of the draft plan of 1843. He suggested that the Committee of Council select pupil-teachers to study under a master; both masters and pupil-teachers would receive modest annual grants from the State, and the latter could also compete for scholarships for one year's study at a normal college. A pension plan was tacked on to the programme.[16]

Wharncliffe sent the plan on to Peel at the end of November; Kay-Shuttleworth told Blomfield early in 1845 that the question was 'waiting at the threshold for discussion'; in the House in July, Peel acknowledged the importance of 'a proper provision for the masters'. The government, however, did nothing. Although supporters of Church education would have welcomed State subvention of salaries, financial apprehensions, Wharncliffe's death, and the corn law crisis prevented any action. Peel, unhappy with the growth of the education budget, was even more dismayed at the estimated cost of Wharncliffe's plans; Goulburn, a financial conservative, resisted any extension of the State's role unsanctioned by legislation. Without the wherewithal Wharncliffe could not pursue his plans, and his death in December removed the architect of Tory education policy; the Duke of Buccleuch, his successor, was less interested in the question.[17]

The ministerial crisis of December 1845 raised Kay-Shuttleworth's hopes; he hurriedly prepared a memorandum, 'The Present Condition of the Administration of the Parliamentary Grant', in the expectation that Lord Lansdowne would take office. Kay-Shuttleworth advocated that the Whigs adopt and carry out two schemes that Wharncliffe had proposed: the endowment of elementary schools (plans for which he had shown the Bishop of

London) and 'the general adaptation of the plan pursued in the Diocese of London'—the pupil-teacher system. The paper continued with concrete suggestions about the terms of apprenticeships, stipends for both pupils and masters, exhibitions for a year's stay at a normal college, and a plan for retiring pensions. After it had become clear that Peel's Ministry could not engage in educational experimentation Kay-Shuttleworth had his memorandum printed and circulated it to friends in January 1846. The government dragged on, the Committee of Council met only twice, and nothing was done until the Whigs returned to power in July.[18]

Yet they were strangely reticent. Lord John Russell evaded questions about teacher training on the 17th, and five weeks later the Committee of Council issued a sketchy outline, but delayed the final minute until December. The government's concern was religious rather than educational: the minutes' educational content was taken for granted in the internal discussions; Ministers were more concerned with the religious implications. Since neither Church-controlled nor combined education was feasible, the government produced a programme that it hoped would be acceptable to the school societies. The minutes, presented to Parliament on 5 February 1847, provoked the hostility of both Radicals and the Bainesocracy. In the House, Thomas Duncombe, J. A. Roebuck, and Sir William Clay denounced the measure on almost every possible ground. It invaded civil and religious liberty; it would prove expensive; its provisions for industrial training would put children into competition with skilled artisans; it confused secular and religious training. They realised that the minutes were a further block to national education. In the provinces, Edward Baines attempted to duplicate his success of 1843, raising the spectres of Continental bureaucratic despotism and creeping popery. Bainesites fought the education question at the general election in the summer, scoring some notable triumphs. Roebuck lost at Bath, William Aldam at Leeds, Hobhouse at Nottingham and Macaulay at Edinburgh; other Whigs retained their seats only by promising to vote against future education grants. Nevertheless the Whigs did well, considering the enmity of 'political Dissent'.[19]

III   WHIG POLICY: THE MINUTES OF 1847

The attitude of the Wesleyans was a major factor in the government's success. This time they supported the State as they had not in 1839 and 1843. Russell told the House that the Wesleyans wanted their education committee to have the same status as that of the British Society, but his enemies accused him of having made a deal. J. A. Roebuck and Sir Benjamin Hall understood the government to have promised that Roman Catholics would be excluded from the grant, that the Wesleyans would be allowed to use their own catechism, and that inspectors of Wesleyan schools would themselves be Wesleyans. His enemies were correct. The Wesleyans wanted a concordat in order to obtain aid for their schools, but like the dog in the manger they also wished to exclude Roman Catholics from the State's largesse. They could not hold out indefinitely, however, against the blandishments of State aid; their educational arm, the Wesleyan Education Committee, had never been rich and was now quite short of funds. Hence it actively sought State aid, approaching the Committee of Council in 1843, and some of its schools actually received money grants from factory inspectors. Throughout 1846, moreover, it carefully monitored the government's educational activities. Thus the dual influences of the Wesleyans' own needs and Lord Ashley's careful preliminary negotiations brought the Wesleyan Education Committee to accept the government's views.[20]

Russell and Lansdowne obtained Wesleyan support for the minute of 1846 by arriving at a compromise. The Committee of Council agreed to recognise the Wesleyan Education Committee as the superintending body for Wesleyan schools, to consult it before appointing inspectors, and to issue its inspectors instructions similar to those of the British inspectors. The government coupled with this concordat a stipulation to the effect that aid under the minute of 1846 was limited to schools that used the Authorised Version of the Scriptures. But accompanying this public concordat was a private statement to the effect that the government planned eventually to draft a minute extending aid to Roman Catholics. In return for abandoning 'political Dissent' the Wesleyans received a concordat and a public statement of Roman Catholic inferiority.[21]

Nevertheless, the exclusion of Roman Catholics from the minute of 1846 provoked opposition and Russell was forced to state publicly what he had told the Wesleyans in private. He declared on 26 April 1847 that there was 'no intention whatever of excluding the Catholics from the benefits of the grant', but was vague about when the government would prepare a special minute. Roman Catholics wanted State aid so long as they exercised 'the *unfettered* command of such temporal means', and, like the Wesleyans, had approached the State earlier. The government's chief concern, however, was to avoid enraging Protestants. Kay-Shuttleworth suggested four conditions to any offer of aid: lay inspectors, aid for secular teaching only, a mandatory conscience clause, and support for the salaries of lay teachers and pupil-teachers only. Russell and Lansdowne accepted most of these stipulations when they drafted the Education Minute of 18 December 1847. It provided that no inspector would be appointed without the concurrence of the Roman Catholic Poor School Committee; the inspectors, who in practice were laymen, were to examine only secular training, and no person in holy orders was eligible for government stipends.[22]

By the same minute the Committee of Council extended the range of grants offered by the State to include the purchase of secular textbooks, more expensive and less easily obtainable than the Bible, the traditional reader. It is at first attractive to think that Kay-Shuttleworth might have been responsible for this minute, since he had an interest in textbooks. He had encouraged workhouse schools to use books from the Edinburgh Sessional School and the Irish education commissioners, and himself published two phonic readers for Battersea in 1843. But other people than Kay-Shuttleworth wanted cheap textbooks. Sir George Grey recommended in 1842 that the Committee of Council follow the example of the Irish education commissioners and publish schoolbooks; the factory inspectors Saunders and Horner and the school inspectors Tremenheere, Noel, Allen, Gibson, Fletcher, Moseley, and Cook repeatedly recommended that schools under their purview be helped to buy good books. (Wharncliffe's Committee of Council actually granted such aid to one school.) Most important, Wharncliffe himself discussed the possibility of grants to help schools buy books from an approved list with Lord Sandon, a former Young Gentleman, and John Sinclair, the National Society's secretary. Thus Wharncliffe and his Conservative Committee of Council had considered the essence of the book minute four years before Russell and Lansdowne adopted it. The expansion of teacher training meant that these precedents had to be translated into stated policy. In July 1847 Kay-Shuttleworth requested the inspectorate to submit recommended texts for 'a list of books combining cheapness with merit'; the Committee of Council issued a minute in December explaining the conditions on which it would provide one-third of the purchase price of books from the official list. Added to this was the privilege of purchasing the books from the committee's distributor at substantially reduced rates.[23] Thus the minutes of 1847 further extended the role of the State by bringing two more groups within the pale and adding another strand to the Committee of Council's financial web. These policies, one must keep in mind, had their roots in Tory thinking.

IV   RELIGIOUS FRAGMENTATION

The extension of the government's role threw both the British and the National societies into disarray. Both had factions that suspected any move towards secular control, and the extension of the State's role in 1846–47 was for many the last straw.

The strains in the British Society appeared over the issue of government aid and non-denominationalism. After the society's General Committee had accepted a government grant of £750 per annum for the Borough Road School in 1845, Congregationalists, Presbyterians, and Unitarians rejected the decision and recommended that its members support denominational schools. This turn to denominationalism was serious, for it struck at the heart of the British ideal, non-sectarian education. Other Dissenters such as Samuel Morley and Edward Miall, founders of the Liberation Society, and the editors of the *Eclectic Review* reacted to the government's encroachments by advocating the separation of Church and State. Disturbed at this tendency, the moderate Congregationalist Robert Vaughan founded in 1845 his own journal, the *British Quarterly Review*, which supported the government's role in education. The minutes of 1846, however, alienated the moderates. Despite the precautions the government had taken, the rights of conscience, Vaughan believed, were damaged; Dissenters had to pay for the support of Anglican religious training. Dissent must insist on a conscience clause for all schools in receipt of State aid.[24]

Concerned to defuse hostility, the government gladly adopted Benjamin Hawes's suggestion not to require reports on religious training in schools employing pupil-teachers. By a 'supplementary minute' of July 1847 the Committee of Council decreed that school managers who objected to such reports would still be eligible for aid under the minute of 1846. The tactic worked, at least partially. Vaughan welcomed the minute as 'a valuable concession'; John Bright, although supporting voluntaryism in theory, declined to take any active part in the public discussions. The concession came too late, however, to help the British Society. In April 1847 a group of ultra-voluntaryists led by Joseph Sturge, the Bainesite parliamentary candidate from Leeds, requested a special general meeting of the British Society to scrutinise the government proposals. The Congregationalists attempted to place the society on record as against State aid of any kind, but the moderates, led by Lord Monteagle and Dr Stephen Lushington, a long-time supporter of State aid, defeated them by a majority of two to one. The result was that the Congregationalists and their supporters left the British Society to operate their own schools purely with voluntary contributions. The society lost about £1,700 in annual donations.[25]

The National Society also had deep fissures, although these took longer to reveal themselves. That society's immediate response to the failure of Graham's Factory Bill was to launch a special fund for schools in the manufacturing areas. To be sure, the working-class riots of 1842 provided a mighty stimulus, but it is equally certain that the fund was a response to the failure of Graham's attempt at national education. The society's literature abounds with references to the Bill's failure, the Queen was told that that was the stimulus for the fund, and Thomas Tancred, the fund's main instigator, testified that its failure had prompted him to act. The special fund of 1843 was in a sense the last fruit of the seeds which the Young Gentlemen had planted in 1838. (Tancred and Sir Robert Peel, who edited the public appeal, consulted Gladstone, Acland, Wood, Sinclair, and Mathison.) But the Young Gentlemen broke up under the impact of State intervention.[26]

Gladstone at first held strictly to his earlier defence of the Church's right to educate the nation, opposing Acland's suggestion of 1840 that the Tories propose an increase in the education estimate, because he feared 'the dangerous character of the Committee of Council', which might give aid to 'every creed alike'. The Factory Bill of 1843, however, made him face a conundrum: he did not want to limit the Church's right to teach, but he recognised that Dissenters must be allowed a conscience clause. (Thus he kept his own school at Oak Farm independent, because he opposed the National Society's strict requirement that the Catechism be used.) By 1853 he had concluded that 'separate and independent subsidies to the various religious denominations' was the only solution. Other supporters of Anglican education, such as W. F. Hook and Thomas Dyke Acland, came to similar conclusions. By 1848, moreover, strains caused by the rise of ritualism within the Oxford Movement had made themselves felt in the National Society. St Mark's College, Chelsea, the training school for men, was in financial trouble and had received adverse reports from the school inspector. Its chapel service, moreover, was suspect. Rumours grew that the officiant bowed when saying' 'The Lord be with you', turned eastward for the Creed, and intoned the *Te Deum*. Concerned, Acland, Sinclair, and the Bishops of London and Salisbury tried to prevent a public scandal.[27]

The National Society's troubles came to a head in 1848 over the 'Management Clauses' controversy. In rural areas often only a National school existed; Dissenters had either to send their children to Anglican schools or to no school at all. Hence they applied pressure on the government in 1846 and 1847 to compel all schools receiving State aid, or at least in single-school areas, to adopt a conscience clause. The Committee of Council was not unwilling, for it opposed both exclusive schools and the National Society's policy of giving the Diocesan the authority to mediate disputes within the local school committee. It issued the Management Clauses in 1846; these defined the composition of local school committees and limited the powers of the clergy.[28] The controversy over the clauses precipitated an open split in the National Society in 1848

The moderates in the society—Gladstone, Sandon, Acland, Samuel Wilberforce, Edward Denison, Bishop of Salisbury, and John Bird Sumner, the new Archbishop of Canterbury—were not averse either to management or to conscience clauses if they could write their own, but they were hard pressed from all sides. The National Society needed government aid; the special fund of 1843 had been exhausted and appeals for more donations were unsuccessful. Its right wing, led by the uncompromising G. A. Denison, Vicar of East Brent and brother of the Bishop of Salisbury, objected to any agreement short of absolute independence. In any event, negotiations with the State were difficult, for Lansdowne persisted in not answering his letters. The result was confusion and the loss of a single, strong voice for Church education.[29]

Thus by 1848 the pressures and dilemmas of voluntaryism versus State intervention had destroyed the unity of both school societies. On the one hand, the expansion of the State's role in education, even within the limitations of the schoolhouse grant, threatened their autonomy. On the other, they had not the resources to reject the State's pecuniary support and still operate schools on the scale necessary to meet educational needs. The result was internal disunity, and they found themselves in an even weaker position *vis-à-vis* the State.

V CONTINUITY OF POLICY

There is a continuity of government education policy, whether Tory or Whig, after the failure of Graham's Bill of 1843. Since any legislative programme seemed impossible, Peel's and Russell's Ministries were thrown back on to the grant of 1833 itself, and had to develop its possibilities. They found that the grant was not limited to the building of schoolhouses, that it could be extended to cover books, furnishings, masters' dwellings, playgrounds and gardens, and the salaries of masters and assistant teachers, without departing from the administrative structure laid down in 1839. There were, moreover, precedents for most of the extensions of 1843–47. Although one cannot argue that these precedents were set as part of a conscious policy of covertly extending the State's influence, they indicate that the Committee of Council did not see itself as limited for all time to the Education Minute of 24 September 1839.

The committee certainly knew what it was about, both before and after Graham's Bill, and the image of it rubber-stamping Kay-Shuttleworth's decisions is false. Wharncliffe, for instance, paid close attention to the Education Department's activities. He knew that the committee had aided schools independent of either school society and kept himself informed of its activities and financial position. He negotiated with both school societies himself; he constantly urged an increase in the department's budget. The minute of November 1843 and the policy discussions of 1844 show that he was a creative head of the Committee of Council. Lansdowne was also an able Lord President. His presentation of the minutes of 1846 to the House of Lords demonstrates a firm grasp of the problem and the proposed solution. He and Russell co-operated in negotiating with pressure groups and in drafting the supplementary minute of July 1847. Although the correspondence was sent out over Kay-Shuttleworth's signature, he was by no means the initiator. Generally, he and Lansdowne discussed the outline of a letter; after preparing a draft, he sent it to Lansdowne and Russell for correction and approval. With regard to the minutes of 1846, Kay-Shuttleworth was charged with developing details such as the terms of apprenticeship or the size of stipends, and worked to the orders of his superiors. His only known independent act was to print and circulate his memorandum to Lord Lansdowne in December 1845. It seems fair to conclude that Lansdowne was no more a pawn in Kay-Shuttleworth's hands than was Wharncliffe.[30]

Politicians, not administrators, made educational policy after 1843. The basic line was laid down to a Cabinet council, and politicians guided its development. The influence of educational pressure groups had relatively little to do with shaping the several minutes between 1843 and 1847. Only the Church participated in the actual drafting of minutes such as those of 1846; the government consulted other groups only when the minutes were completed (save when a minute referred specifically to a particular group, as did the concordats with the Wesleyans and the Roman Catholics).

Dissension within the societies strengthened the government's hand. The education budget tripled in size between 1844 and 1848, from £40,000 to £125,000; the money went largely to supplement stipends. Although the financial benefits of the minutes of 1846 did not reach the training colleges until about 1852 (when the education budget doubled again), they almost immediately increased the income of local schools.[31] It was difficult to forego these benefits, simply to prevent the school inspector from examining the pupils and enquiring more closely than before into a school's affairs. Substantial groups, however, did turn their backs to the State, and the school societies, which had treated with the State as equals since 1833, now found themselves weakened.

Chapter X

CONCLUSION

Since Kitson Clark's call of 1960 for the restoration of religion to its central role in Victorian history our understanding of that great age of faith has increased. Still, it is difficult in our secular age to understand the religious concerns and hostilities that plagued the education question, and some may be tempted to conclude with F. A. Cavanagh that the Church 'constantly impeded the progress of education'. Such a conclusion combines malignant unwillingness to understand an alien ideology with uncritical acceptance of the idea of progress. James Murphy's observation is much more sensible: 'It would be extremely wrong to think of the state as continually straining to establish an admirable system of education, but being thwarted by the churches.'[1]

The Church did not object to State intervention as such. In 1839, for instance, it believed that the Central Society of Education and political Radicals in general were behind a government move to import into England the Irish system, which limited sectarian training to the last hour of the school day. Such compartmentalisation denied that Christian values should pervade all education, implied that doctrinal differences were not central to Christianity, and downgraded the importance of catechising in the minds of both teachers and students. The denials of Lansdowne, Russell, and Kay-Shuttleworth were of no avail, and churchmen remained suspicious until Conservatives were in power and it appeared that the Committee of Council posed no great threat. This may explain why most churchmen accepted the minutes of 1846. They knew by then that there was no subtle plot to destroy Anglican education; they had at last accepted the principle that other sects had the right to public funds.

To the government as well, the education question was primarily religious. The Education Minutes of 13 April and 3 December 1839 and the minutes of 1846 concentrated on religious issues; the first two school inspectors were selected primarily for their religious qualifications. Even the process of inspection itself was a religious exercise, as Seymour Tremenheere, the inspector of British schools, believed:

> Four quiet days of preparation for my first Tour of Inspection; employed chiefly with Divinity;—Beveridge's Catechism, & the Bible;—fixing facts & dates.[2]

The latent power of the Church of England, although great, required a proper climate, leadership, and issue to be released. In the 1830s all three necessary elements converged. Militant denominationalism provided an electrified climate of conflict; the Young Gentlemen and Bishop Blomfield were leaders who combined the purity of the dove with the wisdom of the serpent; the education question was the point at which sacred and secular issues met. In such circumstances, as G. F. A. Best has pointed out, the common ground for a national system of education can exist if one of three conditions obtains: a population adhering generally to a single denomination; a State strong enough to force all sects into a universal system; a tradition of co-operation allowing diverse sects to work together.[3] Britain had none of these preconditions in the 1830s and '40s; hence it is not surprising that there, as in Ireland, schools were divided along denominational lines.

Why, in this cauldron of religious rivalries, can one find no hint of anti-clericalism, at least before 1870, save among a few Chartists and Philosophical Radicals? Why did middling-class liberals, confronted with a powerful Established Church and growing clerical pretensions, not reply in the same manner as did the petty bourgeoisie elsewhere? After all, Anglicanism, the majority Church in a day of Church–State tensions, claimed the monopoly of education, maintained a privileged clergy, and attempted to exercise its traditional prerogatives in an urban and industrialising age. Similar claims in similar settings elsewhere resulted in great anti-clerical movements, and in Spain, Mexico, France, and Italy liberalism and anti-clericalism were almost synonymous.[4]

This is not the place to discuss the history of British anti-clericalism. The English Church, however, seems to stand somewhere between Germanic Protestantism, in which anti-clericalism was irrelevant, and the Latin Churches, plagued by anti-clericalism in the nineteenth century. The Prussian State was strong enough to bureaucratise its clergy, and, indeed, to merge Lutherans and Reformed in the State Church. Anglican clergy, of course, were far more independent than that, but they did not constitute a separate and mysterious caste, and their Church did not take an uncompromising stand against reform. Perhaps more important, the presence of a strong Nonconformist interest meant a three-way tussle, not a sharp line of battle between Church and State. Hence the conflict over education did not result in anti-clericalism, as it did in the Latin world, where the Church was more monolithic and less ready to adjust to nineteenth-century realities. In the late nineteenth century, however, Irish disestablishment encouraged similar movements in Wales and England; the departure of the Hartington Whigs enhanced the position of Nonconformity within the Liberal Party; the growth of working-class electoral politics added a new element to late Victorian religious strife. These factors, and others, may well have fostered anti-clericalism after 1870.

Nor is this the place to discuss the consequences of government policy on its putative beneficiaries. Just as research on the new poor law has demonstrated that the Benthamite vision was not always translated into reality at the local level, so recent work on education (such as that of Jacqueline Grayson at Birmingham) may well show that what actually went on in the classroom bore little relation to the advice churned out by the Committee of Council, or, for that matter, by the training colleges. One suspects that the answers to crucial questions posed by the social history of education—its purpose, ideological content, and beneficiaries—will be found to vary according to time, place, and the personnel offering the schooling. In any case, the vanguard of working-class opinion seems to have been more concerned with other forms of learning—an unstamped press, adult education, and Sunday schools—as Patricia Hollis, T. W. Laqueur and John Hurt have shown.

In its religious dimensions the education question differed from most other social questions of the day. The debates over factory regulation or the new poor law, although touching on moral problems, were concerned primarily with political and economic differences. Those parties interested in creating regulatory agencies for other areas—railways, factories, emigration, salmon fisheries—did not have to meet religion and doctrine at the heart of the issue. One must keep this in mind when considering the development of educational administration. Neither MacDonagh's 'self-generating bureaucratic growth' nor Parris's Benthamite ideology provides a satisfactory explanation for the dynamics of policy for working-class education in the 1830s and '40s, for our analysis has uncovered neither an irresistible engine of administrative change nor a well articulated philosophy of public administration.

The influence of Benthamites and Utilitarians has probably been overrated. Roberts calls Utilitarians and Evangelicals 'the creative minority' who initiated and defined the basic reforms that led to the Victorian administrative State; Johnson believes that the Philosophical Radicals stimulated the Whigs to educational reform in the late 1830s; Parris comments that Radical reformers favoured grants-in-aid as a way of promoting their policies.[5] But it is difficult, as we have seen, to point to a single initiative in our period that is attributable to Radicals. Rather, the 'creative minority' seem to have been moderate Whigs and Conservatives, as Gertrude Himmelfarb guessed:

it may be necessary to reexamine the conventional image of Bentham as the father of reform and of Philosophical Radicalism as the fount of reform. It may then emerge that the actual history of reform . . . [was] brought about by other men under the impulse of other ideas . . . .[6]

As overestimated is the extent to which inspection and reports of 'experts' stimulated reform. The improvement of teacher training had been a concern of the State since 1834, long before there were any inspectors' reports or blue books to show the need for reform. The National Society became aware of the need to improve its teaching training in 1838, before it had its own inspectors. Nor can one assume that the reports of enforcing officers of necessity point to increased intervention; G. F. A. Best observes that both W. F. Hook and Edward Baines, Jr., bolstered their cases with data from the blue books—but the one used them to support State intervention, the other to oppose it.[7] William Ewart probably exaggerated when he declared that blue books

were only accessible to a few, and their ponderous proportions made them formidable to all. If they wanted to hide a thing from the public, the surest way to do it would be to put it in a blue book; for, once entombed there, the chances of resurrection were very trifling.[8]

(But we should not assume that Victorians read blue books as carefully as do historians.) So far as education was concerned, reports from experts were concomitants, not prerequisites, of reform.

Nevertheless, Richard Johnson argues that agitation by educational experts for moral engineering through State auspices started the chain of events that led to the expansion of education in the 1840s. The experts—an older generation of Edwin Chadwick, Leonard Horner, G. R. Porter, and Nassau Senior; a younger of H. S. Tremenheere, B. F. Duppa, W. E. Hickson, and E. C. Tufnell—shared philosophies with London intellectuals and Radical politicians and wanted to transform working-class behaviour by using education 'in the broad Gramscian meaning of the word'. They pushed the aristocratic politicians to act, and supplied them with policies, because they feared the threat to class hegemony posed by independent working-class organisation and knowledge. Johnson believes that the experts' failure to reach their goals was relative, not absolute. A 'major expert victory' would have meant a significant defeat for the Established Church and the landed interest. But such a victory might have divided the ruling class, and at the same time intensified class conflict, for working-class radicals might have seen it as an act of tyranny like the new poor law. Therefore, politically, 'none of this could have happened'. Rather, what emerged was 'a necessary compromise between fractions of the dominant class' designed to protect class hegemony.[9]

This is not the place to assess the Gramscian idea of hegemony, although variants of the social control hypothesis are often encountered in British and American history.[10] Some applications of that hypothesis verge on reductionism and misapprehend the events they seek to explain.[11] In this instance the argument seems to be that a triumph of the experts would have been evidence of class hegemony because of the nature of their ideological position. But since their triumph would have made the ruling class's task of protecting its hegemony more difficult, it was not allowed to happen, and failure also becomes evidence for hegemony. Suffice it to say that this hypothesis needs extended scrutiny elsewhere.

Turning from experts to politicians, the role of the Committee of Council's ministerial members, especially the Lords President, must be upgraded. I therefore disagree with David Roberts and A.

S. Bishop, who deny that the two Lords President were able administrators and who depict Lansdowne as too indolent and Wharncliffe as too indifferent to deal effectively with the complex education question.[12] Charles Greville, who observed the Education Department from the inside, believed that the Lord President was the Committee of Council's mainstay.

Wharncliffe is mightily pleased with his own management of the Council Office, the principal part of which is the Education Department. He really has reason, for he has taken great pains, and has shown fairness, liberality, and, I believe, firmness too. His intentions are certainly good, and I am inclined to think that justice is done him. He really too does the business *himself*.[13]

Nor do the images of Lansdowne as lazy and Wharncliffe as bored match the available evidence, which suggests that policy was made at Cabinet level by Ministers who kept abreast of departmental activities.

These politicians should not be underrated as administrators. Graham, for instance, had distinguished himself in the 1830s as a reforming First Lord of the Admiralty; Arvel Erickson calls him 'essentially a man of business, a tireless worker, a superb administrator . . . '.[14] Wharncliffe, although less distinguished, paid attention to his duties.[15] Russell was less successful an administrator—he tended to lose official documents—and the civilised, tolerant, and cultivated Lansdowne did not pay close attention to the details of administration.[16] Nevertheless, both men in 1839 had more experience than Kay-Shuttleworth at running departments of state. Kay-Shuttleworth, to be sure, matured in office, as his sensible contributions to the debate over State aid to Roman Catholics suggest, and it would be unfair to write him out of the story. His expertise in details did contribute to the smooth functioning of the Education Department. It is equally unfair, however, to dismiss his political masters as aristocratic amateurs who only toyed with education.

Graham, indeed, was disturbed at the growing tendency to transfer the administration of government from the hands of the landed interest to those of paid administrators, a tendency that he feared would render the gentry idle and useless.[17] Hence he retained discretionary powers in his own hands. He rejected the factory inspectors' proposal to establish formulas for the automatic disbursement of fines under the Factory Act of 1844; rather he insisted that each proposed grant be submitted for his sanction. Although Graham and his successors Sir George Grey and Spencer H. Walpole approved most suggestions, they did not rubber-stamp them. The Home Secretaries also regulated the operation of the School Sites Acts, monitored the factory inspectors' twice-yearly meetings, and served as the channel for interdepartmental correspondence on education.[18] Nor did civil servants act in their masters' names; the docketing on a surviving Horner in-letter shows that the Home Secretary and his under-secretary actually made the decisions.[19]

Other departments of state that lacked such close political supervision were generally less effective. The railway department of the Board of Trade never gained the political credibility necessary for efficient operation. Hence its replacement, the Railway Commission of 1846, included members who might sit in Parliament. Similarly the transformation of the Poor Law Commission into the Poor Law Board (with its president an M.P., a Minister of State, and ultimately a member of the Cabinet) demonstrates that questions of administrative reform were also questions of politics. 'Political credibility', Lubenow explains, 'was an important consideration in an age when government growth and the use of central agencies was coming into its own as a means for organising and ordering an industrial society'.[20] Consequently it was impracticable to leave decision-making authority in the hands of individuals or bodies isolated from the political process, particularly when education was moving from the periphery to the centre of debate.

Yet despite the crucial role of politicians in the determination and implementation of policy, party had little to do with the direction of development, and Bishop's assertion 'that periods of advance occurred when Whigs and Liberals were in power, while periods of stagnation or regression coincided with Tory and Conservative governments' is dubious.[21] Rather, there was broad continuity of policy from Ministry to Ministry. Politicians, of course, were not all agreed on the direction and timing of government: Conservatives were rather more sympathetic than were Whigs to the claims of the Established Church. (But Peel, Graham, and Wharncliffe were less sympathetic than some of their backbenchers wished.) There were also divisions within each Cabinet. Within Melbourne's government Monteagle, afraid of conflicts with the Church, restrained the more sanguine Russell, while Lansdowne played the role of conciliator. Later, Peel and Graham moderated between the more adventurous Wharncliffe, always pressing for a larger education budget, and the more cautious Goulburn, always resisting an increase lest the religious issue be raised. Thus the important division between the politicians was not between those who favoured and those who deplored State intervention, but between those more and those less willing to risk conflict with religious bodies in the pursuit of government policy.

My conclusions complement the studies of other scholars who have examined the inner workings of the Education Department after 1850. They have suggested that the educational administrators were no innovators. While some administrators used their powers to curb the authority of local school boards and others favoured voluntary schools, they exercised their judgement within narrowly circumscribed limits. Those limits were defined by the politicians, particularly the vice-presidents of the council, for policy-making was essentially a political activity.[22]

Victorian reform flowed through many channels, had many motives, and attempted to answer diverse social problems. Hence it is foolish to think that a single, simple hypothesis might explain all. Nevertheless, it is certain that to understand the genesis of Victorian reform we must look to the words and actions of moderate Whig and Tory Ministers, even minor Ministers, rather than to bureaucratic spectres lurking in the background.

Notes

INTRODUCTION

[1] Gillian Sutherland, 'The Study of the History of Education', *History*, LIV (1969), 49–59; Asa Briggs, 'The Study of the History of Education', *History of Education*, I (1972), 5–22.

[2] O. R. McGregor, 'Social Research and Social Policy in the Nineteenth Century', *British Journal of Sociology*, VIII (1957), 152; Eric Midwinter, 'A Tory Interpretation of History: Some Comments', *Past and Present*, No. 34 (1966), pp. 130–3.

[3] Richard Johnson, 'Educating the educators: "Experts" and the State, 1833–9', A. P. Donajgrodzki (ed.), *Social Control in Nineteenth Century Britain* (London and Totowa, N.J., 1977), pp. 78–9.

CHAPTER I

[1] W. R. Ward, *Religious and Society in England, 1790—1850* (London, 1972), chs. ii, iv.

[2] *Ibid.*, pp. 4, 125, 177–8; Olive J. Brose, *Church and Parliament: The Reshaping of the Church of England, 1828–1860* (Stanford, Cal., and London, 1959), pp. 7–16.

[3] *Ibid.*, pp. 17–21; David M. Thompson, 'The Liberation Society, 1844–1868', in Patricia Hollis (ed.), *Pressure from Without in Early Victorian England* (New York, 1974), pp. 210–38.

[4] W. Ward, *Religion and Society*, pp. 54, 114; Josef L. Altholz, *The Churches in the Nineteenth Century* (Indianapolis and New York, 1967), pp. 191–3; J. E. Pinnington, 'The Consular Chaplaincies and the Foreign Office Under Palmerston, Aberdeen, and Malmesbury. Two Case Studies: Rome and Funchal', *Journal of Ecclesiastical History*, XXVII (1976), 277–84.

[5] M. G. Jones, *The Charity School Movement* (Hamden, Conn., 1964); T. W. Laqueur, *Religion and Respectability: Sunday Schools and Working-class Culture, 1780–1850* (New Haven and London, 1976), pp. 65–74; Henrietta Jennings, *The Political Theory of State-supported Elementary Education in England, 1750–1833* (Lancaster, Penna., 1928), pp. 3–7; Harold Silver, *The Concept of Popular Education* (London, 1965), pp. 25–33; Michael Sanderson, 'Education and the Factory in Industrial Lancashire,

1780–1840', *Economic History Review*, 2nd ser., XX (1967), 266; S. E. Maltby, *Manchester and the Movement for National Elementary Education, 1800–1870* (Manchester, 1918), pp. 12–14; David Wardle, *Education and Society in Nineteenth-century Nottingham* (Cambridge, 1971), ch. vii. David Salmon (ed.), *The Practical Parts of Lancaster's 'Improvements' and Bell's 'Experiment'* (Cambridge, 1932), is a concise summary of the monitorial method.

⁶ J. M. Goldstrom, *The Social Content of Education, 1808–1870* (Shannon, 1972), pp. 13–15; Jennings, *Political Theory*, pp. 57–72; Chester W. New, *The Life of Henry Brougham to 1830* (Oxford, 1961), pp. 203–4, 208; H. B. Binns, *A Century of Education* (London, 1908), pp. 34–5, 73–6; A. B. Webster, *Joshua Watson* (London, 1954), pp. 18–32; H. J. Burgess, *Enterprise in Education* (London, 1958), p. 22; H. J. Burgess, 'The Educational History of the National Society, 1811–1833' (unpublished M. A. thesis, London University, 1949), pp. 1–28; Edward Churton, *Memoir of Joshua Watson*, 2 vols. (London, 1861), I, 82; *DNB*, XX, 928–30.

⁷ Burgess, 'National Society', pp. 179–90.

⁸ Sanderson, 'Education and the Factory', pp. 267–9; M. W. Thomas, *The Early Factory Legislation* (Leigh on Sea, 1948) pp. 10–26; A. H. Robson, *The Education of Children Engaged in Industry in England, 1833–1876* (London, 1931), pp. 4–5; 1 *Hansard*, IX (1807), 798, 802, 1174–8.

⁹ *Ibid.*, XXXIV (1816), 636, 1230–5, XXXVII (1818), 815, XXXVIII (1818), 585–91; A. M. Gilbert, *The Work of Lord Brougham for Education in England* (Chambersburg, Penna., 1922), pp. 42–9.

¹⁰ Thomas, *Factory Legislation*, pp. 27–31, 49–58; Robson, *Education of Children*, pp. 17–8.

¹¹ See Donald H. Akenson's comprehensive study, *The Irish Education Experiment* (London and Toronto, 1970).

¹² Oliver MacDonagh, 'The Nineteenth-century Revolution in Government: a Reappraisal', *Historical Journal*, I (1958), 53, 58; Oliver MacDonagh, *A Pattern of Government Growth, 1800–60* (London, 1961), pp. 8, 16, 320–1.

¹³ Henry Parris, 'The Nineteenth-century Revolution in Government: a Reappraisal Reappraised', *Historical Journal*, III (1960), 17–37; Henry Parris, *Constitutional Bureaucracy: the Development of British Central Administration since the Eighteenth Century* (London, 1969), pp. 138–40.

¹⁴ L. J. Hume, 'Jeremy Bentham and the Nineteenth-century Revolution in Government', *Historical Journal*, X (1967), 361–75; Jennifer Hart, 'Nineteenth-century Social Reform: a Tory Interpretation of History', *Past and Present*, No. 31 (1965), pp. 39–61.

¹⁵ David Roberts, 'Tory Paternalism and Social Reform in Early Victorian England', *AHR*, LXIII (1957–58), 323–7; David Roberts, 'Jeremy Bentham and the Victorian Administrative State', *Victorian Studies*, II (1958–59), 193–210; David Roberts, *Victorian Origins of the British Welfare State* (New Haven, Conn., 1960); G. Kitson Clark, *The Making of Victorian England* (London, 1962); W. L. Burn, *The Age of Equipoise* (New York, 1965); William C. Lubenow, *The Politics of Government Growth*

(Newton Abbot and Hamden, Conn., 1971).

¹⁶ For the historiography of the 'revolution', see Valerie Cromwell, 'Interpretations of Nineteenth-century Administration: an Analysis', *Victorian Studies*, IX (1965–66), 245–55; Geoffrey Finlayson, *England in the Eighteen Thirties: Decade of Reform* (London, 1969); Roy M. Macleod, 'Statesmen Undisguised', *AHR*, LXVIII (1973), 1386–1405; Gillian Sutherland (ed.), *Studies in the Growth of Nineteenth-century Government* (London, 1972); Derek Fraser, *The Evolution of the British Welfare State* (London, 1973), pp. 1–9, 91–114; Gertrude Himmelfarb, 'The Writing of Social History: Recent Studies of 19th Century England', *Journal of British Studies*, XI (1971), 152–5.

CHAPTER II

¹ 3 *Hansard*, XV (1833), 758–61, XVII (1833), 593–5; *Mirror*, 1833, I, 276, 750, II, 2011; J. Alexander and D. G. Paz, 'The Treasury Grants, 1833–1839', *BJES*, XXII (1974), 78–80.

² *Commons Journal*, LXXXVIII (1833), 692–3.

³ *Mirror*, 1833, IV, 3889–90, 3896–8.

⁴ *Ibid.*, p. 3898.

⁵ 3 *Hansard*, XX (1833), 735–7.

⁶ *Ibid.*, cols. 152–5, 163–6; *Mirror*, 1833, IV, 3433.

⁷ 3 *Hansard*, XVI (1833), 638–9.

⁸ Brougham to Napier, 28 Sept. 1833, Macvey Napier Papers, BM, Add. MS. 34,616, ff. 160–1; Spring Rice to Brougham, [Mar. 1834], and Russell to Brougham, 4 Aug. 1853, Brougham Papers, UCL; Brougham to Russell, 3 Aug. 1853, Brougham Papers, WLCL (in which he stresses Althorp's support); John, Earl Russell, *Recollections and Suggestions* (Boston, Mass., 1875), pp. 122–3, 309; 3 *Hansard*, XXIX (1835), 73, 77, LXXXIX (1847), 871, CIX (1850), 306; *Mirror*, 1835, III, 1649.

⁹ 3 *Hansard*, XXII (1834), 760–1.

¹⁰ *Mirror*, 1834, II, 1037.

¹¹ *Ibid.*, I, 243; 3 *Hansard*, XXI (1834), 761.

¹² 3 *Hansard*, XXII (1834), 843–52.

¹³ *Mirror*, 1834, II, 1074.

¹⁴ *Report of the Committee of the General Assembly for Increasing the Means of Education and Religious Instruction in Scotland* (1834), p. 16; National Society, General Committee Minute, 23 Apr. 1834, III, 283; *Times*, 27 Jan., 18 Apr. 1834.

¹⁵ Alexander and Paz, 'Treasury Grants', p. 84.

¹⁶ Russell to Brougham, 29 Aug. 1834, Brougham Papers, UCL.

¹⁷ Roebuck to Brougham, 5 Mar. 1835, *ibid.*; *Mirror*, 1834, III, 1992, 1837–38, I, 254; memorandum, 'Education Committee of 1834', [*c.* 2 Mar. 1835], Gladstone Papers, BM, Add. MS. 44,723, f. 312; 3 *Hansard*, XXIV (1834), 134–8.

18 *PP*, 1834, IX (572), 18–30.
19 *Ibid.*, pp. 4–6, 145–6.
20 *Ibid.*, p. 60.
21 *Ibid.*, pp. 60–1, 67.
22 *Ibid.*, pp. 45–6, 72–3, 195 *et seq.*
23 See, e.g., *ibid.*, pp. 21, 43, 48, 57, 87, 88, 105, 219.
24 *Ibid.*, p. 220.
25 See *ibid.*, Q. 2829.
26 Brougham to Althorp, [*c.* 3–12 June 1834], Spencer Papers, Althorp, Box 8; Duppa to Brougham, 28 May 1835, Brougham Papers, UCL; memorandum, 'Edn. Comm'ee a Comm'n?', 2 June 1835, Gladstone Papers, BM, Add. MS. 44,724, f. 77; M. R. D. Foot and H. C. G. Matthew (eds.), *The Gladstone Diaries*, 4 vols. (Oxford, 1968–74), II, 173; Kerry to Spring Rice, [2 Dec. 1835], Monteagle Papers, NLI, MS. 13,381 (5).
27 For another view, see Richard Johnson, 'The Education Department, 1839–1864: a Study in Social Policy and the Growth of Government' (unpublished Ph.D. dissertation, Cambridge University, 1968), p. 41; and P. H. Butterfield, 'The Educational Researches of the Manchester Statistical Society, 1830–1840', *BJES*, XXII (1974), 340–59. For Francis Place's famous 'packing' of the select committee on the combination laws in 1824, see E. P. Thompson, *The Making of the English Working Class*, rev. ed. (London, 1968), pp. 516–21.
28 *Mirror*, 1835, III, 1836; 3 *Hansard*, XXIX (1835), 73; *Commons Journal*, XC (1835), 460.
29 Alexander and Paz, 'Treasury Grants', pp. 85–6; D. G. Paz, 'The Politics of Public Education in Britain, 1833–1848: a Study of Policy and Administration' (unpublished Ph.D. dissertation, University of Michigan, 1974), p. 41.
30 *Mirror*, 1837–38, VI, 4776.
31 John Sinclair (ed.), *Correspondence of the National Society with the Lords of the Treasury and with the Committee of Council on Education* (London, 1839), pp. 4–5 (italicised in the original).
32 *Ibid.*, pp. 1–2, 5, 7–14; *PP*, 1839, XLI (216), 372–9; Spring Rice to Wigram, 19 Apr. 1839, Monteagle Papers, NLI, MS. 536, f. 172.
33 Kerry to J. P. Kay, 23 May 1834, Kay-Shuttleworth Papers, JRL.
34 R. W. Rich, *The Training of Teachers in England and Wales during the Nineteenth Century* (Cambridge, 1933), p. 50; Alexander and Paz, 'Treasury Grants', pp. 86–7; Melbourne to Spring Rice, 19 June 1835, Monteagle Papers, NLI, MS. 13,381 (4); Melbourne to Brougham, 22 June 1835, Brougham Papers, UCL; Brougham to Melbourne, [22 June 1835], Broadlands Archives, NRA, MEL/BR/23/1.
35 E.g. Lord David Cecil, *Lord M.* (London, 1954), pp. 129–30, 234; John Prest, *Lord John Russell* (London, 1972), p. 137.
36 Spring Rice to William Allen, 9 Dec. 1835, Monteagle Papers, NLI, MS. 551, pp. 268–70; A. Y. Spearman to Henry Dunn, 7 July 1838, *PP*, 1839, XLI (216), 373; Spring Rice to Kerry, 8 Dec. 1835, Monteagle

Papers, NLI, MS. 551, pp. 266–7; Spring Rice to Brougham, 16 Nov. [1835], Brougham Papers, UCL; Spring Rice to Wigram, 1 Apr. 1839, Sinclair, *Correspondence*, pp. 12–13.

[37] There is no published study of Slaney, but see his journal in the Morris-Eyton Collection, Shrewsbury Public Library. For Wyse, see Akenson, *Irish Education Experiment*, pp. 108–115; James J. Auchmuty, *Sir Thomas Wyse, 1791–1862: the Life and Career of an Educator and Diplomat* (London, 1939); Olga Bonaparte-Wyse, *The Spurious Brood: Princess Letitia Bonaparte and her Children* (London, 1969); Thomas Wyse, *Education Reform; or, the Necessity of a National System of Education* (London, 1836), *passim*.

[38] *Commons Journal*, XCIII (1837–38), 699; *Mirror*, 1837–38, VII, 5370–1; TM, 5 July 1838, *PP*, 1837–38, XXXVIII (695), 365.

[39] Johnson, 'Education Department', p. 51.

[40] Roberts, *Victorian Origins*, pp. 35–45; T. K. Djang, *Factory Inspection in Great Britain* (London, 1942), p. 31; Nancy Ball, *Her Majesty's Inspectorate, 1839–1849* (Edinburgh and London, 1963), pp. 3, 6–11, 15–19; E. L. Edmonds, *The School Inspector* (London, 1962), pp. 20–3; Akenson, *Irish Education Experiment*, pp. 143–6; Gaelic School Society, *Annual Report*, XXIV (1835), 37–8; TM, 23 Feb. 1837, Treasury Board Minutes, PRO, T. 29/386, p. 388.

[41] Patricia Hollis, *The Pauper Press: a Study in Working-class Radicalism of the 1830s* (Oxford, 1970), pp. 55–9, 65–75, 89–90.

CHAPTER III

[1] J. R. Torrance, 'Sir George Harrison and the growth of bureaucracy in the early nineteenth century', *EHR*, LXXXIII (1968), 65.

[2] J. Stewart to Rev. William Wright, 27 Sept. 1833, Treasury Out-letters, General, PRO, T. 27/95, p. 74; TM, 30 Aug. 1833, *PP*, 1834, XLII (178), 527.

[3] TM, 10 Dec. 1833, *ibid.*, pp. 527–9; TM, 7 Mar. 1834, *ibid.*, p. 531; TM, 11 July 1834, *PP*, 1835, XL (236), 680.

[4] TM, 16 and 23 May 1834, PRO, T. 29/353, pp. 382, 524.

[5] TM, 14 and 18 Feb. 1834, PRO, T. 29/350, pp. 279, 345, 9 May 1834, T. 29/353, p. 219; J. Stewart to Dunn, 18 and 21 Feb. 1834, PRO, T. 27/95, pp. 277–8, 281.

[6] Spring Rice to Parker, 9 Sept. 1835, Monteagle Papers, NLI, MS. 551, pp. 120–1.

[7] Baring to Spring Rice [*c.* 5 Oct. 1835], *ibid.*, MS. 561, f. 93. (This series of MSS. are registers of in-letters with notes of their disposition, rather than actual correspondence, and will hearafter be indicated by the word 'Register' in parentheses.) Keasley to Spring Rice, 29 Nov. 1835 (Register), *ibid.*, f. 107, and 14 Dec. 1835 (Register), MS. 555, f. 6; Abstract of Correspondence, 26 Nov. 1835, PRO, Ed. 103/138, p. 597; Keasley to Baring, 14 Dec. 1835, *ibid.*, p. 599; TM, 16 Sept. 1836, *PP*, 1837, XLI (372), 465.

⁸ Its technical status as a British school had been forgotten by 1845 (Commitee of Council minutes, *PP*, 1845, XXV [622], 541). I thank the late Professor A. C. F. Beales, the Rev. George Bradley, Leeds Diocesan archivist, and Mr. Osmund Mallinder, Hon. Sacristan, St. Marie's Roman Catholic Church, Sheffield, for their help in this matter.

⁹ James E. Handley, *The Irish in Scotland, 1798–1845* (Cork, 1943).

¹⁰ TM, 7 Mar. 1834, PRO, T. 29/351, p. 167.

¹¹ Documents in PRO, T. 1/4208, bdl. 1833–4–6, file 4295.

¹² TM, 30 Jan. 1838, PRO, T. 29/397, p. 522.

¹³ D. Chambers, 'The Church of Scotland's Highlands and Islands Education Scheme, 1824–1843', *Journal of Educational Administration and History*, VII (1975), 8–9; George H. Baird to the Treasury, 28 Aug. 1833, PRO, T. 1/4208, bdl. 1833–4–6, doc. 17,071; TM, 24 Sept. 1833, PRO, T. 29/345, p. 446, 29 Nov. 1833, T. 29/347, p. 619; *PP*, 1834, XLII (178), 536; *PP*, 1839, XLI (282), 391.

¹⁴ H. G. Roseveare, *The Treasury* (London, 1969), p. 156; see also the docketing on, e.g., PRO, Ed. 103/135, pp. 66, 160; PRO, T. 1/3152, doc. 21, 478, 3230, doc, 24,658, 3299, bdl. 21,140, doc. 11,941.

¹⁵ Maurice Wright, *Treasury Control of the Civil Service* (Oxford, 1969), p. xxviii; PRO, Ed. 103/135, pp. 66, 160, 496, 632; *ibid.*, 136, p. 374; *ibid.*, 139, p. 238.

¹⁶ The Treasury Board transacted its business in five functional divisions; the fourth division, charged with Irish and Home Office affairs, also handled schools. In only one case, apparently, another division, the Revenue Department, appropriated money for a school (TM, 11 Oct. 1837, PRO, T. 29/394, p. 187).

¹⁷ Wright, *Treasury Control*, pp. 7–8; J. C. Sainty, *Treasury Officials* (London, 1972), p. 17; Torrance, 'Sir George Harrison', p. 60; 'Report from the Select Committee on Miscellaneous Expenditure', *PP*, 1847–48, XVIII, Pt. I (543), 2–3, 75–92, 101–25.

¹⁸ PRO, T. 1/3254, doc. 5802; TM, 3 Oct. 1834, PRO, T. 29/359, pp. 50–1, 26 Mar. 1838, T. 29/399, pp. 630–1; George Cranstone to Baring, 26 Sept. 1834, PRO, T. 1/3000, doc. 18,694, Edward Dawson to Baring, 29 Sept. 1834, 3001, doc. 18,880.

¹⁹ TM, 10 and 27 Dec. 1833, PRO, T. 29/348, pp. 190, 530–1, 3 Feb. 1835, T. 29/362, p. 81, 8 Nov. 1836, T. 29/383, p. 188, 11 Oct. 1837, T. 29/394, p. 182, 12 Dec. 1837, T. 29/396, pp. 265–6, 27 July 1838, T. 29/403, pp. 635–6; John Harrison to Treasury, 17 Oct. 1835, memorandum of Baring, 5 Mar. 1839, PRO, Ed. 103/135, pp. 565–8, 833; memorial, Rector and inhabitants, St Paul's Covent Garden [late Mar. 1838], Ed. 103/136, p. 851; A. Y. Spearman to Wigram, 17 Dec. 1836, PRO, T. 27/137, p. 52.

²⁰ Howard Elphinstone to Spring Rice, 10 Aug. 1835 (Register), Monteagle Papers, NLI, MS. 561, f. 65.

²¹ Palmerston to Spring Rice, 15 May 1835 (Register), Mrs Gaskell to Spring Rice, 2 July 1835, *ibid.*, ff. 18, 43, Spring Rice to the Bishop of Durham, 31 Aug. 1837, MS. 532, f. 257, Spring Rice to Rev. T. Grylls, 18

Sept. 1838, MS. 543, p. 87, Spring Rice to Baring, 18 Nov. 1838, MS. 535, f. 57.

22 TM, 21 Oct. 1834, *PP*, 1835, XL (236), 686–7; TM, 14 Feb. 1837, PRO, T. 29/386, p. 241.

23 See the marginalia on, e.g., PRO, T. 1/4208, bdl. 1833–4–6, doc. 15,002, bdl. 1837–8, doc. 27,053; Spring Rice to Steuart, 31 Dec. 1838, Monteagle Papers, NLI, MS. 543, p. 179; TM, 12 Sept. 1838, PRO, T. 29/405, pp. 208–9, 14 June 1836, T. 29/378, p. 266; Baring to Rev. A. Lyne, 19 Jan. 1836, PRO, T. 17/34, p. 277, Baring to Rev. J. M. MacCullock, 5 Dec. 1837, T. 17/35, p. 159; 'Applications made from Scotland for participation in the Grants', *PP*, 1837, XXIX (304), 239–46; 'Account of the Expenditure of £10,000, granted 1834 to 1838, for . . . Scotland", *PP*, 1839, XLI (282), 383–407.

24 PRO, Ed. 103/135, pp. 87, 95–100, 345–7; TM, 14 Aug. 1838, PRO, T. 29/404, pp. 350–1.

25 Memorial, inhabitants of Barnard Castle, 28 Dec. 1833, PRO, Ed. 103/135, p. 563, memorial, Rev. William H. Vale, 23 Oct. 1833, Ed. 103/136, pp. 271–2, 'Y.Z.' to the Treasury, 14 Oct. 1836, Ed. 103/138, pp. 235–6, memorial, inhabitants of Great Torrington, 19 Dec. 1833, pp. 751–2, W. W. Howard to R. R. W. Lingen, 9 Apr. 1864, pp. 749–51; John Sinclair to C. E. Trevelyan, 11 Feb. 1840, PRO, T. 1/4550, doc. 28,273; Ball, *Her Majesty's Inspectorate*, p. 72.

26 *PP*, 1834, XLII (178), 528–30; *PP*, 1836, XLVII (502), 53–7.

27 H. M. Knox, *Two Hundred and Fifty Years of Scottish Education* (Edinburgh and London, 1953), pp. 3–25; John Tawse, 'Report of a Visit to the Society Schools in Orkney & Caithness', July–Aug. 1834, Records of the Society in Scotland for the Propagation of Christian Knowledge, SRO, GD 95/9/5, f. 24 (hereafter cited as 'SSPCK Records'); Christopher Smout, 'Demographic Crises in Scotland from the Seventeenth to the Nineteenth Centuries' (paper presented at the Comparative Studies in History Colloquium, University of Michigan, March 1975); Gaelic School Society, *Annual Report*, XXII (1833), 9–10, 19; *Report of the Committee of the General Assembly* (1832), p. 11; General Assembly's Education Committee, *Educational Statistics of the Highlands and Islands of Scotland* (Edinburgh, 1833), pp. 23–4.

28 *Report of the Committee of the General Assembly* (1834), pp. 16–18; Baird to Althorp, 2 Aug. 1834 [copy], Seaforth Papers, SRO, GD 46/12/68(7); Gordon to J. A. Stewart Mackenzie, 13 Feb. 1836, *ibid.*, 148(2); James Ewing to Thomas Chalmers, 8 Aug. 1834, Gordon to Chalmers, 14 Sept. 1834, Colquhoun to Chalmers, [11 Oct. 1834], J. J. H. Johnstone to Chalmers, 16 May 1836, all in Chalmers Papers, NCE; Steuart to Spring Rice, 11 Dec. 1835 (Register), Monteagle Papers, NLI, MS. 555, f. 4; *Report of the Committee of the General Assembly* (1836), pp. 9–11; *Times*, 14 May 1836, p. 4e.

29 Committee minute, 2 June 1836, SSPCK Records, SRO, GD 95/2/17, p. 361; memorial, inhabitants, Burgh of Oban [early June 1836], PRO, T. 1/4208, bdl. 1833–4–6, doc. 5002; memorial, Knock Kirk

Session, to Mackenzie, Seaforth Papers, SRO, GD 46/12/148(1); *PP*, 1836, XXXVIII (525), 436; Treasury Minute, 28 Oct. 1836, *PP*, 1837, XLI (372), 471.

30 Baring to Commissioners, Highland Churches, 1 Nov. 1836, PRO, T. 1/4208, bdl. 1833–4–6, doc. 22,015; Rickman to Baring, 15 Dec. 1836, *ibid.*, doc. 25,543; Mackenzie to Rickman, 20 Dec. 1836, *ibid.*, doc. 26,035; Baird to Baring, 20 Mar. 1837, *ibid.*, bdl. 1837–8, doc. 7128; Baring to Rickman, 21 Jan. 1837, PRO, T. 17/35, p. 44; Baring to Baird, 1 Apr. 1837, *ibid.*, 35, p. 69; Treasury Minute, 31 Mar. 1837, *PP*, 1837, XLI (372), 471.

31 Memorandum, General Assembly's Education Committee, 10 Apr. 1837, encl. in Gordon to Baring, 12 Apr. 1837, PRO, T. 1/4208, bdl. 1837–8, file 8378; Spiers to Steuart, 15 Apr. 1837, *ibid.*

32 The custom was to appoint one junior lord from each of the three kingdoms; they sometimes handled business relating to their country.

33 Steuart, 'Highland Schools' [*c.* Apr.–May 1837], PRO, T. 1/4208, bdl. 1837–8, file 8378.

34 Rutherford to Spring Rice, 21 Apr. 1837, *ibid.*, Spring Rice to Gordon, 26 Mar. 1837, Monteagle Papers, NLI, MS. 545, p. 113.

35 Baird to Baring, 16 Oct. 1837, PRO, T. 1/4208, bdl. 1837–8, doc. 21,704; Richardson to Steuart, 16 and 17 Nov. 1837, *ibid.*, unnumbered documents; text of the Schools (Scotland) Bill in *PP*, 1837–38, VI (114), 31–5; *Mirror*, 1837–38; II, 1612–16. The Select Committee on Scottish Education merely circulated printed queries to schoolmasters. Its report is in *PP*, 1837–38, VI (715), 439; the digest of returns is in *ibid.*, 1841, XIX (64), 1.

36 Dickson to Baring, 12 Oct. 1838, PRO, T. 1/4208, bdl. 1837–8, doc. 22,607; Spring Rice to Steuart, 31 Dec. 1838, Monteagle Papers, NLI, MS. 543, pp. 177–9; Treasury Minute, 11 Jan. 1839, *PP*, 1840, XL (382), 357–8.

37 The Glasgow Educational Society had been founded in 1834 to enlist popular support and parliamentary interest for Scottish educational needs in general and David Stow's model schools in particular. Although not officially connected with the Kirk, the society had close ties with it and required clerical references from its students. (Marjorie Cruickshank, *A History of the Training of Teachers in Scotland*, London, 1970, pp. 42–5).

38 Mackenzie to Spring Rice, 31 July 1835 (Register), Monteagle Papers, NLI, MS. 561, f. 62; Spring Rice to Mackenzie, 26 Sept. 1835, *ibid.*, MS. 551, pp. 171–2; Hope Johnstone to Spring Rice, 4 Mar. 1836 (Register), *ibid.*, MS. 555, f. 89; Colquhoun to Spring Rice, 21 Mar. 1836 (Register), *ibid.*, f. 86; Pillans to Spring Rice [*c.* 4 June 1836] (Register), *ibid.*, MS. 562, f. 7.

39 *Report of the Committee of the General Assembly* (1835), pp. 14–17.

40 J. J. H. Johnstone to Thomas Chalmers, 16 May 1836, Chalmers Papers, NCE.

41 Buchanan to Chalmers, 18 Oct. 1837, *ibid.*

42 Spring Rice to Jeffrey, 21 Oct. 1836, Monteagle Papers, NLI, MS.

542, pp. 147–8.

⁴³ The unexpectedly mild response of Colquhoun and the General Assembly to the Bill is surprising. In autumn 1837 Spring Rice had spoken to both Chalmers and Colquhoun on Scottish education; any barter might have taken place then (Spring Rice to Chalmers, 26 Aug. 1837, Monteagle Papers, NLI, MS. 532, ff. 203–4; Spring Rice to Colquhoun, 17 Oct. 1837, *ibid.*, MS. 543, p. 39). But restraint might have been applied from outside. Colquhoun had been hot since February 1837 to bring forward a motion attacking Whig policy towards the Kirk (Colquhoun to Chalmers, 25 Feb. [1837], Chalmers Papers, NCE). Sir James Graham, however, told him that the Church question was an important card in the Tories' hand and ought not to be played without consulting the party leaders. Graham also asked Peel to cool him down. (Graham to Peel, 15 Nov. 1837, Peel Papers, BM, Add. MS. 40,318, ff. 103–4.) A combination of these two influences may have led Colquhoun to support the Ministry's measure.

⁴⁴ The reports are in *PP*, 1840, XL (382), 368; *PP*, 1841, Sess. 2, II (29), 393; *PP*, 1842, XXXIII (543), 419. (I cannot explain why the Treasury ceased to report.) *PP*, 1843, **XXXI** (91), 433; Committee of Council Minutes, *PP*, 1845, **XXV** [622], 507; Knox, *Two Hundred and Fifty Years*, p. 56. The short debate on the appropriation never alluded to the schools (*Times*, 8 Apr. 1843, p. 4f).

CHAPTER IV

¹ Leonard Horner, *The Factories Regulation Act Explained, with some remarks on its Origin, Nature, and Tendency* (Glasgow, 1834), p. 21; Thomas, *Early Factory Legislation*, pp. 64–5; see also Gertrude Ward, 'The Education of Factory Child Workers, 1833–1850', *Economic History*, III (1935), 110–11; S. E. Finer, *The Life and Times of Sir Edwin Chadwick* (London, 1952), p. 65; 3 *Hansard*, XX (1833), 449.

² 3 *Hansard*, XIX (1833), 222–3.

³ Robson, *Education of Children*, pp. 32–3.

⁴ G. Ward, 'Factory Child Workers', pp. 112–13; Thomas, *Early Factory Legislation*, pp. 83, 161–3; Robson, *Education of Children*, pp. 35–7, 42, 72–3; Sanderson, 'Education and the Factory in Industrial Lancashire', *Economic History Review*, 2nd ser., XX (1967), 275–8; W. C. R. Hicks, 'The Education of the Half-timers: as shown Particularly in the Case of Messrs. McConnel and Co. of Manchester', *Economic History*, III (1939), 225–32.

⁵ E. L. Edmonds, 'Education and Early Factory Inspectors', *Vocational Aspect of Secondary and Further Education*, X (1958), 85–95; Sanderson, 'Education and the Factory', p. 274; G. Ward, 'Factory Child Workers', p. 115; Factory Inspectors' Minute Book, PRO, Lab. 15/1, n.p. (2 Feb. 1841), 4–5 (10 Sept. 1836).

⁶ Hicks, 'Half-timers', p. 224; G. Ward, 'Factory Child Workers', pp. 114–16, 122; Thomas, *Early Factory Legislation*, pp. 80–1.

⁷ Fox Maule to Mr Trimmer, 7 June 1837, Home Office Entry Books: Factories, PRO, H.O. 87/1, pp. 66–7.

⁸ S. M. Phillipps to R. J. Saunders, 17 Dec. 1839, *ibid.*, pp. 183–4; Fox Maule to R. J. Saunders, 28 Dec. 1839, *ibid.*, pp. 185–92; Factory Inspectors' Minute Book, PRO, Lab. 15/1, pp. 28–9 (22 Sept. 1836), 38 (4 Oct. 1836), 76 (22 July 1837); Horner to Chadwick, 28 Dec. 1837, Chadwick Papers, UCL; Nassau W. Senior, *Letters on the Factory Act, as it affects the Cotton Manufacture* (London, 1837), pp. 19, 22.

⁹ S. M. Phillipps to factory inspectors, 25 Jan. 1837, PRO, H.O. 87/1, p. 38; Fox Maule to James Stewart, 21 Mar. 1838, *ibid.*, p. 110; Fox Maule to factory inspectors, 24 Apr. 1838, *ibid.*, pp. 121–2; Thomas, *Early Factory Legislation*, pp. 166–7; Robson, *Education of Children*, pp. 49, 56–9.

¹⁰ 'Reports on the Effects of the Educational Provisions of the Factories Act', *PP*, 1839, XLII (42), 357.

¹¹ *Ibid.*, pp. 424–6.

¹² 3 *Hansard*, XLV (1839), 881–5, 889, 893; Thomas, *Early Factory Legislation*, pp. 172–3; Robson, *Education of Children*, pp. 59–61.

¹³ 3 *Hansard*, XLVIII (1839), 1077–8, 1090–4, 1416–18; *ibid.*, XLIX (1839), 914.

¹⁴ Robson, *Education of Children*, pp. 61–4, 67–8; Thomas, *Early Factory Legislation*, pp. 187–90; Chadwick to Russell, 1 Aug. 1840, Chadwick Papers, UCL.

¹⁵ Leonard Horner, *On the Employment of Children, in Factories and other Works in the United Kingdom, and in some Foreign Countries* (London, 1840), p. 6.

¹⁶ Francis Duke, 'The Education of Pauper Children: Policy and Administration, 1834–1855' (unpublished M.A. thesis, Manchester University, 1968), pp. 21–3.

¹⁷ Sir George Nicholls, *A History of the English Poor Law, in connexion with the legislation and other circumstances affecting the Condition of the People*, 2 vols. (London, 1854), II, 248; 'Appendix (A.) Reports of Assistant Commissioners. Part II', *PP*, 1834, XXIX (44), 76.

¹⁸ 'Appendix (A.) Reports of Assistant Commissioners. Part I', *ibid.*, XXVIII (44), 648.

¹⁹ *Ibid.*, pp. 99, 169, 531–9.

²⁰ *Ibid.*, p. 400.

²¹ 'Report from His Majesty's Commissioners for inquiring into the Administration and Practical Operation of the Poor Laws', *ibid.*, XXVII (44), 176–7, 209; Anthony Brundage, *The Making of the New Poor Law: the Politics of Inquiry, Enactment, and Implementation* (New Brunswick, N.J., 1978), pp. 15, 47–52; 'Poor Law Amendment Bill', *PP*, 1834, III (211), 239; Thomas Mackay, *A History of the English Poor Law from 1834 to the Present Time* (New York and London, 1900), pp. 117–31; 3 *Hansard*, XXI (1834), 896; *ibid.*, XXII (1834), 806, 1345.

²² *ibid.*, XXIV (1834), 719, 926.

²³ *Mirror*, 1834, III, 2494.

²⁴ *Ibid.*, IV, 2940–1, 2960–1, 3192.

25   *Ibid.*, pp. 3352, 3358–62, 3374–5; 'Poor Law Amendment Act', 4 and 5 Wm. IV, cap. 76, sects. xv, xix, *Public General Statutes* (1834), pp. 380–2.
26   Brundage, Nicholls, and Mackay do not mention it at all; the Webbs give it a footnote.
27   Sidney and Beatrice Webb, *English Local Government*, 9 vols. (London, 1929), VIII, 96; Brundage, *Poor Law*, pp. 54, 64–6, 71–3; 'Poor Law Amendment Bill (Lords' Amendments)', *PP*, 1834, III (581), 359.
28   Brundage, *Poor Law*, pp. 79–80, 86; Webb, *English Local Government*, VIII, 109–10; Finer, *Chadwick*, pp. 109–23.
29   Graham to DeGrey, 12 Dec. 1842, Graham Papers, NL, reel 8, bdl. 56A; S. M. Phillipps to Poor Law Commissioners, 8 Nov. 1839, PRO, H.O. 34/3, pp. 15–16; J. E. Drinkwater Bethune to Chadwick, 8 July 1839, Chadwick Papers, UCL; Chadwick to Napier, 17 Dec. 1835, Napier Papers, BM, Add. MS. 34,617, ff. 288–9; Finer, *Chadwick*, pp. 132–9.
30   'First Annual Report of the Poor Law Commissioners for England and Wales', *PP*, 1835, XXXV (500), 1–66, 98–9, 101, 104–5; Webb, *English Local Government*, VIII, 110–19.
31   *Ibid.*, pp. 127–33; Duke, 'Education of Pauper Children', pp. 21–31.
32   Finer, *Chadwick*, pp. 151–2; Alexander M. Ross, 'Kay-Shuttleworth and the training of Teachers for Pauper Schools', *BJES*, XV (1967), 275–83; Johnson, 'Education Department', pp. 19–20; Duke, 'Education of Pauper Children', pp. 32–48.
33   Slaney Committee Report, *PP*, 1837–38, VII (589), 185.
34   Draft circular, Kay to Poor Law Guardians, [*c.* 19 Aug.] 1837, PRO, M.H. 32/49; Poor Law Commissioners to Aubin, 23 Oct. 1838, *ibid.*, 50 (drafted by Kay); J. P. Kay, 'Minute showing the Duties of the Chaplains of a Union Workhouse', 28 May 1838, *ibid.*, 50; Henry Biggs, *Report on the Industrial Plan of Education, Under the Direction of the Poor Law Commissioners, in England* (Cork, 1841), pp. 10–14.
35   'Second Annual Report of the Poor Law Commissioners for England and Wales', *PP*, 1836, XXIX, Pt. I (595), 28–9, 477; 'Fourth Annual Report of the Poor Law Commissioners for England and Wales', *PP*, 1837–38, XXVII [147], 311, 315; Duke, 'Education of Pauper Children', pp. 37–8, 50–1, 55–6.
36   G. C. Lewis to Melbourne, 23 Aug. 1839, Melbourne Papers, RA MP 51/161; Nicholls, *Poor Law*, II, 287–8; Hickson to Chadwick, 14 Aug. 1838, Chadwick Papers, UCL; Duke, 'Education of Pauper Children', p. 39.
37   The best and most recent research on the local workings of the poor law is Brundage, *Poor Law*, pp. 75–144; Rhodes Boyson, 'The New Poor Law in North-east Lancashire, 1834–1871', *Transactions of the Lancashire and Cheshire Antiquarian Society*, LXX (1960), 35–56; Norman McCord, 'Implementation of the 1834 Poor Law Amendment Act on Tyneside', *International Review of Social History*, XIV (1969), 90–108; Maurice Caplan, 'The Poor Law in Nottinghamshire, 1836–71', *Transactions of the Thoroton Society of Nottinghamshire*, LXXIV (1970), 82–98; Vincent Joseph Walsh, 'The Administration of the Poor Laws in Shropshire, 1820–1855'

(unpublished Ph.D. dissertation, University of Pennsylvania, 1970); Anthony Brundage, 'The Landed Interest and the New Poor Law: a Reappraisal of the Revolution in Government', *EHR*, LXXXVII (1972), 27–48; and Eric Midwinter, *Social Administration in Lancashire, 1830–1860* (Manchester, 1969).

³⁸ Duke, 'Education of Pauper Children', pp. 57–9; 4th report PLC, *PP*, 1837–38, XXVII [147], 208; 'Fifth Annual Report of the Poor Law Commissioners for England and Wales', *PP*, 1839, XX (239), 17–20; 'Report of the Poor Law Commissioners on the Continuation of the Poor Law Commission', *PP*, 1840, XVII [226], 208–10; 'Seventh Annual Report of the Poor Law Commissioners', *PP*, 1841, XI [327], 228; 'Ninth Annual Report of the Poor Law Commissioners', *PP*, 1843, XXI [468], 16.

³⁹ 3 *Hansard*, XLIX (1839), 970–2; *ibid.*, L (1839), 98; Webb, *English Local Government*, VIII, 173–6; Finer, *Chadwick*, p. 181.

⁴⁰ 3 *Hansard*, LVII (1841), 9, 573–4, 677–97, 720–32; *PP*, 1840, III (230), 260–1; *PP*, 1841, III (7), 41; *ibid.*, (110), 57–8; *ibid.* (220), 75–6.

⁴¹ 4th report PLC, *PP*, 1837–38, XXVIII [147], 208; 'Continuation of the Commission', *PP*, 1840, XVII [226], 208; 'Poor Law Amendment Bill: Clauses to be moved in Committee by Lord John Russell', *PP*, 1841, III (0.54), 106; *PP*, 1836, XLV (254), 204–13.

⁴² Tufnell to Poor Law Commissioners, 20 Feb. 1839, PRO, M.H. 32/70.

⁴³ Brundage, *Poor Law*, pp. 14, 21–3.

CHAPTER V

¹ British Society, *Annual Report*, XXIX (1834), 6; *ibid.*, XXX (1835), 11; *ibid.*, XXXII (1837), 10; *ibid.*, XXXIII (1838), 14; General Committee Minute, 5 Mar. 1834, National Society Minute Book, III, 265; National Society, *Annual Report*, XXIV (1835), 14; *ibid.*, XXV (1836), 10; *ibid.*, XXVI (1837), 18.

² Anonymous memorandum, 5 July 1835, Monteagle Papers, NLI, MS. 13,381(13).

³ W. E. Gladstone to John Gladstone, 13 June 1833, Gladstone–Glynn Papers, Flint CRO; Memorandum, 'Slavery', [2 June 1831), Gladstone Papers, BM, Add. MS. 44,649, f. 30; Harrison to Gladstone, 10 Nov. [1834], *ibid.*, MS. 44,204, f. 11; Harrison to Gladstone, 29 Nov. [1834], *ibid.*, f. 55; Arthur Acland to T. D. Acland, 6 July 1834, A. H. D. Acland, *Memoir and Letters of the Right Honourable Sir Thomas Dyke Acland* (London, 1902), p. 73–5.

⁴ 'Heads of a Plan for promoting the Education of Youth in the British West Indies', [*c.* 2 Apr. 1834], Original Correspondence, West Indies, PRO, C.O. 318/118; circular, Spring Rice to West Indian Governors, 1 Nov. 1834, *ibid.*, 119; memorandum, 'West Indian Education', 7 Apr.

1835, *ibid.*, 122, ff. 521–35; Gladstone's copy is in his papers, BM, Add. MS. 44,724, ff. 4 *et seq.*

⁵ 'Secret Political Memoranda', 13 Apr. 1835, John Brooke and Mary Sorensen (eds.), *The Prime Ministers' Papers: W. E. Gladstone*, 2 vols. (London, 1971–72), II, 50–1.

⁶ Blomfield to Gladstone, 21 May 1835, Gladstone Papers, BM, Add. MS. 44, 354, ff. 197–8; Henry Phillpotts to Gladstone, 25 Mar. 1837, *ibid.*, 44,355, f. 212; Acland to Gladstone, 20 Mar. 1835, Acland, *Acland*, pp. 77–8; Foot and Matthew, *Gladstone Diaries*, II, *passim.*

⁷ *Ibid.*, pp. 343, 352, 353, 355; Hook to Gladstone, 26 Mar. 1838, Gladstone Papers, BM, Add. MS. 44,213, f. 5; Goulburn to Gladstone, 7 Apr. 1838, *ibid.*, 44,162, ff. 3–4, Acland, *Acland*, pp. 88–9; Lincoln to Gladstone, 9 Apr. 1838, Newcastle Papers, University of Nottingham Library, NeC 11,669.

⁸ Memorandum, 'A Third Order', 9 Mar. 1838, D. C. Lathbury (ed.), *Correspondence on Church and State of William Ewart Gladstone*, 2 vols. (New York, 1910), II, 433–7; Gladstone to Hook, 14 Apr. 1838, Gladstone Papers, BM, Add. MS. 44,213, ff. 13–15.

⁹ Foot and Matthew, *Gladstone Diaries*, II, 302; Churton, *Watson*, II, 190–1; General Committee Minute, 11 Apr. 1838, National Society Minute Book, IV, 25–6; General Committee Minute, 12 May 1838, *ibid.*, p. 39; 'Suggestions Tendered to the Sub-committee of the National Society', May 1838, Gladstone Papers, BM, Add. MS. 44,563, f. 61; 'Heads of Inquiry Referred to the Committee of Inquiry and Correspondence', *ibid.*, f. 65; Gladstone's memoranda are in *ibid.*, 44,728, ff. 80–94; Acland to Gladstone, [June 1838], *ibid.*, 44,088, ff. 9–11; Acland, *Acland*, pp. 89–90; A. Isham to John Kaye, Bishop of Lincoln, 24 Sept. 1838, Kaye Deposit, Lincs. CRO, Cor. B/5/3/34; see also Burgess, *Enterprise in Education*, pp. 68–9; he treats this in greater detail in his 'Work of the Established Church in the Education of the People, 1833–1870' (unpublished Ph.D. dissertation, University of London, 1954), pp. 108–13.

¹⁰ *National Education in the Principles of the Established Church* (London, 1839), pp. 3 *et seq.*; *Times*, 29 May 1839, p. 5a. The best assessment of the Young Gentlemen is J. L. Alexander, 'Collegiate Teacher Training in England and Wales: a Study in the Historical Determinants of Educational Provision and Practice in the Mid-nineteenth Century' (unpublished Ph.D. dissertation, University of London, 1977), pp. 59–107.

¹¹ M. J. Lynch, 'Was Gladstone a Tractarian? W. E. Gladstone and the Oxford Movement, 1833–45', *Journal of Religious History*, VIII (1974–75), 364–89.

¹² David Newsome's *Parting of Friends* (London, 1966) distorts the relationship between Gladstone and Manning. Newsome contends that Henry Edward Manning was one of the three 'most prominent members' of the Young Gentlemen—the others were S. F. Wood and Gladstone (p. 219). Manning 'revealed his vision to the world' in a sermon at Chichester

Cathedral on 31 May 1838, 'and with S. F. Wood and Gladstone the details were more fully worked out' (p. 220). This account misapprehends Manning's role in the affair. The future cardinal was but a minor member of the ginger group. His sermon was hardly original or unusual, and he was not present at the meeting with Howley. His proposal to revive the teaching functions of the cathedrals in his tract *The Presentation of the Unendowed Canonries* (1840), an important piece of evidence for Newsome, is ante-dated by Gladstone's and Acland's correspondence on that subject. Manning's role was not central and Newsome's evaluation cannot be accepted.

13 *Mirror*, 1837–38, I, 252, 393–5.

14 *Commons Journal*, XCIII (1837–38), 90, 195; 3 *Hansard*, XXXIX (1837–38), 1022–3.

15 'Report from the Select Committee on Education of the Poorer Classes in England and Wales', *PP*, 1837–8, VII (589), 173–5, 215–16, 222, 238–50, 276, 311.

16 *Ibid.*, pp. 189, 224, 230–4.

17 *Ibid.*, pp. 213–14, 225–7, 243–4, 260–1.

18 *Ibid.*, p. 258.

19 *Ibid.*, pp. 216–19.

20 Slaney to Sir Thomas Dyke Acland senior, 6 Jan. [1838], Acland of Broadclyst Papers, Devon CRO, 1148 M/8/5; Slaney Journal, May 1838, Morris-Eyton Collection, Shrewsbury Public Library, VIII; Slaney Committee Report, *PP*, 1837–38, VII (589), 168–71.

21 Hickson to Brougham, 1 Dec. 1837, Brougham Papers, UCL.

22 Gladstone to Hook, 12 Mar. 1838, Gladstone Papers, BM, Add. MS. 44,213, f. 3.

23 Cruickshank, *Training of Teachers in Scotland*; James Murphy, *The Religious Problem in English Education: the Crucial Experiment* (Liverpool, 1959), pp. 81–2, 104–7; V. G. Toms, 'Secular Education in England, 1800–1870' (unpublished Ph.D. dissertation, London University, 1972), pp. 234–8; John Cosgrove, 'The Educational Aims and Activities of Sir Thomas Wyse (1791–1862)' (unpublished Ph.D. dissertation, University of Manchester, 1975).

24 See the membership lists in the *First, Second, and Third Publications* of the Central Society of Education (1837–39).

25 B. F. Duppa, 'Objects of the Society', *First Publication* (1837), p. 14; Central Society of Education, *Schools for the Industrious Classes; or, The Present State of Education among the Working People of England* (London, 1837), pp. 6–30, 53–4.

26 Thomas Wyse, 'Education in the United Kingdom', *First Publication* (1837), p. 63.

27 *Morning Chronicle*, 16 Sept. 1837, p. 3a, 29 Sept. 1837, p. 3a.

28 Murphy, *Religious Problem*, pp. 107–17; Maltby, *Manchester*, pp. 47–55; *Mirror*, 1837, III, 2062; *ibid.*, 1837–38, III, 2289; 3 *Hansard*, XLIII (1837–38), 714, 717–27.

29 *Ibid.*, cols. 728–35.

30 *House of Commons Divisions*, 1837–38, pp. 322–3; Akenson, *Irish Education Experiment*, pp. 207–10.

31 Garratt, *Brougham*, pp. 226–7; New, *Brougham*, pp. 414–16; Arthur Aspinall, *Lord Brougham and the Whig Party* (Manchester, 1927), pp. 184–9, 202–21.

32 *Lords Journal*, LXIX (1837), 12; 'Education and Charities Bill', *PPL*, 1837, II (2), 277–93; 3 *Hansard*, XXXVIII (1837), 1683; Brougham to Napier, [22 Mar. 1837], Macvey Napier Papers, BM, Add. MS. 34,618, f. 77; Brougham to Napier, [20 Apr. 1837], *ibid.*, f. 113; memorandum in Brougham's hand, 'Substance of the Education Bill', July 1837, Brougham Papers, UCL.

33 Allen to Spring Rice, 9 Jan. 1837 (Register), Monteagle Papers, NLI, MS. 557, f. 2; Allen to Brougham, 22 May 1837, 8 and 14 Aug. 1837, Dunn, 'Observations on certain portions of Lord Brougham's Bill on Education', Feb. 1837, encl. in Allen to Brougham, 8 Aug. 1837, all in Brougham Papers, UCL.

34 Dunn to Allen, 6 Sept. 1837, *ibid.*

35 Dunn to Brougham, 23 Oct. 1837, and Allen to Brougham, 29 Oct. 1837, *ibid.*; Henry Dunn, *National Education, the Question of Questions* (London, 1838), pp. 7–9; British Society, *Annual Report*, XXXIII (1838), 1–2.

36 William Empson, 'State of parties', *Edin. Rev.*, LXV, 280; Brougham to Russell, 7, 18 Aug., 8 Oct. 1837, Brougham Papers, WLCL; Russell to Melbourne, 11 Aug. 1837, Broadlands Archives, NRA, MEL/RU/38/1–2; Melbourne to Russell, 13 Aug. 1837, *ibid.*, MEL/RU/387/1; Russell to Brougham, 15, 24, 27 Aug., 2 Oct. 1837, all in Brougham Papers, UCL; Brougham to Russell, 6 Sept. 1837, R. Russell, *Early Correspondence*, II, 20–2.

37 Russell to Brougham, 17 Sept. 1837, Russell to Brougham, 3 Oct. and 25 Nov. 1837, and Hickson to Brougham, 28 Nov. 1837, all in the Brougham Papers, UCL; *Lords Journal*, LXX (1837–38), 27; 'Education Bill', *PPL*, 1837–38, II (9), 647–63; 'Brougham's Clause', *ibid.* (9a), p. 665; 3 *Hansard*, XXXIX (1837–38), 445–58, 464–6; *ibid.*, XLIV (1837–38), 1174–5.

38 The government had considered making a statement of the extent to which it would support general education on the Bill's second reading, but when the Bill died it remained silent (Lansdowne to Gladstone, [Apr. 1838], Gladstone Papers, BM, Add. MS. 44,356, ff. 66–7).

39 Melbourne to Russell, 13 Aug. 1837, Broadlands Archives, NRA, MEL/RU/387/1.

40 Russell to Melbourne, 17 Feb. 1835, *ibid.*, MEL/RU/4; Melbourne to Russell, 8 Aug. 1837, *ibid.*, MEL/RU/383/2; Slaney journal, Nov. 1837, Morris-Eyton Collection, Shrewsbury Public Library, VIII; Holland to Althorp, 2 Nov. 1834, Spencer Papers, Althorp, Box 11; Napier to Monteagle, 27 Feb. [1840], Monteagle Papers, NLI, MS. 13,392(5); Spring Rice to W. Fisher, 17 Nov. 1838, *ibid.*, MS. 533, f. 42; journal entry, 8 Dec. 1837, Lytton Strachey and Roger Fulford (eds.), *The*

Greville Memoirs, 8 vols. (London, 1938), III, 404.

41 Brougham to Napier, [25 Sept. 1837], Macvey Napier Papers, BM, Add. MS. 34,618, f. 277.

42 Henry, Lord Brougham, 'The Education Bill', *Edin. Rev.*, LXVI (1838), 442–3; Brougham to Napier, 29 Dec. 1837, Macvey Napier (ed.), *Selection from the Correspondence of the late Macvey Napier, Esq.* (London, 1879), p. 223.

43 Brougham to Napier, 23 Dec. 1837, *ibid.*, p. 216.

44 3 *Hansard*, LXVI (1843), 928.

45 Melbourne supported voluntary schools, but objected to public education; the latter was appropriate for Germany, but not for the free-born English. He also questioned the hypothesis that education could suppress crime. (Viscount Esher, ed., *The Girlhood of Queen Victoria*, 2 vols., London, 1912, II, 117, 148). He made an exception for Ireland, however, where he supported Stanley's and Spring Rice's ideas on State intervention (Melbourne to E. G. Stanley, 7 Jan. 1831, Lloyd C. Sanders, ed., *Lord Melbourne's Papers*, London, 1889, pp. 171–2). For Melbourne's cynicism, see Philip Ziegler, *Melbourne* (London, 1976).

46 Wyse, *Education Reform*, p. 19.

47 *Reaction and Reconstruction*, p. 76.

48 Palmerston to Russell, 22 Jan. 1835, Russell Papers, PRO, P.R.O. 30/22/1E, ff. 10–11; Duncannon to Melbourne, 20 Oct. 1838, Sanders, *Melbourne's Papers*, pp. 380–1; Spring Rice to Edward Ellice, [May 1839], Ellice Papers, National Library of Scotland, E 45, f. 189.

49 Duncannon to Melbourne, 20 Oct. 1838, Melbourne Papers, RA, MP 3/53.

50 Ronald Hugh Cameron, 'Lord Melbourne's Second Administration and the Opposition, 1837–1841' (unpublished Ph.D. dissertation, University of London, 1970), p. 15.

CHAPTER VI

1 Spencer Walpole, *The Life of Lord John Russell*, 2 vols. (London, 1889), I, 333.

2 This pamphlet does not exist in the major collections. His *Reports of the House of Commons on the Education (1838), and on the Health (1840), of the Poorer Classes in Large Towns; with some Suggestions for Improvement* (London, 1840; 2nd ed., 1841), merely repeats parliamentary testimony.

3 Allen to Russell, 14 Apr. 1838, *PP*, 1839, XLI (216), 373–4; Allen to Brougham, 14 Aug. 1838, Brougham Papers, UCL; Russell to Allen, 13 Aug. 1838, Russell Papers, PRO, P.R.O. 30/22/3B, ff. 250–1.

4 Spring Rice to Russell, 17, 27 Aug. 1838, Monteagle Papers, NLI, MS. 534, ff. 52–7, 106–7; Russell to Spring Rice, 19, 30 Aug. 1838, *ibid.*, MS. 13,390(6); Spring Rice to Melbourne, 5 Sept. 1838, *ibid.*, MS. 543, pp. 55–6; Melbourne to Spring Rice, 10 Sept. 1838, *ibid.*, MS. 13,390(10).

⁵ Russell to Poor Law Commissioners, 25 Aug. 1838, Poor Law Commission, Correspondence and Papers, PRO, M.H. 19/63. Russell later admitted that the returns were inaccurate and useless (3 *Hansard*, XLV [1839], 274). The census was in fact impracticable, owing to the lack of adequate machinery and to the opposition of local guardians (E. C. Tufnell to J. G. S. Lefevre, 22 Oct. 1838, Assistant Poor Law Commissioners, Correspondence, PRO, M.H. 32/70).

⁶ Russell to Spring Rice, 27 Oct. 1838, Monteagle Papers, NLI, MS. 13,390(6).

⁷ *Ibid.* See also Cottenham to Russell, 25 Oct. 1838, Russell Papers, PRO, P.R.O. 30/22/3B, ff. 340–3; and Spring Rice to Russell, 29 Oct. 1838. *ibid.*, ff. 346–7.

⁸ Spring Rice to Russell, 29 Oct. 1838, *ibid.*, ff. 348–9; Melbourne to Russell, 27 Nov. 1838, Sanders, *Melbourne's Papers*, pp. 384–5; Russell to Spring Rice, 9 Dec. 1838, Monteagle Papers, NLI, MS. 13,390(6); Russell to Melbourne, 28 Nov. 1838, R. Russell, *Early Correspondence*, II, 234–6; John, Lord Broughton, *Recollections of a Long Life*, (ed.) Lady Dorchester, 6 vols. (London, 1911), V, 168.

⁹ *Times*, 6 Oct. 1838, p. 4e.

¹⁰ *Ibid.*, 16 Aug. 1838, pp. 3f, 4c, 25 Aug. 1838, p. 5c, 29 Aug. 1838, p. 4a, 5 Sept. 1838, p. 4b, 8 Oct. 1838, p. 5f, 13 Dec. 1838, p. 6a. Close's letters are in *ibid.*, 26 Jan.–5 Feb. 1838.

¹¹ Fremantle to Peel, 25 Oct. 1838, Peel Papers, BM, Add. MS. 40,425, f. 291.

¹² Peel to Croker, 12 Nov. [1838], Louis J. Jennings (ed.), *The Croker Papers*, 3 vols. (London, 1885), II, 321.

¹³ Allen to Brougham, 22 Jan. 1839, Brougham papers, UCL; see also Allen to Brougham, 16 Jan. 1839, *ibid.*, wherein Allen comments that Russell did not know how to deal with the Establishment.

¹⁴ Alfred Blomfield, *A Memoir of Charles James Blomfield, D.D., Bishop of London*, 2 vols. (London, 1863), I, 260; Spring Rice to Russell, 6 Feb. 1839, Monteagle Papers, NLI, MS. 536, ff. 6–8.

¹⁵ The *Times* called it 'not a measure, but a step to avoid a measure' (13 Feb. 1839, p. 5e).

¹⁶ Russell to Lansdowne, 4 Feb. 1839, *PP*, 1839, XLI (16), 255–6.

¹⁷ 3 *Hansard*, XLV (1839), 275–83.

¹⁸ *Ibid.*, col. 301.

¹⁹ *Mirror*, 1839, I, 181. While this last sentence does not appear in *Hansard*, the *Times* (13 Feb. 1839, p. 4c) confirms *Mirror*.

²⁰ 3 *Hansard*, XLV (1839), 287, 301–8; *Mirror*, 1839, I, 181–3.

²¹ Order in Council, 10 Apr. 1839, *PP*, 1839, XLI (287), 265.

²² Education Minute (hereinafter EM), 13 Apr. 1839, *ibid.* (177), pp. 259–61; EM, 20 Apr. and 15 May 1839, Education Department, Miscellanea, PRO, Ed. 9/1, pp. 8–9, 11; James Simpson to J. P. Kay, 1 May 1839, Kay-Shuttleworth Papers, JRL.

²³ 3 *Hansard*, XLVII (1839), 680–1, 756, 1381; *Report of the Select Committee of the House of Commons on Public Petitions* (1839); *Morning Chronicle*,

4 June 1839, p. 6d; Howick journal, 17 May 1839, Grey Papers, Durham University; EM, 1 June 1839, PP, 1839, XLI (284), 263; David N. Hempton, 'Wesleyan Methodism and Educational Politics in Early Nineteenth-century England', *History of Education*, VIII (1979), 210–11.
   24 Graham to Wharncliffe, 3 Jan. 1839, Wharncliffe Muniments, Sheffield City Library, Wh.M. 516(i).
   25 Graham to Stanley, 6 and 7 June 1839, Graham Papers, NL, reel 6, bdl. 37F; Peel to Gladstone, 22 May 1839, Peel Papers, BM, Add. MS. 44,275, ff. 28–9; Clerk to Peel, 21 May 1839, *ibid.*, 40,427, ff. 20–2; Mahon's 'Proposed Resolutions', 14 June 1839, *ibid.*, f. 60 (and Peel's pencilled comments); Order paper No. 75 (14 June 1839), *Votes and Proceedings of the House of Commons* (1839), II, 869; Lansdowne to Russell [12 June ?] 1839, Russell Papers, PRO, P.R.O. 30/22/3D, ff. 157–8; Russell to Victoria, 14 June 1839, Victorian Archive, RA, A 6/89.
   26 *Commons Journal*, XCIV (1839), 345, 366, 376, 386; Croker to the King of Hanover, 16 [June] 1839, Jennings, *Croker Papers*, II, 346; Diary of the Fourth Duke of Newcastle, 15 June 1839, Newcastle Papers, University of Nottingham Library, Ne 2F/6.
   27 H. D. Goring, R. Ingham, the Hon. A. F. Kinnaird, and Lord A. Lennox; of the four, Goring and Lennox also voted against the government on Peel's motion of no confidence in June 1841.
   28 The eight were Radicals—T. Duncombe, G. Grote, J. Jervis, J. T. Leader, Sir W. Molesworth, W. S. O'Brien, W. Turner, and T. Wakley.
   29 Graham to Peel, [21 June 1839?], Peel Papers, BM, Add. MS. 40,318, ff. 149–51; 'Draft Resolutions on National Education,' [*c.* 21–23 June] 1839, *ibid.*, ff. 377–8. Two drafts in Ellenborough's hand are in his papers, PRO, P.R.O. 30/12/24/1. For the discussions, see Peel's memorandum of 17 July 1839 (Peel Papers, BM, Add. MS. 40,427, f. 78), which minimises Ellenborough's role; and Graham to Ellenborough, 3 July 1839, Ellenborough Papers, PRO, P.R.O. 30/12/21/3; Wellington to Ellenborough, 3 July 1839, *ibid.*, 24/1. The general content of the resolutions was not decided upon until 2 July (Order Paper No. 75, *Minutes of Proceedings of the House of Lords, Session 1839*, p. 528), and were unveiled to the backbench peers two days later (diary of the Fourth Duke of Newcastle, 4 July 1839, Newcastle Papers, University of Nottingham Library, Ne 2F/6); *Lords Journal*, LXXI (1839), 470–1.
   30 Howick journal, 11 July 1839, Grey Papers, Durham University.
   21 Murphy, *Religious Problem*, pp. 14–16, 20–1, 53–4, 83–135.
   32 *Ibid.*, p. 167.
   33 *Ibid.*, p. 202. For variants of this hypothesis, see V. G. Toms, 'Secular Education', pp. 251–2; Richard Aldrich, 'Education and the Political Parties', pp. 179, 191; and A. S. Bishop, *Central Authority*, p. 19. See also Murphy's *Church, State and Schools*, pp. 17–21, and 'Religion, the State, and Education in England', *History of Education Quarterly*, VIII (1968), 3–34.
   34 3 *Hansard*, XLVIII (1839), 546–8, 1294–5; *Times*, 11 July 1839, p. 4b; *Mirror*, 1839, III, 2263; *Morning Chronicle*, 27 May 1839, p. 3b–c.
   35 'Education Department', pp. 55–7; 'Administrators in education

before 1870', in Gillian Sutherland (ed.), *Studies in the Growth of Nineteenth-century Government* (London, 1972), p. 117; 'Educating the Educators', pp. 82–3, 98–9.

³⁶ Johnson, 'Education Department', p. 49; Kay to T. Frankland Lewis, 9 Dec. 1837, PRO, M.H. 32/49; Slaney Committee Report, *PP*, 1837–38, VII (589), 173; Poor Law Committee Report, *ibid.*, XVIII, Pt. I (202), 463.

³⁷ Kay to Lewis, 19 Mar. 1838, PRO, M.H. 32/49.

³⁸ B. C. Bloomfield (ed.), 'The Autobiography of Sir James Kay Shuttleworth', *Education Libraries Bulletin*, Supplement Seven (1964), p. 59. The passage appears as well in Smith, *Kay-Shuttleworth*, p. 82.

³⁹ But see J. L. Alexander, 'Lord John Russell and the Origins of the Committee of Council of Education', *Historical Journal*, XX (1977), 414, for another view.

⁴⁰ J. P. Kay, 'Minute shewing the Duties of the Chaplain of a Union Workhouse', 28 May 1838, PRO, M.H. 32/50; Kay to Russell, 29 Oct. 1838, Russell Papers, PRO, P.R.O. 30/22/3B, ff. 350–2; Kay to Russell, 24 May 1839, *ibid.*, 3C, f. 315.

⁴¹ Slaney journal, 21 Oct. 1838, Jan., Feb. 1839, Morris-Eyton Collection, Shrewsbury Public Library, VIII; Slaney to Spring Rice, 16 Jan. 1839 (Register), Monteagle Papers, NLI, MS. 559, f. 5; Spring Rice to Slaney, 29 Jan. 1839, *ibid.*, MS. 533, ff. 330–1; Slaney to Spring Rice, 5 Feb. 1839 (Register), *ibid.*, MS. 559, f. 9; Slaney to Peel, 25 Nov. 1844, Peel Papers, BM, Add. MS. 40,554, f. 344.

⁴² Johnson, 'Education Department', pp. 77–8; *Morning Chronicle*, 13 Feb. 1839, p. 4f. For Slaney's role in the 1838 grant, see *supra*, pp. 21–3.

⁴³ Johnson, 'Education Department', p. 53; Johnson, 'Educating the Educators', pp. 99–100; Burgess, *Enterprise in Education*, pp. 70–1; Burgess, 'Work of the Established Church', p. 113; circular, Committee of Inquiry and Correspondence, Aug. 1838, Russell Papers, PRO, P.R.O. 30/22/3B, ff. 236–7; Spring Rice to Russell, 29 Oct. 1838, *ibid.*, f. 348; 3 *Hansard*, XLV (1839), 277–8; Russell to Spring Rice, 27 Oct. 1838, Monteagle Papers, NLI, MS. 13,390(6).

⁴⁴ J. L. Alexander ('Origins of the Committee of Council', p. 406) finds greater significance.

⁴⁵ Lansdowne to Russell, 18 Sept. 1837, Lansdowne Papers, Bowood House; Russell to Brougham, 3 Oct. 1837, Brougham Papers, UCL; Brougham to Russell, 8 Oct. 1837, Brougham Papers, WLCL; Brougham to Napier, 18 Aug. 1837, Napier, *Napier*, p. 198, Lansdowne to Russell, n.d., Russell Papers, PRO, P.R.O. 30/22/3C, ff. 111–12; Maltby to Russell, 31 May 1839, *ibid.*, f. 329; journal entries, 14 June and 2 July 1839, RA, Queen Victoria's Journals, XXVI, ff. 52–3, 55–6, 138.

⁴⁶ Russell, *Recollections*, pp. 118, 122, 124, 375.

⁴⁷ *Essays in English History* (London, 1976), p. 72.

⁴⁸ Howick to Edward Ellice, Sr., 6 Sept. 1839, Ellice Papers, National Library of Scotland, E 22, ff. 47–8.

CHAPTER VII

¹ 3 *Hansard*, LVII (1841), 937–49, LVIII (1841), 799, 1012, 1054, 1077.
² EM, 15 Aug., 29 Nov. 1839, 14 Jan. and 6 Aug. 1840, PRO, Ed. 9/1, pp. 15, 46–7, 91, 226; Ball, *Her Majesty's Inspectorate*, p. 29.
³ Otter to Allen, [*c.* 23] Nov. 1839, R. M. Grier, *John Allen, a Memoir* (London, 1889), pp. 80–1; Allen to Otter, 27 Nov. 1839, *ibid.*, pp. 82–5; Anna Otter Allen, *John Allen and his Friends* (London, 1922), pp. 93–105; E. L. and O. P. Edmonds, *I Was There: The Memoirs of H. S. Tremenheere* (Eton, 1965), pp. 34–5; R. K. Webb, 'A Whig Inspector', *JMH*, XXVII (1955), 354–5; Lansdowne to Russell, May 1839, Russell Papers, PRO, P.R.O. 30/22/3C, ff. 247–8; Russell to Melbourne, Nov. 1839, Broadlands Archives, NRA, MEL/RU/114/1. E. L. and O. P. Edmonds believe that J. P. Kay, the committee's secretary, got Tremenheere his job by mentioning his name to Lansdowne ('Hugh Seymour Tremenheere, Pioneer Inspector of Schools', *BJES*, XII, 1963, 66–8); Tremenheere's own testimony does not substantiate this.
⁴ As the committee was part of the Privy Council, Charles Greville, the Clerk of the Council, was its secretary *ex officio*; he of course played no role in its actual work.
⁵ Russell, *Recollections*, p. 309; A. V. Judges, 'Sir James Kay-Shuttleworth, Pioneer of National Education', in *Pioneers of English Education*, ed. A. V. Judges (London, 1952), p. 111; Smith, *Kay-Shuttleworth*, pp. 1–2, 15, 25–6; Hugh M. Pollard, *Pioneers of Popular Education, 1760–1850* (London, 1956), pp. 215–16; Kay to Brougham, 27 Sept. 1833, Brougham Papers, UCL; Finer, *Chadwick*, p. 151; Kerry to Kay, 10 Aug. 1834 and 25 Nov. 1835, both in Kay-Shuttleworth Papers, JRL.
⁶ Smith, *Kay-Shuttleworth*, pp. 68, 81,138–9, 154–5; Paz, 'Public Education', pp. 191–3; see also the perceptive comments of Peter Searby in *History of Education*, II (1973), 216–20.
⁷ Prest, *Russell*, p. 225; Brougham to Melbourne, [April 1835], RA, MP 2/41; Gash, *Peel*, p. 288.
⁸ F. W. Stretton to Kay, 19 July 1839, Kay to Stretton, 24 July 1839, W. Johnson to Kay, 31 July 1839, Kay to Wigram, 17 Aug. 1839, all in Sinclair, *Correspondence*, pp. 16–22; Russell to Kay, 16 Aug. 1839, Kay-Shuttleworth Papers, JRL; *Times*, 15 Oct. 1839, p. 4a.
⁹ General Committee Minutes, 30 Oct., 26 Nov. 1839, National Society Minute Book, IV, 210–11, 233–5; Lansdowne to Russell, n.d. [late 1839], Russell Papers, PRO, P.R.O. 30/22/3D, ff. 161–2; National Society, *Annual Report*, XXVIII (1839), 13; *ibid.*, XXIX (1840), 5, 15–16.
¹⁰ *Ibid.*, XXVIII (1839), 88–9; General Committee Minutes, 30 Oct. 1839, 29 Apr. and 23 May 1840, all in National Society Minute Book, IV, 211, 253, 257; Leonard Horner to his wife, 30 Apr. 1840, Katherine M. Lyell, *Memoirs of Leonard Horner*, 2 vols. (London, 1890), II, 13; H. Gally Knight to John Kaye, Bishop of Lincoln, 8 Jan. 1840, Kaye Deposit, Lincs. CRO, Cor. B/5/8A/36/1; '[Report of the] Archidiaconal Board',

Nottingham, 28 Apr. 1840, *ibid.*, Cor. B/5/8A/36/3.

¹¹ 'Return of Applications for Portions of the Sum granted for the Promotion of Public Education in 1839', *PP*, 1840, XL (124), 2–7, 11–12, 16; Burgess, *Enterprise in Education*, p. 89; Burgess, 'Work of the Established Church', pp. 159–60; E. L. Edmonds, 'School Inspection: the Contribution of Religious Denominations', *BJES*, VII (1958), 19–23.

¹² *Times*, 30 Sept. 1839, p. 4a, 3 Oct. 1839, p. 4c. 11 Oct. 1839, p. 3d, 16 Oct. 1839, p. 5b, 26 Oct. 1839, p. 3f. 19 Nov. 1839, p. 3d, 26 Nov. 1839, p. 5f, 6 Dec. 1839, p. 3f, 17 Dec. 1839, p. 3e; 3 *Hansard*, LI (1840), 652–3, 1039; Harry Chester to Macvey Napier, 7 Sept. 1839, Napier Papers, BM, Add. MS, 34,620, ff. 354–5.

¹³ *Report of the Committee of the General Assembly* (1840), pp. 22–3; Kay to Chalmers, 19 Aug. 1839, Chalmers Papers, NCE; Gordon to Kay, 19 Dec. [1839], *PP*, 1840, XL (490), 385.

¹⁴ Lansdowhe to Kay, 31 Dec. 1839, Smith, *Kay-Shuttleworth*, p. 97, n. 1; EM, 4 Jan. 1840, *PP*, 1840, XL (18), 399–402.

¹⁵ Kay to Gordon, 4 Jan. 1840, *ibid.* (490), pp. 385–6; Minute of the General Assembly's Education Committee, 12 Feb. 1840, *PP*, 1841, XX (392), 224–5; Gordon to Kay, 22 May 1840, and Kay to Gordon, 4 July 1840, *ibid.*, p. 232.

¹⁶ Monteagle to Napier, 22 Mar. 1840, Napier Papers, BM, Add. MS. 34,621, f. 81.

¹⁷ Ball, *Her Majesty's Inspectorate*, pp. 37–42. My account of the compromise, unless otherwise documented, is based on this source.

¹⁸ Blomfield, *Blomfield*, I, 270–1.

¹⁹ Howley to Peel, 4 July 1840, Peel Papers, BM, Add. MS. 40,428, f. 215.

²⁰ Sinclair also claimed that he had initiated the discussions in the first place through Sir Henry Thompson, Sir George Grey's brother-in-law and a friend of Kay's. There is no corroborating evidence for this assertion. (John Sinclair, *Sketches of Old Times and Distant Places*, London, 1875, pp. 208–10.)

²¹ Howley to Peel, 15 July 1840, Peel Papers, BM, Add. MS. 40,428, ff. 235–6.

²² EM, 15 July 1840, *PP*, 1840, XL (490), 386–7.

²³ Having accepted the Concordat, the National Society attempted to have the State inspect schools along diocesan lines. Lasdowne, however, refused. (Kay to Edward Denison, Bishop of Salisbury, 18 Feb. 1841 [copy], and Sinclair to Kay, 11 March 1841 [copy], both in the Lansdowne Papers, Bowood House.)

²⁴ For the contents of the Treasury minutes, see *supra*, pp. 26–31; for the education minute, *supra*, p. 84.

²⁵ J. P. Kay, *Recent Measures for the Promotion of Education in England*, reprinted with emendations in Sir James Kay-Shuttleworth, *Four Periods of Public Education as Reviewed in 1832–1839–1846–1862* (London, 1862), p. 238.

²⁶ Kay to Lansdowne, 12 Aug. 1839, Russell Papers, PRO, P.R.O. 30/22/3C, ff. 399–403.

27 See the marginalia on *ibid.*; Thomas Spring Rice, Lord Monteagle, 'Ministerial Plan of Education—Church and Tory Misrepresentations', *Edin. Rev.*, LXX (1839), 166, 171; Monteagle to Russell, 1 Sept. 1839, Monteagle Papers, NLI, MS. 547, pp. 36–7; *DNB*, XVIII, 836–7, puts it more gently.

28 S. M. Phillipps to Kay, 23 Aug. 1839, PRO, H.O. 34/2, p. 459.

29 EM, 24 Sept. 1839, *PP*, 1840, XL (18), 389–90.

30 Kay to Russell, 11 Oct. 1839, Kay-Shuttleworth Papers, JRL. Nancy Ball's shrewd comments on the scheme are worth noting (*Her Majesty's Inspectorate*, p. 33).

31 *PP*, 1841, XX [317], 116–32; EM, 20 Nov. 1839, *PP*, 1840, XL (18), 391–4; 'Instructions Respecting the Mode of Answering the Questions,—Form (A)', *PP*, 1841, XX [317], 111–12.

32 EM, 20 Feb. 1840, *PP*, 1840, XL (254), 409; Supplementary Minute, Dec. 1840, *PP*, 1841, XX [317], 111; D. G. Paz, 'A Note on the Quarto and Octavo Minutes of the Committee of Council, 1839/40–1857/8', *History of Education Society Bulletin*, No. 14, (autumn 1974), p. 55.

33 EM, 3 Dec. 1839, *PP*, 1840, XL (18), 395.

34 EM, 24 Sept., 29 Nov. 1839, 14 Jan., 16 May, 4 June 1840, PRO, Ed. 9/1, pp. 23, 49, 94–5, 109, 206–7; 'Copy of Minutes of the Committee of Council on Education (1841–2)', *PP*, 1842, XXXIII (442), 400–17; *PP*, 1840, XL (124), 13; *PP*, 1841, XX [317], 138–9.

35 Grey advocated a State normal school and gratuities for schoolmasters. See his 'Committee of Council on Education', *Edin. Rev.*, LXXV (1842), 136–9. For the committee's membership, see D. G. Paz, 'The Composition of the Education Committee of the Privy Council, 1839–1856', *Journal of Educational Administration and History*, VIII (1976), 1–8.

36 30 Apr., 1843, Smith, *Kay-Shuttleworth*, pp. 147–8.

37 Journal, 11 May 1840, Tremenheere Papers, Morrab Library, Album IV, pp. 41–2.

38 Glasgow Educational Society to the Treasury, Mar. 1839, *PP*, 1839, XLI (216), 371–2; Kay to Glasgow Educational Society, 4 Dec. 1839, *PP*, 1842, XXXIII (442), 119–20; John Leadbitter *et al.* to the Committee Council, 7 Feb. 1840, *ibid.*, p. 122; Kay to David Stow, 22 Feb. 1840, *ibid.*, pp. 122–3; Stow to Kay, 5 May 1841, *ibid.*, pp. 123–4; James Buchanan to Kay, 30 Mar. 1841, Kay-Shuttleworth Papers, JRL.

39 Report of John Gibson, 3 July 1841, *PP*, 1842, XXXIII (442), 129.

40 Gibson to Kay, Dec. 1841, *ibid.*, pp. 147–8; EM, Dec. 1841, *ibid.*, pp. 149–50; Kay to John Gordon, 28 Feb. 1842, *ibid.*, p. 153.

41 EM, 20 Apr. 1839, 5 Feb. 1841, PRO, Ed. 9/1, pp. 9–10, 314–16; 'National Education on Comprehensive Principles' [printed paper dated 12 July 1839], Gladstone Papers, BM, Add. MS. 44,728, f. 101; Russell to Melbourne, 31 July 1839, Russell Papers, PRO, P.R.O. 30/22/3C, ff. 393–4; Melbourne to Russell, 31 July 1839, Melbourne Papers, RA, MP 14/51; British Society, *Annual Report*, XXXV (1840), 11.

⁴² Dunn to Committee of Council, 11 Jan. 1841, *PP*, 1843, XL (217), 596–9; Kay to Dunn, 8 Feb. 1841, *ibid.*, pp. 600–2; Tremenheere, 'Report on British Schools in London', 1 July 1842, *ibid.*, pp. 614–54; Dunn to Wharncliffe, 20 Aug. 1842, *ibid.*, p. 657; Webb, 'Whig Inspector', p. 356; Edmonds, *I Was There*, pp. 44–6; British Society, *Annual Report*, XXXVII (1842), 24.
⁴³ Wharncliffe to Kay-Shuttleworth, 20 Dec. [1842], Kay-Shuttleworth Papers, JRL; 'Inspection of Schools by Government', *Eclectic Review*, new ser., XII (1842), 486, 490, 492, 500.
⁴⁴ Wharncliffe to Peel, 9 Jan. 1843, Peel Papers, BM, Add. MS. 40,522, f. 287; Dunn to Wharncliffe, 7 June 1842, *PP*, 1843, XL (217), 610–13; Wharncliffe to Dunn, 13 Jan. 1843, *ibid.*, pp. 660–1.
⁴⁵ Sinclair to Gladstone, 5 Nov. 1841, Gladstone Papers, BM, Add. MS. 44,357, f. 192; Sinclair to Gladstone, 8 Nov. 1841, *ibid.*, f. 195; *Times*, 4 Dec. 1841, p. 2f; *ibid.*, 27 Sept. 1842, p. 4b; Monteagle to Napier, 26 July 1842, Macvey Napier Papers, BM, Add. MS. 34,623, f. 30.

CHAPTER VIII

¹ George Kitson Clark, 'Hunger and Politics in 1842', *JMH*, XXV (1953), 356–7, 360–2; Chadwick, *Victorian Church*, Part I, p. 223; Wortley to Peel, 5 Feb. 1842, Peel Papers, BM, Add. MS. 40,502, ff. 12–13; Peel to Wortley, 6 Feb. 1842, *ibid.*, f. 14; Wortley to Graham, 20 Apr. 1843, Wharncliffe Muniments, parcel V(d); Travis L. Crosby, *Sir Robert Peel's Administration, 1841–1846* (Newton Abbot and Hamden, Conn., 1976), p. 36; Graham to G. G. Manning, 12 June 1834, Graham Papers, NL, reel 4, bdl. 26; Graham to Rev. R. Burgess, 22 Nov. 1842, Charles Stuart Parker, *Life and Letters of Sir James Graham, 1792–1861*, 2 vols. (London, 1907), I, 342.
² Brougham to Graham, 21 Oct. 1841, Parker, *Graham*, I, 337; Graham to Brougham, 24 Oct. 1841, *ibid.*, pp. 338–9; Graham to Brougham, 18 Dec. 1841 and 19 Jan. 1842, Brougham Papers, UCL; Graham to Peel, 16 Jan. 1842, Peel Papers, BM, Add. MS. 40,446, f. 312; Peel to Graham, 18 Jan. 1842, Parker, *Peel*, II, 533–4; Brougham to Napier, 11 Feb. 1842, Macvey Napier Papers, BM, Add. MS. 34,622, f. 407; T. Jones Howell to Graham, 2 Nov. 1841, PRO, H.O. 45/61; Graham to Peel, 28 Dec. 1842, Peel Papers, BM, Add. MS. 40,448, f. 148. Bernice Martin calls Horner 'the most impressive and influential of the first English factory inspectors', although she admits that 'Saunders often ran him close' ('Leonard Horner: a Portrait of an Inspector of Factories', *International Review of Social History*, XIV, 1969, 412, 428).
³ 'Reports of Inspectors of Factories to Her Majesty's Principal Secretary of State for the Home Department. For the Half-year ending 30th June 1839', *PP*, 1839, XIX [201], 551; Horner, *Factories Regulation Act Explained*, p. 20; Leonard Horner, 'Preliminary Observations', in his

translation of Victor Cousin, *On the State of Education in Holland, as Regards Schools for the Working Classes and for the Poor* (London, 1838); Horner to Senior, 23 May 1837, Senior, *Letters on the Factory Act*, p. 37; Horner, *Employment of Children*, pp. 18–19; 'Report of the Inspectors of Factories . . . December 1839', *PP*, 1840, XXIII [218], 6, 14; 'Reports of the Inspectors of Factories . . . June 1840', *ibid.* [261], pp. 42–3; 'Reports of the Inspectors of Factories . . . December 1841', *PP*, 1842, XXII (31), 347–8, 432–3; Robson, *Education of Children*, pp. 65–6; 'Report of Mr. R. J. Saunders, upon the Establishment of Schools in the Factory Districts, in February 1842', *PP*, 1843, XXVII [500], 393–4; G. Ward, 'Factory Child Workers', p. 119; General Committee Minutes, 4 Nov. 1840 and 13 Jan. 1841, National Society Minute Book, IV, 277–83.

⁴ Kay-Shuttleworth to Janet Shuttleworth, 12 Jan. 1842, Kay-Shuttleworth Papers, JRL; Kay-Shuttleworth to Blomfield, Jan. 1842, Smith, *Kay-Shuttleworth*, p. 141; Graham to Peel, 16 Jan. 1842, Peel Papers, BM, Add. MS. 40,446, f. 312; Graham to Blomfield, 21 Jan. 1842, Graham Papers, NL, reel 7, bdl. 46; Graham to Blomfield, 27 Dec. 1842, Parker, *Graham*, I, 342–3.

⁵ Kitson Clark, 'Hunger and Politics', pp. 362–9; Graham to Earl Powis, [31] Aug. 1842, Parker, *Graham*, I, 328–9.

⁶ Graham to Peel, 26 Aug. 1842, Charles Stuart Parker, *Sir Robert Peel from His Private Papers*, 3 vols. (London, 1891–99), II, 541.

⁷ Chadwick to Russell, 1 Nov. 1837, Chadwick Papers, UCL; Graham to Kay-Shuttleworth, 30 Aug. 1842, Parker, *Graham*, I, 329; Graham to Peel, 8 Sept. 1842, Parker, *Peel*, II, 546–7.

⁸ The causal relationship between the riots of 1842 and the Bill of 1843 is not as clear as some scholars argue (e.g., J. T. Ward and J. H. Treble, 'Religion and Education in 1843: Reaction to the "Factory Education Bill"', *Journal of Ecclesiastical History*, XX, 1969, 81). I agree with Richard Johnson, who contends that they 'strengthened the arguments of those already committed to further legislative action' ('Education Department', p. 121).

⁹ National Society, *Annual Report*, XXXIII (1844), 1–3; John Sinclair (ed.), *Correspondence on the Subject of the Late Disturbances in the Manufacturing and Mining Districts* (London, 1842).

¹⁰ Graham to Kay-Shuttleworth, 10 Dec. 1842, Smith, *Kay-Shuttleworth*, p. 142.

¹¹ Graham to Blomfield, 27 Dec. 1842, Parker, *Graham*, I, 342–3; Graham to Peel, 28 Dec. 1842, Peel Papers, BM, Add. MS. 40,448, f. 148; Graham to Peel, 28 Dec. 1842, *ibid.*, f. 152; Graham to Kay-Shuttleworth, 29 Dec. 1842, Graham Papers, NL, reel 8, bdl. 57; Factory Inspectors' Minute Book, 7 Feb. 1843, PRO, Lab. 15/1; 'Factory Bill, 1843', *PP*, 1843, II (182), 499–501, 512–17, 522.

¹² Robson, *Education of Children*, pp. 74–5; Smith, *Kay-Shuttleworth*, pp. 142–3; Kay-Shuttleworth to Russell, 30 Apr. 1843, *ibid.*, p. 149; Saunders to Kay-Shuttleworth, 30 Dec. 1842, *ibid.*, pp. 144–5.

¹³ Graham to the Bishop of Chester, 19 Jan. 1843, Graham Papers, NL,

reel 8, bdl. 57; Lansdowne to Kay-Shuttleworth, 16 Dec. 1842, Kay-Shuttleworth Papers, JRL.

[14] Ward and Treble, 'Religion and Education in 1843', p. 80; Edward Baines, Jr., *On the Social, Educational, and Religious State of the Manufacturing Districts*, 3rd ed. (London, 1843), p. 6.

[15] Journal of the Seventh Earl of Shaftesbury, 14 April, 6 Sept. 1842, 13 Feb. 1843, Broadlands Archives, NRA, SHA/PD/2; Shaftesbury Journal, 13, 23 Mar., 1, 2 May, 30 June 1843, 11 Mar. 1845, *ibid.*, PD/3. In his most notorious entry he called Peel and Russell 'the most criminal of mankind', and declared that Graham 'has contrived to render himself so thoroughly odious that I cannot find one human being who will speak a word on his behalf' (Shaftesbury journal, 8 July 1843, Edwin Hodder, *The Life and Work of the Seventh Earl of Shaftesbury*, 3 vols., London, 1887, I, 477–80).

[16] 3 *Hansard*, LXVII (1843), 75, 77–90.

[17] *Ibid.*, cols. 91–3, 99–100, 102–5, 112–14.

[18] *Ibid.*, cols. 1430, 1433–8, 1442–50, 1454–62, 1469–70; Peel to Victoria, 25 Mar. 1843, Peel Papers, BM, Add. MS. 40,436, f. 138; Ashley to Graham, 28 Mar. 1843, Graham Papers, NL, reel 9, bdl. 59; Shaftesbury journal, 28 Mar. 1843, Broadlands Archives, NRA, SHA/PD/3.

[19] *Times*, 25 Mar. 1843, p. 3c, 31 Mar. 1843, p. 5d, 8 Apr. 1843, p. 5f, 21 Apr. 1843, p. 6a, 27 Apr. 1843, p. 6f; *Spectator*, 15 Apr. 1843, pp. 341–3, 29 Apr. 1843, pp. 390–2, 6 May 1843, p. 416; *Examiner*, 8 Apr. 1843, p. 218, 13 Apr. 1843, p. 231, 22 Apr. 1843, p. 246, 29 Apr. 1843, p. 266; *Leeds Mercury*, 25 Mar. 1843, p. 5a, 29 Apr. 1843, pp. 6a, 7e; *Sheffield Mercury*, 1 Apr. 1842; British Society, *Annual Report*, XXXVIII (1843), 24–5.

[20] Graham to Peel, 13 Apr. 1843, Parker, *Peel*, II, 560.

[21] 1 Shaftesbury journal, 26 Apr. 1843, Broadlands Archives, NRA, SHA/PD/3; *Sheffield and Rotherham Independent*, 29 Apr. 1843; Leeds Wesleyan Deputation, *On the Educational Clauses of Sir James Graham's Factory Bill* (Leeds, 1843), pp. 3–4; Hempton, 'Methodism and Educational Politics', pp. 214–18

[22] G. D. H. Cole, *Chartist Portraits* (London, 1965), pp. 184, 223; H. U. Faulkner, *Chartism and the Churches: a Study in Democracy* (New York, 1916), pp. 28–30, 46–7; James H. Treble, 'The Reaction of Chartism in the North of England to the Factory Education Bill of 1843', *Journal of Educational Administration and History*, VI, No. 2 (July 1974), 1–9; *Leeds Mercury*, 22 Apr. 1843, p. 6a–b, 20 May 1843, p. 6; *Times*, 27 Mar. 1843, p. 4f, 30 Mar. 1843, p. 4e, 13 Apr. 1843, p. 4b, 20 Apr. 1843, p. 3e, 29 Apr. 1843, p. 6e; *Examiner*, 13 Apr. 1843, p. 231; *Spectator*, 22 Apr. 1843, pp. 364–5; *Sheffield Mercury*, 3 June 1843.

[23] *Report, Public Petitions* (1843); 3 *Hansard*, LXVIII (1843), 745–6; Monteagle to Napier, 6 Apr. 1843, Macvey Napier Papers, BM, Add. MS. 34,623, f. 536.

[24] Graham to Blomfield, 20 Apr. 1843, Graham Papers, NL, reel 9, bdl. 60B; Graham to Peel, 13 Apr. 1843, Peel Papers, BM, Add. MS. 40,448, f.

269; Kay-Shuttleworth to Russell, 30 Apr. 1843, Smith, *Kay-Shuttleworth*, pp. 147–50; Russell to Kay-Shuttleworth, 2 May 1843, *ibid.*, p. 151; 'Factory Bill, 1843 (Amended)', *PP*, 1843, II (220), 556, 568–74; James Stansfeld to Charles Wood, 3 May 1843, Hickleton Papers, A4/50 (reel 1); 3 *Hansard*, LXVIII (1843), 1119–21, 1123–4, 1126–8; *Report, Public Petitions* (1843); *Times*, 3 May 1843, p. 6b, 10 May 1843, p. 7d, 11 May 1843, p. 7f, 12 May 1843, p. 5c, 26 May 1843, pp. 4f–5a, 6 June 1843, p. 6b; *Spectator*, 6 May 1843, p. 416; *Examiner*, 6 May 1843, p. 282, 13 May 1843, p. 299, 20 May 1843, p. 313, 27 May 1843, p. 330, 10 June 1843, p. 362; *Leeds Mercury*, 20 May 1843, p. 5b; *Sheffield Mercury*, 20 May 1843.

[25] Ever concerned about resistence to such pressure, Peel had declared in 1841 that '. . . it is dangerous to admit any other recognized organ of public opinion than the House of Commons. It is dangerous to set up the implied or supposed opinions of constituencies against their declared and authorized organ, the House of Commons' (3 *Hansard*, LVIII, 1841, 817).

[26] 'Secret Political Memoranda', 13 May 1843, Gladstone Papers, BM, Add. MS. 44,819, ff. 92–3; 'Secret Political Memoranda', 15 June 1843, Brooke and Sorensen, *Prime Ministers' Papers*, II, 206–8.

[27] 'Review of the Session', *Eclectic Review*, new ser., XIV (1843), 459; 'The Government Education Bill: Conduct of Dissenters', *ibid.*, pp. 576, 590–1, 594; Leeds Wesleyan Deputation, *Graham's Factory Bill*, pp. 6–7; Edward Baines, Jr., *The Factory Education Bill, Original and Amended* (London, 1843), p. 7.

[28] 'Sir Robert Peel', *Eclectic Review*, new ser., XIV (1843), 710.

[29] 'I might even conjecture that the bill was a joint production, having its birth in this very town, and that it is one fruit of the many visits which Mr Saunders pays at the *Leeds Vicarage*.' Baines, *Education Bill*, pp. 4, 61; Leeds Wesleyan Deputation, *Graham's Factory Bill*, p. 5.

[30] 'Factories Education Bill', *Eclectic Review*, new ser., XIII (1843), 577–8, 580–1; 'Review of the Session', pp. 473–4; Baines, *Education Bill*, p. 14; Baines, *Manufacturing Districts*, p. 6.

[31] *Examiner*, 13 Apr. 1843, p. 231; John Howard Hinton, *A Plea for Liberty of Conscience* (London, 1843), pp. 6–7; 'Factories Education Bill', pp. 578–9, E. G. West, 'Private Versus Public Education: a Classical Economic Dispute', *Journal of Political Economy*, LXXII (1964), 466–7; Thomas, Lord Monteagle, 'Distress of the Manufacturing Districts—Causes and Remedies', *Edin. Rev.*, LXVII (1843), 217; Leeds Wesleyan Deputation, *Graham's Factory Bill*, p. 10; Baines, *Education Bill*, pp. 9, 45–7; *Leeds Mercury*, 4 Mar. 1843, p. 4e, 22 Apr. 1843, p. 4b.

[32] R. A. Soloway, *Prelates and People* (London and Toronto, 1969), pp. 413–14; *Times*, 6 Mar. 1843, p. 5e; Shaftesbury journal, 11 May 1843, Hodder, *Shaftesbury*, I, 457–8; 'Political Diary', 25 Mar. 1843, Gladstone Papers, BM, Add. MS. 44,819, ff. 89–90; Graham to Gladstone, 25 Mar. 1843, *ibid.*, MS. 44,163, f. 19; Foot and Matthew, *Gladstone Diaries*, III, 276 (1 May 1843).

[33] Cecil Wray, *The Suppression of any Portion of the Truth in the Work of Education Unjustifiable* (London and Liverpool, 1843), pp. 8–9, 19; Derwent

Coleridge, *The Teachers of the People: a Sermon Preached at the Opening of the Chapel of St. Mark's College, Chelsea* (London, 1843), p. 15; George W. Sandys, *A Letter to the Right Honourable Sir James R. G. Graham, . . . on the Subject of National Education* (London, 1843), p. 13; Tenax, *A Letter to the Right Hon. the Lord Wharncliffe, on the Unconstitutional Character of his late Declarations with Respect to National Education* (London, 1842); Charles Lloyd, *A Calm Inquiry into all the Objections made to the Educational Provisions of the Factory Bill* (London, 1843), p. 5.

[34] 'Returns of the Number of Children Employed, under 14 Years of Age', *PP*, 1836, XLV (254), 204, 205, 213; 'Returns Relative to Factories', *PP*, 1839, XLII (41), 55–6, 90, 200, 289.

[35] Graham to the Rev. G. R. Gleig, 6 Mar. 1843, Parker, *Graham*, II, 344.

[36] Slaney journal, Aug. 1843, Morris-Eyton Collection, Shrewsbury Public Library, IX; Ashley to Peel, 17 June 1843, Parker, *Peel*, II, 561–2; Shaftesbury journal, 16 June 1843, Hodder, *Shaftesbury*, I, 459–60; 3 *Hansard*, LXXVI (1844), 1077–9; Kay-Shuttleworth to Russell, 30 Apr. 1843, Smith, *Kay-Shuttleworth*, p. 150.

[37] Two good examples of orchestrated meetings are the quarterly meeting of the Sheffield Sunday School Union, 27 March (*Sheffield and Rotherham Independent*, 1 Apr. 1843), and the extraordinary town meeting at Leeds, 11 April (*Leeds Mercury*, 8 Apr. 1843, p. 4a, 15 Apr. 1843, p. 6a–d).

[38] *Reaction and Reconstruction*, p. 89.

CHAPTER IX

[1] 3 *Hansard*, XLVIII (1839), 1267.

[2] Peel to Graham, 18 Jan. 1842, Parker, *Peel*, II, 533–4; Graham to Peel, 17 Sept. 1842, *ibid.*, pp. 548–9; Graham to Gladstone, 25 Mar. 1843, Gladstone Papers, BM, Add. MS. 44,163, ff. 19–20.

[3] Thomas, *Early Factory Legislation*, pp. 213–14; Robson, *Education of Children*, pp. 79–80, 101–3; Duke, 'Education of Pauper Children', pp. 67–76; Francis Duke, 'The Poor Law Commission and Education', *Journal of Educational Administration and History*, III (1970), 7–13; Gladstone's memorandum of 25 July 1843, Brooke and Sorensen, *Prime Ministers' Papers*, II, 215–17.

[4] Sandon to Wharncliffe, 3 Oct. 1843, Harrowby Papers, Sandon Hall, vol. XVIII, ff. 200–2; Hurt, *Education in Evolution*, p. 49; Webb, 'Whig Inspector', p. 356; Ball, *Her Majesty's Inspectorate*, pp. 49–57; Wharncliffe to Dunn, 30 Nov. 1843, *Minutes of the Committee of Council on Education: with Appendices, and Plans of School-houses, 1842–43* (London, 1844), p. 537.

[5] EM, 22 Nov. 1843, *PP*, 1844, XXXVIII (84), 219–20; Raymond Pallister, 'Educational Capital in the Elementary School of the Mid-nineteenth Century', *History of Education*, II (1973), 147–57; 'Minutes of the Committee of Council, 1839–40', *PP*, 1840, XL (254), 623; 'Minutes of

the Committee of Council, 1840–1', *PP*, 1841, XX [317], 152–3; 'Minutes of the Committee of Council, 1841–2', *PP*, 1842, XXXIII (442), 367, 388–9, 402–17; Sandon to Wharncliffe, 3 Oct. 1843, Harrowby Papers, vol. XVIII, ff. 200–2; Sandon to Maltby, 6 Oct. 1843, *ibid.*, f. 43; Kay-Shuttleworth to Patrick Graham, 19 Jan. 1844, *ibid.*, XLII (309), 691; Minute Book of the SSPCK for 1843–44, SRO, GD 95/2/19, *passim*; 'A Return of the Number and Locality of Schools in *Scotland* to which Aid has been granted by the Educational Committee of the Privy Council', *PP*, 1844, XLII (309), 676–85; 'Return of all Sums which have been granted under Authority of the Committee of Privy Council for Educational Purposes in *Scotland*', *PP*, 1847–48, L (197), 649–52.

⁶ D. G. Paz, 'Working-class Education and the State, 1839–1849: the Sources of Government Policy', *Journal of British Studies*, XVI (1976), 142; Kay-Shuttleworth to Sir R. Peel and William Yates Peel, 5 Nov. 1844, Peel Papers, BM, Add. MS. 40,537, f. 263; Allen's reports are in 'Minutes of the Committee of Council, 1842–3', *PP*, 1843, XL [500], 220, 226–7.

⁷ Circular to school inspectors, 13 Aug. 1843, *Minutes of the Committee of Council on Education: with Appendices, 1844*, 2 vols. (London, 1845), I, 122; circular to school inspectors, 16 Dec. 1844, *ibid.*, pp. 127–30; Kay-Shuttleworth to Poor Law Commissioners, 14 Dec. 1846, PRO, M.H. 19/14; 'Scheme of Periodical Inspection for England and Wales', *Minutes of the Committee of Council, 1842–43*, pp. 23–36; EM, 22 Nov. 1843, *PP*, 1844, XXXVIII (84), 220; Ball, *Her Majesty's Inspectorate*, pp. 87–90; Hurt, *Education in Evolution*, pp. 50–1; Privy Council minute, 6 Jan. 1845, Privy Council Minute Book, PRO, P.C. 4/19, pp. 279–82; Goulburn to Peel, 16 Jan. 1845, Peel Papers, BM, Add. MS, 40,445, ff. 20–2; Crosby, *Peel's Administration*, pp. 51–2.

⁸ 3 *Hansard*, LXXII (1844), 334–5, LXXVI (1844), 1075–6, LXXX (1845), 171–2, LXXXII (1845), 1140–3, LXXXVII (1846), 1232, 1257–8, CXII (1850), 797.

⁹ Strachey and Fulford, *Greville Memoirs*, V, 269 (22 Dec. 1845).

¹⁰ *PP*, 1847, XLV [866], 13–18.

¹¹ Kay-Shuttleworth, *Four Periods*, pp. 287–91; 'First Report on the Training School at Battersea' (1841), *ibid.*, p. 310; Tufnell to Chadwick, 5 Sept. 1867, Chadwick Papers, UCL; Slaney Committee Report, *PP*, 1837–38, VII (589), 190; Kay to Poor Law Commissioners, [14 Jan. 1839], PRO, M.H. 32/50.

¹² Maltby to Committee of Council, 9 Jan. 1840, PRO, Ed. 9/1, p. 93; Edmonds, *I Was There*, p. 28; General Assembly's Education Committee, *Report on the Returns from Presbyteries on the State of Schools in the Year 1841*, pp. 12–13; Horner to Graham, 21 Jan. 1845, and Saunders to Graham, 22 Jan. 1845, PRO, H.O. 45/1290; references to pupil-teachers and the salaries of schoolmasters in the inspectors' reports: *PP*, 1841, XX [317], 152, 176; *PP*, 1842, XXXIII (442), 334, 370, 390, 394–5; *PP*, 1843, XL [500], 419; *PP*, 1845, XXV [622], 344, 381, 410, 425, 451, 476–7, 561–2, 587; *PP*, 1846, XXXII [741], 272–3, 315, 375; National Society, *Annual Report*, XXV (1836), 54–6; *ibid.*, XXVIII (1839), 67–9; *ibid.*, XXIX

(1840), 125; *ibid.*, XXX (1841), 18–19; *Times*, 4 Dec. 1841, p. 2e; *Minutes of the Committee of Council, 1845*, I, viii–x; London Diocesan Board of Education, *Inspector's Report* (London, n.d.), p. 5; Burgess, *Enterprise in Education*, pp. 98–9; Burgess, 'Work of the Established Church', pp. 171–208; Alexander, 'Collegiate Teacher-training', pp. 108–51; Dunn, *National Education*, pp. 43–6; Binns, *Century of Education*, pp. 137–8, 160–3.

¹³ Buccleuch to Kay-Shuttleworth, 12 Feb. 1847, Kay-Shuttleworth Papers, JRL.

¹⁴ EM, 22 Nov. 1843, *PP*, 1844, XXXVIII (84), 220; EM, 16 Jan. 1844, *ibid.*, p. 221; Smith, *Kay-Shuttleworth*, p. 152; Alexander, 'Collegiate Teacher-training', pp. 192–7.

¹⁵ Smith, *Kay-Shuttleworth*, p. 163.

¹⁶ *Ibid.*, p. 162.

¹⁷ *Ibid.*, p. 164; Wharncliffe to Peel, 29 Nov. 1844, Peel Papers, BM, Add. MS. 40,554, ff. 449–50; Peel to Wharncliffe, 30 Nov. 1844, *ibid.*, ff. 451–2; Goulburn to Peel, 22 Aug. 1849, *ibid.*, 40,445, ff. 473–4; 3 *Hansard*, LXXII (1845), 1145; *Minutes of the Committee of Council on Education: with Appendices, 1845*, 2 vols. (London, 1846), I, viii–xxiv; for a differing view, see Johnson, 'Education Department', pp. 191–6, and Hurt, *Education in Evolution*, pp. 91–2.

¹⁸ 'Present Condition', Kay-Shuttleworth Papers, JRL; Lady Lorne to Kay-Shuttleworth, 22 Jan. 1846, and the Duke of Buccleuch to Kay-Shuttleworth, 23 Mar. 1846, both in *ibid.*; Johnson, 'Education Department', pp. 189–99; Gladstone to Hook, 12 July 1846, Smith, *Kay-Shuttleworth*, p. 178; Foot and Matthew, *Gladstone Diaries*, III, 539, 546.

¹⁰ 3 *Hansard*, LXXXVII (1846), 1251–4; *ibid.*, LXXXIX (1847), 859; *ibid.*, XCI (1847), 979–80, 1028–9, 1082–3, 1109–10, 1273; Alexander, 'Collegiate Teacher-training', pp. 203–45, shows drawn-out consultation with the Church; Edward Baines, Jr., *An Alarm to the Nation on the Unjust, Unconstitutional and Dangerous Measure of State Education Proposed by the Government* (London, 1847); R. E. Leader, *Life and Letters of John Arthur Roebuck* (London, 1897), pp. 148–85; Prest, *Russell*, p. 262; James Stansfeld, Sr., to Charles Wood, 13 Apr. 1847, Hickleton Papers, A. 4/50 (reel 1); Aldam's papers at Frickley Hall; Fraser, *Urban Politics*, p. 188; letters to Russell from Charles Wood, 1 and 14 Aug. 1847, and Lord Fortescue, 5 Aug. 1847, all in the Russell Papers, PRO, P.R.O. 30/22/6E, ff. 33, 43, 108.

²⁰ Kay-Shuttleworth to Russell, 31 Mar. 1847, *ibid.*, 6B, ff. 326–7; Ashley to Russell, 8 Apr. 1847, *ibid.*, 6C, ff. 35–6; Russell to Ashley, 7 Apr. 1847, and Shaftesbury journal, 1 and 15 Apr. 1847, all in Hodder, *Shaftesbury*, II, 214–15; 3 *Hansard*, XCI (1847), 949–51, 1305–7; Foot and Matthew, *Gladstone Diaries*, II, 333; Wesleyan Education Committee, *Annual Report*, V (1843), 16–17; *ibid.*, VII (1845), xiv, xxvi; *ibid.*, VIII (1846), 10–13, 25.

²¹ EM, 28 June 1847, *PP*, 1847, XLV [866], 23 (confirming a decision of 7 April); W. Ward, *Religion and Society*, p. 251; Hempton, 'Methodism and Educational Politics', pp. 219–20; Wesleyan Education Committee,

Annual Report, IX (1847), 49–74. (This interpretation corrects that in my 'Working-class Education and the State', pp. 144–5; for another view, see Machin, *Politics and the Churches*, pp. 183–4.)

[22] 3 *Hansard*, XCI (1847), 1367–8; J. C. Symons, 'Education of the Working Classes', *Dublin Review*, XIV (1844), 177; *Times*, 22 Apr. 1847, p. 7c; Kay-Shuttleworth to Russell, 25 Apr. 1847, Russell Papers, PRO, P.R.O. 30/22/6C, ff. 176–7; EM, 18 Dec. 1847, *PP*, 1847–48, L (488), 613; J. Kitching, 'The Catholic Poor Schools, 1800 to 1845', *Journal of Educational Administration and History*, I, No. 2 (1969), 1–8, and II, No. 1 (1969), 1–12; M. G. Holland, 'The British Catholic Press and the Educational Controversy, 1847–1865' (unpublished Ph.D. dissertation, Catholic University of America, 1975), pp. 58–91.

[23] Duke, 'Education of Pauper Children', pp. 52–3; Goldstrom, *Social Content of Education*, pp. 132–7; J. W. Croker, 'Shuttleworth's Phonics', *Quarterly Review*, LXXIV (1844), 26–39; Grey, 'Committee of Council', pp. 138–9; Horner to Graham, 21 Jan. 1845, and Saunders to Graham, 22 Jan. 1845, both in PRO, H.O. 45/1290; *PP*, 1842, XXXIII (442), 402–17; inspectors' recommendations in *PP*, 1840, XL (254), 623; *PP*, 1841, XX [317], 151–2, 176; *PP*, 1842, XXXII (442), 179, 377–8; *PP*, 1845, XXV [622], 553, 588–9; and *PP*, 1846, XXXII [741], 274, 317, 365–6; Sandon to Wharncliffe, 3 Oct. 1843, Harrowby Papers, Sandon Hall, vol. XVIII, ff. 200–2; Circular to school inspectors, 29 July 1847, PRO, Ed. 9/12, pp. 11–12; EM, 18 Dec. 1847, *PP*, 1847–48, L. [998], 10.

[24] Binns, *Century of Education*, pp. 141–4; R. J. Watson, 'Presbyterian Day Schools', *Journal of the Presbyterian Historical Society of England*, XIV (1969), 67–8 (I am indebted to Mr Watson for this reference); Brougham to Dr Shepherd [1846?], George Armstrong to Brougham, 13 Jan. 1847, Henry Warburton to Brougham, 14 July 1854, and Lord John Russell to Brougham, 6 Aug. 1854, all in the Brougham Papers, UCL; Chadwick, *Victorian Church*, Pt. I, p. 151; Raymond G. Cowherd, *The Politics of English Dissent* (New York, 1956), pp. 153–9; 'National Education—Sectarian and Unconstitutional', *Eclectic Review*, new ser., XXI (1847), 507; 'The New Ministry', *British Quarterly Review*, IV (1846), 266–8; David M. Thompson, 'The Liberation Society, 1844–1868', in *Pressure from Without in Early Victorian England*, ed. Patricia Hollis (New York, 1974), pp. 210–38; Robert Vaughan, 'Popular Education in England', *British Quarterly Review*, IV (1846), 493–501; Robert Vaughan, 'The Education Question', *ibid.*, V (1847), 543–7.

[25] Benjamin Hawes to Russell, 28 May 1847, Russell Papers, PRO, P.R.O. 30/22/6C, ff. 359–61; EM, 10 July 1847, *PP*, 1847, XLV (660), 9; 3 *Hansard*, XCIV (1847), 667; Robert Vaughan, 'The Education Controversy—What has it Done?', *British Quarterly Review*, VI (1847), 534–5; John Bright to Edward Baines, Jr., 1 Feb. and 7 Mar. 1848, both in the Baines Papers, Leeds City Archives, MS. 2; anonymous circular dated London, 27 May 1847, and William Aldam to Mary Aldam, 1 June 1847, Aldam Papers, Frickley Hall; Binns, *Century of Education*, pp. 144–6.

[26] National Society, *Annual Report*, XXXIII (1844), 1–2; Sinclair, *Late*

Disturbances, p. 6; John Grey, *A Sermon, Preached* . . . *in Behalf of the Special Fund for Providing National Schools for the Manufacturing and Mining Districts* (London, 1843), pp. 4, 6, 7–8, 11, 14; National Society, *Annual Report*, XXXII (1843), 16; A. P. Percival, *Two Sermons*, 'Advertisement to the Second Sermon', unpaginated; R. W. Almond, 'Parochial National-Schools Committee for Nottingham', Kaye Deposit, Lincs. CRO, Cor. B/5/8A/36/42; Tancred to Gladstone, 6 Apr. and 3 July 1843, Gladstone Papers, BM, Add. MS. 44,360, ff. 98, 202; George Anson to Prince Albert, 15 July 1843, Victorian Archive, RA, F37/61; Peel to Albert, 24 July 1843, *ibid.*, F37/64; Peel to Albert, 25 July 1843, *ibid.*, F37/67. For another view see Hurt, *Education in Evolution*, pp. 26–7.

[27] 'Secret Political Memoranda', 21 July 1840, Brooke and Sorensen, *Prime Ministers' Papers*, II, 129; Gladstone to Hook, 30 Mar. 1843, Lathbury, *Church and Religion*, II, 133–4; Gladstone to Lord Lyttleton, 24 Mar. 1843, *ibid.*, pp. 130–1; Gladstone to Graham, 25 Mar. 1843, *ibid.*, pp. 131–2; Gladstone to the Bishop of Salisbury, 5 Aug. 1853, *ibid.*, pp. 134–5; Gladstone to Lyttleton, 15 Dec. 1843, Gladstone–Glynn Papers, Flint CRO; Hook to Samuel Wilberforce, 5 July 1843, Arthur R. Ashwell and Reginald G. Wilberforce, *Life of the Right Reverend Samuel Wilberforce, D.D., Lord Bishop of Oxford and afterwards of Winchester*, 3 vols. (London, 1880–82), I, 225–7; Hook to Gladstone, 28 Mar. 1843, W. R. W. Stephens, *The Life and Letters of Walter Farquhar Hook*, 7th ed. (London, 1885), pp. 346–8; Hook to Edward Stanley, Bishop of Norwich, 28 Sept. 1846, *ibid.*, pp. 423–5; Hook to Gladstone, 14 Apr. 1845, Gladstone Papers, BM, Add. MS. 44,213, f. 71; W. F. Hook, *On the Means of Rendering more Efficient the Education of the People* (London, 1846), pp. 3–4, 21–2, 32, 36; 3 *Hansard*, XCI (1847), 1287–90; draft letter from Sinclair, 27 July 1847, and Derwent Coleridge to Acland, 6 Oct. 1847, both in Acland of Broadclyst papers, Devon CRO, 1148 M/21 (iv)23; Benjamin Harrison to Acland, [*c.* 1848], *ibid.* (iv)26; Acland to his wife, 5 Dec. 1848, Acland, *Acland*, p. 158.

[28] Lansdowne to Russell, [1846], Russell Papers, PRO, P.R.O. 30/22/5G, f. 212; John Shipman to Lansdowne, 15 Apr. 1847, *ibid.*, 6C, ff. 96–7; Kay-Shuttleworth to Rev. H. Jeffreys, 30 Aug. 1847, PRO, Ed. 9/12, p. 20; Russell to Sandon, 25 Nov. 1846, Harrowby Papers, Sandon Hall, XVIII, ff. 143–6; 'Minutes of the Committee of Council, 1846', *PP*, 1847, XLV [866], 25–8.

[29] Gladstone to Manning, 6 July 1849, Lathbury, *Church and Religion*, II, 281–2; 3 *Hansard*, XCI (1847), 1064; Acland to his father, 4 June 1848, Acland, *Acland*, pp. 156–7; Samuel Wilberforce to Henry Phillpotts, 15 June 1848, R. K. Pugh and J. F. A. Mason (eds.), *The Letter Book of Samuel Wilberforce*, vol. XLVII of *The Oxfordshire Record Society* (n.p., 1970), p. 127; Ashwell and Wilberforce, *Wilberforce*, II, 9; National Society, *Annual Report*, XXXVIII (1849), 37–8; undated memorandum, Acland Papers, Exeter City Library, 51/12/1; National Society, *Monthly Paper*, No. 19 (30 June 1848), pp. 3–4; J. B. Sumner to Kay-Shuttleworth, 1 June 1848, Kay-Shuttleworth papers, JRL.

[30] 'Secret Political Memoranda', 25 July 1843, Brooke and Sorensen,

Prime Ministers' Papers, II, 216; Grey to Lansdowne, 18 Nov. 1846, PRO, H.O. 34/7, pp. 230–2; Lansdowne to Russell, 7 Apr. 1847, Russell Papers, PRO, P.R.O. 30/22/6C, ff. 29–30; Lansdowne to Russell, May 1847, *ibid.*, f. 198; Russell to Kay-Shuttleworth, 13 Dec. 1846, Kay-Shuttleworth Papers, JRL; Lansdowne to Brougham, 20 Aug. 1846, Brougham Papers, UCL; Kay-Shuttleworth to Lansdowne, 6 Mar. [1847], Lansdowne Papers, Bowood House.

  [31] Alexander, 'Collegiate Teacher-training', pp. 203–46, shows that the minutes of 1846 were the economic salvation of several Anglican training schools.

CHAPTER X

  [1] Cavanagh, 'State Intervention in English Education', *History*, XXV (1940), 144; Murphy, *Church, State and Schools in Britain* (London, 1971), p. xiii.

  [2] Journal entry, 29 May 1840, Tremenheere Papers, Morrab Library, Album IV, p. 56.

  [3] 'The Religious Difficulties of National Education in England, 1800–70', *Cambridge Historical Journal*, XII (1956), 158–9.

  [4] See Joan Connelly Ullman, *The Tragic Week: a Study of Anticlericalism in Spain, 1875–1912* (Cambridge, Mass., 1968); and José Sánchez, *Anticlericalism: a Brief History* (Notre Dame, Ind., 1972).

  [5] Roberts, *Victorian Origins*, p. 318; Johnson, 'Educational Policy and Social Control in Early Victorian England', *Past and Present*, No. 49 (1970), pp. 96–7; Parris, *Bureaucracy*, p. 206.

  [6] *Victorian Minds* (New York, 1968), p. 81.

  [7] 'Religious Difficulties', p. 157.

  [8] 3 *Hansard*, CXII (1850), 798.

  [9] Johnson, 'Educating the Educators', pp. 83–5, 88–91, 100.

  [10] A. P. Donajgrodzki (ed.), *Social control in Nineteenth Century Britain* (London and Totowa, N.J., 1977); Michael B. Katz, *The Irony of Early School Reform: Educational Innovation in Mid-nineteenth Century Massachusetts* (Boston, Mass., 1970); Clifford S. Griffin, *Their Brothers' Keepers: Moral Stewardship in the United States, 1800–1865* (New Brunswick, N.J., 1960); Phillip McCann (ed.), *Popular Education and Socialization in the Nineteenth Century* (London, 1977).

  [11] Lois W. Banner, 'Religious Benevolence as Social Control: a Critique of an Interpretation', *Journal of American History*, LX (1973), 23–41.

  [12] Roberts, *Victorian Origins*, pp. 141, 145, 245; Bishop, *Central Authority*, p. 24.

  [13] Strachey and Fulford, *Greville Memoirs*, V, 144–5 (29 Nov. 1843).

  [14] *The Public Career of Sir James Graham* (Oxford and Cleveland, O., 1952), p. 157; C. I. Hamilton, 'Sir James Graham, the Baltic Campaign

and War-planning at the Admiralty in 1854', *Historical Journal*, XIX (1976), 89–112; but see A. P. Donajgrodzki, 'Sir James Graham at the Home Office', *ibid.*, XX (1977), 97–120, for a different view.

¹⁵ See Crosby, *Peel's Administration*, pp. 40, 144, for a different view.

¹⁶ Prest, *Russell*, pp. 225, 345–8; Cameron, 'Melbourne's Second Administration', pp. 48–9.

¹⁷ Memorandum, [21?] Nov. 1842, Graham Papers, NL, bdl. 55B (reel 8).

¹⁸ H. Manners Sutton to Saunders, 27 Jan. 1845, PRO, H.O. 87/1, p. 344; H. Manners Sutton to Horner, 27 Jan. 1845, *ibid.*, p. 345; for decisions on suggested grants, see the letters to various factory inspectors in *ibid.*, pp. 373–4, 401, and H.O. 87/2, pp. 28, 170, 178, 367–8, 424, 440; factory inspectors' minute book, 7 June 1840, PRO, Lab. 15/1, n.p., and 12 Aug. 1844, 9 June 1845, 24 June 1846, Lab. 15/2, pp. 34, 170–1, 260–1; Fox Maule to Poor Law Commission, 26 Jan. 1841, PRO, H.O. 34/3, pp. 319/20; H. Waddington to H. Chester, 8 Sept. 1848, *ibid.*, 8, p. 364; H. Waddington to Kay-Shuttleworth, 3 Dec. 1849, *ibid.*, 9, pp. 172–3; H. Waddington to Saunders, 6 Aug. 1849, *ibid.*, 87/2, pp. 179/80.

¹⁹ Horner to Grey, 26 Oct. 1849, PRO, H.O. 45/2866.

²⁰ *Politics of Government Growth*, p. 126.

²¹ *Central Authority*, p. 271.

²² Henry Roper, 'The Education Department for England and Wales, 1865–1885: a Study in Legislation and Administrative Response' (unpublished Ph.D. dissertation, Cambridge University, 1972). Gillian Sutherland, *Policy-making in Elementary Education, 1870–1895* (Oxford, 1973); Gail S. Clark, 'The Exercise of Power: The Influence of the Civil Service on English Educational Policy, 1919 to 1939' (unpublished Ph.D. dissertation, University of Texas, 1977); Alexander, 'Collegiate Teacher training', pp. 246–347.

Bibliography

PRIMARY SOURCES

Private papers

Acland of Broadclyst Papers. Devon County Record Office.
Acland Papers. Exeter City Library.
Aldam Papers. Frickley Hall, near Doncaster, Yorks.
Baines Papers. Leeds City Archives.
Broadlands Archives. National Register of Archives.
Brougham Papers. University College, London.
Brougham Papers. William L. Clements Library, University of Michigan.
Chadwick Papers. University College, London.
Chalmers Papers. New College, Edinburgh.
Ellenborough Papers. Public Record Office, P.R.O. 30/12.
Ellice Papers. National Library of Scotland.
Gladstone Papers. British Museum, Additional Manuscripts 44,086–835.
Gladstone–Glynne Papers. Flint County Record Office.
Gordon and Buckland Collection. Devon County Record Office.
Graham Papers. Newberry Library.
Grey of Howick Papers. Department of Palaeography and Diplomatic, University of Durham.
Haddington Papers. National Register of Archives (Scotland).
Harrowby Papers. Sandon Hall, near Stafford.
Hickleton Papers. Garrowby Hall, near York.
John Kaye Deposit. Lincolnshire Record Office, Cor. B/5.
Kay-Shuttleworth Papers. John Rylands University Library of Manchester.
Lansdowne Papers. Bowood House, near Calne, Wilts.
Macvey Napier Papers. British Museum, Additional Manuscripts 34,611–31.
Melbourne Papers. Royal Archives.
Monteagle Papers. National Library of Ireland.
Morris-Eyton Collection. Shrewsbury Public Library.
Newcastle Papers. University of Nottingham Library.
National Society. General Committee Minute Books, vols. III–IV (1824–47), National Society Archives.
Peel Papers. British Museum, Additional Manuscripts 40,181–617.

Russell Papers. Public Record Office, P.R.O. 30/22.
Seaforth Papers. Scottish Record Office, GD 46.
Society in Scotland for Propagating Christian Knowledge. Scottish
    Record Office, GD 95.
Spencer Papers. Althorp, near Northampton.
Tremenheere Papers. Morrab Library, Penzance.
Victorian Archive. Royal Archives.
Wharncliffe Muniments. Sheffield City Library.

Departmental papers at the Public Record Office

Colonial Office. Original Correspondence, West Indies. C.O. 318.
Education Department. Miscellanea. Ed. 9.
Education Department. Building Grant Applications. Ed. 103.
Home Office. Registered Papers. H.O. 45.
Home Office. Entry Books, Factories. H.O. 87.
Ministry of Labour. H.M. Factory Inspectors' Minute Books. Lab. 15.
Poor Law Commission. Correspondence and Papers. M.H. 19.
Poor Law Commission. Assistant Poor Law Commissioners,
    Correspondence. M.H. 32.
Privy Council Registers. P.C. 2.
Privy Council Minute Books. P.C. 4.
Treasury Board Papers. T. 1.
Treasury Out Letters, North Britain. T. 17.
Treasury Out Letters, General. T. 27.
Treasury Out Letters, Various. T. 28.
Treasury Minute Books. T. 29.

Parliamentary Papers

Legislation
'Poor Law Amendment Bill.' 1834, III (211), 235–90; (581), 357–416.
'Schools (Scotland) Bill.' 1837–38, VI (114), 31–5.
'Poor Law Amendment Bill, 1840.' 1840, III (230), 257–70.
'Poor Law Amendment Bill, 1841.' 1841, III (7), 37–112.
'Factory Bill, 1843.' 1843, II (82), 495–642.
'Education of the Poor Bill'. 1844, II (399), 113–16.

Select committees
'Report from the Select Committee on the State of Education.' 1834, IX
    (572), 1.
'[Second] Report from the Select Committee on Education in England
    and Wales.' 1835, VII (465), 1.
'Report from the Select Committee on the Poor Law.' 1837–38, XVIII,
    Part I (202), 1.

'Report from the Select Committee on Education of the Poorer Classes in England and Wales.' 1837–38, VII (589), 157–343.

'Report from the Select Committee on Scotch Education.' 1837–38, VII (715), 439.

'Digest of Returns to the Select Committee on Scotch Education.' 1841, XIX (64), 1.

'Report from the Select Committee on Miscellaneous Expenditure.' 1847–48, XVIII, Parts I and II (543), 1.

Reports

'Minutes of the Committee of Council on Education, relating to the Condition on which the Parliamentary Grant . . . for the Promotion of Education in Great Britain is distributed . . . .' 1840, XL (18), 389–406.

'Minutes of the Committee of Council on Education, with Appendices and Plans of School Houses.' 1840, XL (254), 407–669. 1841, XX [317], 97–222. 1842, XXXIII (442), 115–418. 1845, XXXV [622], 337–771. 1846, XXXII [741], 209–710. 1847, XLV [866], 11–523.

'Extracts from Minutes of Committee of Council on Education, of 4 January and 15 July 1840.' 1840, XL (490), 385–7.

'Copies of all Minutes in Council containing Regulations as to the Distribution of the Parliamentary Grant for the Promotion of Education in Great Britain, from the close of last Session to the End of January'. 1844, XXXVIII (84), 219–25.

'Copy of Supplementary Minute of the Committee of Council on Education.' 1847, XLV (660), 9.

'Copy of Minutes of the Committee of Council on Education, defining the Conditions of Aid to Roman Catholic Schools.' 1847–48, L (488), 613.

'Reports of the Inspectors of Factories to Her Majesty's Principal Secretary of State for the Home Department'. 1839, XIX [201], 539–60. 1840, XXIII [218], 1–26; [261], 27–47. 1842, XXXII (31), 337–440.

'The Report of Mr. R. J. Saunders, upon the Establishment of Schools in the Factory Districts, in February, 1842.' 1843, XXVII [500], 385–400.

'Report from His Majesty's Commissioners for inquiring into the Administration and Practical Operation of the Poor Laws.' 1834, XXVII–XXIX (44).

'Annual Reports of the Poor Law Commissioners for England and Wales.' 1835, XXXV (500), 107–363. 1836, XXIX, Part I (595), 1. 1837–38, XXVIII [147], 145. 1839, XX (239), 1. 1841, XI [327], 197. 1843, XXI [468], 1.

'Report of the Poor Law Commissioners on the Continuation of the Poor Law Commission.' 1840, XVII [226], 167.

Returns

'Sums of Money granted in aid of the Erection of Schools in England and Scotland, and of Model Schools in England, stating places in which Schools are situated, Description of Schools, Amount Contributed.'

1834, XLII (178), 527. 1835, XL (236), 679. 1836, XLVII (502), 52. 1837, XLI (372), 463.

'Returns of the Number of Children Employed, under 14 Years of Age.' 1836, XLV (254), 203–14.

'Applications made from Scotland for participation in the Grants.' 1837, XXXIX (304), 239.

'Sums granted by Parliament, 1834 to 1837, for the Advancement of Education in England and Wales.' 1837–38, XXXVIII (395), 325.

'Treasury Minute, 5 July 1838.' 1837–38, XXXVIII (695), 365.

'Papers on Education.' 1839, XLI (16), 255—7.

'Returns relative to Factories.' 1839, XLII (41), 1–351.

'Reports on the Effects of the Educational Provisions of the Factories Act.' 1839, XLII (42), 353–428.

'Minute of Proceedings of Committee of Privy Council on Education of the 11th April 1839'. 1839, XLI (177), 259–61.

'Return of Expenditure of the Grant for Model Schools, and Applications for Aid.' 1839, XLI (216), 371–9.

'Account of the Expenditure of £10,000, Granted 1834 to 1838, for . . . Scotland.' 1839, XLI (282), 383.

'A Copy of the Report of the Committee of Council appointed to superintend the Application of any Sums voted by Parliament for the purpose of promoting public Education, of 3rd June 1839.' 1839, XLI (284), 263.

'A Copy of any Order in Council, appointing a Committee of Council . . . .' 1839, XLI (287), 265.

'Return of Applications for Portions of the Sum granted for the Promotion of Public Education in 1839.' 1840, XL (124), 1–18.

'Proceedings of the Treasury for facilitating the Foundation and Endowment of additional Schools in Scotland.' 1840, XL (382), 355–70.

'A Return of Applications for Portions of the Sum granted for the Promotion of Public Education in 1839.' 1840, XL (470), 19–24.

'Correspondence between Her Majesty's Government and the General Assembly of the Church of Scotland, respecting the Appointment, &c., of Inspectors of Schools for Scotland.' 1841, XX (392), 223–72.

'An Account of Schools in the Highlands and Islands of Scotland.' 1841, Sess. 2, II (29), 393; 1842, XXXII (543), 419.

'Copies of Extracts of Correspondence . . . between the Committee of Council on Education and the Committee of the British and Foreign School Society, relative to . . . the Normal School in the Borough Road, and the Question of School Inspection.' 1843, XL (217), 593–669.

'A Return of the Number and Locality of Schools in Scotland to which Aid has been granted by the Educational Committee of the Privy Council.' 1844, XLII (309), 675–94.

'Return of all Sums which have been granted under Authority of the Committee of Privy Council for Educational Purposes in Scotland'. 1847–48, L (197), 649–52.

Estimates

'To aid in the Erection of Schoolhouses in Great Britain'. 1833, **XXIV** (654), 505.

'To aid in the Erection of Schoolhouses in England.' 1834, **XLII** (183), 433. 1835, **XXXVIII** (143), 511. 1836, **XXXVIII** (159), 416. 1837, **XXXVIII** (148), 367. 1837–38, **XXXVII** (313), 384.

'To aid in the Erection of Schoolhouses in Scotland.' 1834, **XLII** (311), 445. 1836, **XXXVIII** (525), 436. 1837, **XXXVIII** (148), 367. 1837–38, **XXXVII** (313), 384.

'To aid in the Erection of Model Schools in England.' 1835, **XXXVIII** (418), 541.

'For Education in Great Britain.' 1839, **XXXI** (309), 755. 1840, **XXX** (179), 850. 1841, **XIV** (224), 451. 1841, Sess. 2, **II** (14), 145. 1842, **XXVII** (130), 519. 1842, **XXVII** (492), 439. 1843, **XXXI** (91), 433. 1844, **XXXIII** (108), 539. 1845, **XXIX** (257), 371. 1846, **XXVI** (266), 695. 1847, **XXXV** (229), 331. 1847–48, **XL** (327), 355. 1849, **XXXI** (268), 377.

Other printed public records

Parliamentary proceedings
Hansard's Parliamentary Debates. First Series, vols. **IX, XXXIV–XXXVIII** (1807, 1816–18).
Hansard's Parliamentary Debates. Third Series, vols. **XV–CXII** (1833–50).
House of Commons Divisions, 1837–38.
Journal of the House of Commons. Vols. **LXXXVIII–CII** (1833–47).
Journal of the House of Lords. Vols. **LXV–LXXI** (1833–39).
Minutes of Proceedings of the House of Lords, Session 1839.
Mirror of Parliament, 1833–39.
Reports of the Select Committee of the House of Commons on Public Petitions, 1839, 1843.
Votes and Proceedings of the House of Commons (1839).

Legislation
A Collection of the Public General Statutes. Passed in the Fourth and Fifth Years of the Reign of His Majesty King William IV. London, 1834.
A Collection of the Public General Statutes, Passed in the First and Second Years of the Reign of Her Majesty Queen Victoria. London, 1838.
'Education and Charities Bill, 1835.' *House of Lords Papers,* 1835, I (95), 487–98.
'Education and Charities Bill, 1837.' *House of Lords Papers,* 1837, II (2), 277–93.
'Education Bill, 1838.' *House of Lords Papers,* 1837–38, II (9), 647–65.
'Schools (Scotland) Bill.' *House of Lords Papers,* 1837–38, IV (295), 621–5.
'Education Bill, 1839.' *House of Lords Papers,* 1839, III (108), 391–408.

Reports

Minutes of the Committee of Council of Education; with Appendices, and Plans of School-houses, 1839–40. London, 1840.

Minutes of the Committee of Council on Education; with Appendices, and Plans of School-houses, 1842–43. London, 1844.

Minutes of the Committee of Council on Education; with Appendices, 1844. 2 vols. London, 1845.

Minutes of the Committee of Council on Education; with Appendices, 1845. 2 vols. London, 1846.

Printed diaries, correspondence, and memoirs

Bloomfield, B. C., editor. 'The Autobiography of Sir James Kay-Shuttleworth.' *Education Libraries Bulletin*, Supplement Seven (1964).

Brooke, John, and Mary Sorensen, editors. *The Prime Ministers' Papers: W. E. Gladstone.* 2 vols. London, 1971–72.

Broughton, John Cam Hobhouse, Lord. *Recollections of a Long Life.* Edited by Lady Dorchester. 6 vols. London, 1911.

Chapple, J. A. V., and Arthur Pollard, editors. *The Letters of Mrs Gaskell.* Manchester, 1966.

Edmonds, E. L. and O. P. *I Was There: The Memoirs of H. S. Tremenheere.* Eton, 1964.

Esher, Viscount, editor. *The Girlhood of Queen Victoria: a Selection from Her Majesty's Diaries between the years 1832 and 1840.* 2 vols. London, 1912.

Foot, M. R. D., and H. C. G. Matthew, editors. *The Gladstone Diaries.* 4 vols. Oxford, 1968–74.

Gooch, G. P., editor. *Later Correspondence of Lord John Russell, 1840–1878.* 2 vols. London, 1925.

Jennings, Louis J., editor. *The Croker Papers: the Correspondence and Diaries of the late Right Honourable John Wilson Croker.* 3 vols. London, 1885.

Lathbury, D. C., editor. *Correspondence on Church and Religion of William Ewart Gladstone.* 2 vols. New York, 1910.

Napier, Macvey, editor. *Selection from the Correspondence of the late Macvey Napier, Esq.* London, 1879.

Pugh, R. K., and J. F. A. Mason, editors. *The Letter Books of Samuel Wilberforce.* Oxfordshire Record Society, vol. XLVII. N.P., 1970.

Russell, John Russell, Earl. *Recollections and Suggestions, 1813–1873.* Boston, Mass., 1875.

Russell, Rollo, editor. *Early Correspondence of Lord John Russell.* 2 vols. London, 1913.

Sanders, Lloyd C., editor. *Lord Melbourne's Papers.* London, 1889.

Sinclair, John, editor. *Correspondence of the National Society with the Lords of the Treasury and with the Committee of Council on Education.* London, 1839.

—. *Sketches of Old Times and Distant Places.* London, 1875.

Strachey, Lytton, and Roger Fulford, editors. *The Greville Memoirs, 1814–1860.* 8 vols. London, 1938.

Contemporary books and pamphlets

Baines, Edward, Jr. *An Alarm to the Nation on the Unjust, Unconstitutional and Dangerous Measure of State Education Proposed by the Government.* London, 1847.

—. *The Factory Education Bill, Original and Amended.* London, 1843.

—. *On the Social, Educational, and Religious State of the Manufacturing Districts.* 3rd ed. London, 1843.

Biggs, Henry. *Report on the Industrial Plan of Education, under the Directions of the Poor Law Commissioners, in England.* Cork, 1841.

Coleridge, Derwent. *The Teachers of the People: a Sermon Preached at the Opening of the Chapel of St. Mark's College, Chelsea.* London, 1843.

Cousin, Victor. *On the State of Education in Holland, as Regards Schools for the Working Classes and for the Poor.* Translated, with preliminary observations, by Leonard Horner. London, 1838.

Dunn, Henry. *National Education, the Question of Questions.* London, 1838.

Grey, the Hon. and Rev. John. *A Sermon, Preached . . . in Behalf of the Special Fund for Providing National Schools for the Manufacturing and Mining Districts.* London, 1843.

Hinton, John Howard. *A Plea for Liberty of Conscience: a Letter . . . on the Educational Clauses of the Factories' Bill.* London, 1843.

Hook, Walter Farquhar. *On the Means of Rendering more Efficient the Education of the People.* London, 1846.

Horner, Leonard. *The Factories Regulation Act Explained, with some Remarks on its Origin, Nature, and Tendency.* Glasgow, 1834.

—. *On the Employment of Children in Factories and other Works in the United Kingdom, and in some Foreign Countries.* London, 1840.

Kay-Shuttleworth, Sir James. *Four Periods of Public Education as Reviewed in 1832–1839–1846–1862.* London, 1862.

Leeds Wesleyan Deputation. *On the Educational Clauses of Sir James Graham's Factory Bill.* Leeds, 1843.

Lloyd, Charles. *A Calm Inquiry into all the Objections made to the Educational Provisions of the Factory Bill.* London, 1843.

Perceval, Arthur P. *Two Sermons.* London, 1843.

Salmon, David editor. *The Practical Parts of Lancaster's 'Improvements' and Bell's 'Experiment'.* Cambridge, 1932.

Sandys, George W. *A Letter to the Right Honourable Sir James R. G. Graham, . . . on the Subject of National Education.* London, 1843.

Senior, Nassau W. *Letters on the Factory Act, as it affects the Cotton Manufacture.* London, 1837.

Sinclair, John, editor. *Correspondence on the Subject of the late Disturbances in the Manufacturing and Mining Districts.* London, 1842.

Slaney, Robert A. *Reports of the House of Commons on the Education (1838), and on the Health (1840), of the Poorer Classes in Large Towns; with some Suggestions for Improvement.* London, 1840.

Tenax. *A Letter to the Right Hon. the Lord Wharncliffe, on the Unconstitutional Character of his late Declarations with Respect to National Education.* London, 1842.

Wray, Cecil. *The Suppression of any Portion of the Truth in the Work of Education Unjustifiable.* London and Liverpool, 1843.
Wyse, Thomas. *Education Reform; or, the Necessity of a National System of Education.* London, 1836.

Contemporary periodicals

Brougham, Henry Brougham, Lord. 'The Education Bill.' *Edinburgh Review,* LXVI (1838), 439–49.
Croker, J. W. 'Shuttleworth's Phonics.' *Quarterly Review,* LXXIV (1844), 26–39.
Empson, William. 'State of Parties.' *Edinburgh Review,* LXV (1837), 265–82.
'Factories Education Bill.' *Eclectic Review,* new series, XIII (1843), 573–94.
'The Government Education Bill: Conduct of Dissenters.' *Eclectic Review,* new series, XIII (1843), 697–715.
Grey, Sir George. 'Committee of Council on Education.' *Edinburgh Review,* LXXV (1842), 105–39.
'Inspection of Schools by Government.' *Eclectic Review,* new series, XII (1842), 481–502.
Monteagle, Thomas Spring Rice, Lord. 'Distress of the Manufacturing Districts—Causes and Remedies.' *Edinburgh Review,* LXXVII (1843), 190–227.
—. 'Ministerial Plan of Education—Church and Tory Misrepresentations.' *Edinburgh Review,* LXX (1839), 149–80.
—. 'The Ministry and the late Session.' *Edinburgh Review,* LXXVIII (1843), 517–49.
'National Education—Sectarian and Unconstitutional.' *Eclectic Review,* new series, XXI (1847), 507–29.
'The New Ministry.' *British Quarterly Review,* IV (1846), 259–76.
'Review of the Session.' *Eclectic Review,* new series, XIV (1843), 458–76.
'Sir Robert Peel.' *Eclectic Review,* new series, XIV (1843), 692–716.
Symons, J. C. 'Education of the Working Classes.' *Dublin Review,* XIV (1844), 141–77.
Vaughan, Robert. 'The Education Controversy—What has it Done?' *British Quarterly Review,* VI (1847), 528–47.
—. 'The Education Question.' *British Quarterly Review,* V (1847), 540–51.
—. 'Popular Education in England.' *British Quarterly Review,* IV (1846), 444-508.

Publications of the school societies

British and Foreign School Society. *Annual Reports,* XXIX–XXXVII (1834–42).
—. *Strictures on the Publications of the Central Society of Education.* London, 1837.
Central Society of Education. *Schools for the Industrious Classes; or, The Present*

State of Education among the Working People of England. London, 1837.
—. *First, Second, Third Publications* (1837–39).
Gaelic School Society. *Annual Reports*, XXII–XXXIII (1833–43).
General Assembly's Education Committee. *Educational Statistics of the Highlands and Islands of Scotland.* Edinburgh, 1833.
—. *Report on the Returns from Presbyteries on the State of Schools in the Year 1841.*
—. *Report of the Committee of the General Assembly for Increasing the means of Education and Religious Instruction in Scotland, particularly in the Highlands and Islands* (1832–43).
London Diocesan Board of Education. *Inspectors' Report.* London, n.d.
National Society. *Annual Reports*, XXII–XXXVIII (1833–49).
—. *Monthly Paper*, No. 19 (30 June 1848).
—. *National Education in the Principles of the Established Church.* London, 1839.
Wesleyan Education Committee. *Annual Reports*, V–IX (1843–47).

Contemporary newspapers

Examiner. 1843.
Leeds Mercury. 1843.
Morning Chronicle. 1837–39
Sheffield Mercury and Hallamshire Advertiser. 1843.
Sheffield and Rotherham Independent. 1843.
Spectator. 1843.
The Times. 1833–48.

SECONDARY ACCOUNTS

General histories

Briggs, Asa. *The Age of Improvement, 1783–1867.* London, 1960.
Halévy, Elie. *A History of the English People, 1830–41.* Vol. III of *A History of the English People in the Nineteenth Century.* Translated by E. I. Watkin. London, 1927.
Knox, H. M. *Two Hundred and Fifty Years of Scottish Education, 1696–1946.* Edinburgh and London, 1953.
Woodward, Llewellyn. *The Age of Reform, 1815–1870.* 2nd ed. Oxford, 1962.

Biographies

Acland, A. H. D. *Memoir and Letters of the Right Honourable Sir Thomas Dyke Acland.* London, 1902.
Allen, Anna Otter. *John Allen and his Friends.* London, [1922].
Ashwell, Arthur E., and Reginald G. Wilberforce. *Life of the Right Reverend Samuel Wilberforce, D. D., Lord Bishop of Oxford and afterwards of Winchester.* 3 vols. London, 1880–82.
Auchmuty, James Johnston. *Sir Thomas Wyse, 1791–1862: the Life and Career*

of an Educator and Diplomat. London, 1939.

Blomfield, Alfred. *A Memoir of Charles James Blomfield, D. D., Bishop of London, with Selections from his Correspondence*. 2 vols. London, 1863.

Bonaparte-Wyse, Olga. *The Spurious Brood: Princess Letitia Bonaparte and her Children*. London, 1969.

Cecil, Lord David, *Lord M*. London, 1954.

Churton, Edward. *Memoir of Joshua Watson*. 2 vols. London, 1861.

The Dictionary of National Biography.

Finer, S. E. *The Life and Times of Sir Edwin Chadwick*. London, 1952.

Garratt, G. T. *Lord Brougham*. London, 1935.

Gash, Norman. *Sir Robert Peel*. London, 1972.

Grier, R. M. *John Allen, a Memoir*. London, 1889.

Hodder, Edwin. *The Life and Work of the Seventh Earl of Shaftesbury*. 3 vols. London, 1887.

Leader, R. E. *Life and Letters of John Arthur Roebuck*. London, 1897.

Lyell, Katherine M., editor. *Memoir of Leonard Horner*. 2 vols. London, 1890.

New, Chester W. *The Life of Henry Brougham to 1830*. Oxford, 1961.

Parker, Charles Stuart. *Life and Letters of Sir James Graham, 1792–1861*. 2 vols. London, 1907.

——. *Sir Robert Peel from his Private Papers*. 3 vols. London, 1891–99.

Pollard, Hugh M. *Pioneers of Popular Education, 1760–1850*. London, 1956.

Prest, John. *Lord John Russell*. London, 1972.

Smith, Frank. *The Life and Work of Sir James Kay-Shuttleworth*. London, 1923.

Stephens, W. R. W. *The Life and Letters of Walter Farquhar Hook*. 7th ed. London, 1885.

Walpole, Spencer. *The Life of Lord John Russell*. 2 vols. London, 1889.

Webster, A. B. *Joshua Watson: the Story of a Layman, 1771–1855*. London, 1954.

Ziegler, Philip. *Melbourne*. London, 1976.

Monographs

Akenson, Donald H. *The Irish Education Experiment: the National System of Education in the Nineteenth Century*. Studies in Irish History, second series, no. VII. London and Toronto, 1970.

Altholz, Josef L. *The Churches in the Nineteenth Century*. Indianapolis and New York, 1967.

Aspinall, Arthur. *Lord Brougham and the Whig Party*. Manchester, 1927.

Ball, Nancy. *Her Majesty's Inspectorate, 1839–1849*. Edinburgh and London, 1963.

Binns, Henry Bryan. *A Century of Education: being the Centenary History of the British and Foreign School Society, 1808–1908*. London, 1908.

Bishop, A. S. *The Rise of a Central Authority for English Education*. Cambridge, 1971.

Brose, Olive J. *Church and Parliament: the Reshaping of the Church of England,*

1828–1860. Stanford, Cal., and London, 1959.

Brown, Lucy M. *The Board of Trade and the Free Trade Movement, 1830–42.* Oxford, 1958.

Brundage, Anthony. *The Making of the New Poor Law: the Politics of Inquiry, Enactment, and Implementation, 1832–1839.* New Brunswick, N. J., 1978.

Burgess, Henry James. *Enterprise in Education: the Story of the Work of the Established Church in the Education of the People Prior to 1870.* London, 1958.

Burn, W. L. *The Age of Equipoise.* New York, 1965.

Chadwick, Owen. *The Victorian Church,* Part I. *An Ecclesiastical History of England,* vol. V. Edited by J. C. Dickenson. 2nd ed. London, 1970.

Cowherd, Raymond G. *The Politics of English Dissent.* New York, 1956.

Crosby, Travis L. *Sir Robert Peel's Administration, 1841–1846.* Newton Abbot and Hamden, Conn., 1976.

Cruickshank, Marjorie. *A History of the Training of Teachers in Scotland.* London, 1970.

Djang, T. K. *Factory Inspection in Great Britain.* London, 1942.

Edmonds, E. L. *The School Inspector.* London, 1962.

Erickson, Arvel B. *The Public Career of Sir James Graham.* Oxford and Cleveland, O., 1952.

Finlayson, Geoffrey. *England in the Eighteen-thirties: Decade of Reform.* London, 1969.

Fraser, Derek. *The Evolution of the British Welfare State: a History of Social Policy since the Industrial Revolution.* London, 1973.

—. *Urban Politics in Victorian England: the Structure of Politics in Victorian Cities.* Leicester, 1976.

Gash, Norman. *Reaction and Reconstruction in English Politics, 1832–1852.* Oxford, 1965.

Gilbert, Amy M. *The Work of Lord Brougham for Education in England.* Chambersburg, Penna., 1922.

Goldstrom, J. M. *The Social Content of Education, 1808–1870: a Study of the Working Class School Reader in England and Ireland.* Shannon, 1972.

Handley, James E. *The Irish in Scotland, 1798–1845.* Cork, 1943.

Himmelfarb, Gertrude. *Victorian Minds.* New York, 1968.

Hurt, John. *Education in Evolution: Church, State, and Popular Education, 1800–1870.* London, 1971.

Jennings, Henrietta Cooper. *The Political Theory of State-supported Elementary Education in England, 1750–1833.* Lancaster, Penna., 1928.

Jones, M. G. *The Charity School Movement: a Study of Eighteenth Century Puritanism in Action.* Hamden, Conn., 1964.

Kitson Clark, George. *Churchmen and the Condition of England, 1832–1885: a study in the development of social ideas and practice from the Old Regime to the Modern State.* London, 1973.

—. *The Making of Victorian England.* London, 1962.

Laqueur, T. W. *Religion and Respectability: Sunday Schools and Working-class Culture, 1780–1850.* New Haven and London, 1976.

Lubenow, William C. *The Politics of Government Growth: Early Victorian Attitudes toward State Intervention, 1830–1848.* Newton Abbot and Hamden,

Conn., 1971.

MacDonagh, Oliver. *A Pattern of Government Growth, 1800–60*. London, 1961.

Mackay, Thomas. *A History of the English Poor Law from 1834 to the Present Time*. London, 1900.

Machin, G. I. T. *Politics and the Churches in Great Britain, 1832 to 1868*. Oxford, 1977.

Maltby, S. E. *Manchester and the Movement for National Elementary Education, 1800–1870*. Manchester, 1918.

Murphy, James. *Church, State and Schools in Britain, 1800–1970*. London, 1971.

—. *The Religious Problem in English Education: the Crucial Experiment*. Liverpool, 1959.

Newsome, David. *The Parting of Friends: a Study of the Wilberforces and Henry Manning*. London, 1966.

Nicholls, Sir George. *A History of the English Poor Law, in connexion with the legislation and other circumstances affecting the Condition of the People*. 2 vols. London, 1854.

Parris, Henry. *Constitutional Bureaucracy: the Development of British Central Administration since the Eighteenth Century*. London, 1969.

Rich. R. W. *The Training of Teachers in England and Wales during the Nineteenth Century*. Cambridge, 1933.

Roberts, David. *Victorian Origins of the British Welfare State*. New Haven, Conn., 1960.

Robson, Adam Henry. *The Education of Children Engaged in Industry in England, 1833–1876*. London, 1931.

Roseveare, H. G. *The Treasury: the Evolution of a British Institution*. London, 1969.

Sainty, J. C. *Treasury Officials, 1660–1870. Office-holders in Modern Britain*, vol. I. London, 1972.

Sanchez. José. *Anticlericalism: a Brief History*. Notre Dame, Ind., 1972.

Silver, Harold. *The Concept of Popular Education: a Study of Ideas and Social Movements in the Early Nineteenth Century*. London, 1965.

Soloway, R. A. *Prelates and People: Ecclesiastical Social Thought in England, 1783–1852*. London and Toronto, 1969.

Sutherland, Gillian. *Policy-making in Elementary Education, 1870–1895*. Oxford, 1973.

Taylor, A. J. P. *Essays in English History*. London, 1976.

Thomas, Maurice Walton. *The Early Factory Legislation*. Leigh on Sea, 1948.

Thompson, E. P. *The Making of the English Working Class*. Rev. ed. London, 1968.

Ullman, Joan Connelly. *The Tragic Week: a Study of Anticlericalism in Spain, 1875–1912*. Cambridge, Mass., 1968.

Ward, W. R. *Religion and Society in England, 1790–1850*. London, 1972.

Wardle, David. *Education and Society in Nineteenth-century Nottingham*. Cambridge, 1971.

Webb, Sidney and Beatrice. *English Local Government.* 9 vols. London, 1929.
Wright, Maurice. *Treasury Control of the Civil Service, 1854–1874.* Oxford, 1969.

Articles

Aldrich. R. E. 'Radicalism, National Education and the Grant of 1833.' *Journal of Educational Administration and History,* V (1973), 1–5.
Alexander, J. L. 'Lord John Russell and the Origins of the Committee of Council on Education.' *Historical Journal,* XX (1977), 395–415.
—. and D. G. Paz. 'The Treasury Grants, 1833–1839.' *British Journal of Educational Studies,* XXII (1974), 78–92.
Best, G. F. A. 'The Religious Difficulties of National Education in England, 1800–70.' *Cambridge Historical Journal,* XII (1956), 155–73.
Boyson, Rhodes. 'The New Poor Law in North-east Lancashire, 1834–1871.' *Transactions of the Lancashire and Cheshire Antiquarian Society,* LXX (1960), 35–56.
Briggs, Asa. 'The Study of the History of Education.' *History of Education,* I (1972), 5–22.
Brundage, Anthony. 'The Landed Interest and the New Poor Law: a Reappraisal of the Revolution in Government.' *English Historical Review,* XC (1975), 27–48.
Butterfield, P. H. 'The Educational Researches of the Manchester Statistical Society, 1830–1840.' *British Journal of Educational Studies,* XXII (1974), 340–59.
Caplan, Maurice. 'The Poor Law in Nottinghamshire, 1936–71.' *Transactions of the Thoroton Society of Nottinghamshire,* LXXIV (1970), 82–98.
Cavanagh, F. A. 'State Intervention in English Education.' *History,* XXV (1940), 143–56.
Chambers, D. 'The Church of Scotland's Highlands and Islands Education Scheme, 1824–1843.' *Journal of Educational Administration and History,* VIII, No. 1 (1975), 8–17.
Cromwell, Valerie. 'Interpretations of Nineteenth-century Administration: an Analysis.' *Victorian Studies,* IX (1965–66), 245–55.
Donajgrodzki, A. P. 'Sir James Graham at the Home Office.' *Historical Journal,* XX (1977), 97–120.
Duke, Francis. 'The Poor Law Commissioners and Education.' *Journal of Educational Administration and History,* III, No. 1 (1970), 7–13.
Edmonds, E. L. 'Education and Early Factory Inspectors.' *Vocational Aspects of Secondary and Further Education,* X (1958), 85–95.
—. 'School Inspection: the Contribution of Religious Denominations.' *British Journal of Educational Studies,* VII (1958), 12–76.
— and O. P. 'Hugh Seymour Tremenheere, Pioneer Inspector of Schools.' *British Journal of Educational Studies,* XII (1963), 65–76.
Hamilton, C. I. 'Sir James Graham, the Baltic Campaign and War-planning at the Admiralty in 1854.' *Historical Journal,* XIX (1976),

89–112.

Hart, Jennifer. 'Nineteenth-century Social Reform: a Tory Interpretation of History.' *Past and Present*, No. 31 (1965), pp. 39–61.

Hempton, David N. 'Wesleyan Methodism and Educational Politics in early Nineteenth-century England.' *History of Education*, VIII (1979).

Hicks, W. C. R. 'The Education of the Half-timers: as shown Particularly in the case of Messrs. McConnel and Co. of Manchester.' *Economic History*, III (1939), 222–39.

Himmelfarb, Gertrude. 'The Writing of Social History: Recent Studies of 19th Century England.' *Journal of British Studies*, XI (1971), 148–70.

Hume, L. J. 'Jeremy Bentham and the Nineteenth-century Revolution in Government.' *Historical Journal*, X (1967), 361–75.

Johnson, Richard. 'Administrators in education before 1870: patronage, social position and role.' *Studies in the Growth of Nineteenth-century Government*. Edited by Gillian Sutherland. London, 1972.

——. 'Educating the Educators: "Experts" and the State, 1833–9.' *Social Control in Nineteenth Century Britain*. Edited by A. P. Donajgrodzki. London and Totowa, N.J., 1977.

——. 'Educational Policy and Social Control in Early Victorian England.' *Past and Present*, No. 49 (1970), pp. 96–119.

Kitching, J. 'The Catholic Poor Schools, 1800 to 1845.' *Journal of Educational Administration and History*, I, No. 2 (1969), 1–8, and II, No. 1 (1969), 1–12.

Kitson Clark, G. 'Hunger and Politics in 1842.' *Journal of Modern History*, XXV (1953), 355–74.

——. ' "Statesmen in Disguise": Reflexions on the History of the Neutrality of the Civil Service.' *Historical Journal*, II (1959), 19–39.

Lynch, M. J. 'Was Gladstone a Tractarian? W. E. Gladstone and the Oxford Movement, 1833–45.' *Journal of Religious History*, VIII (1974–5), 364–89.

MacDonagh, Oliver. 'The Nineteenth-century Revolution in Government: a Reappraisal.' *Historical Journal*, I (1958), 52–67.

McGregor, Oliver R. 'Social Research and Social Policy in the Nineteenth Century.' *British Journal of Sociology*, VIII (1957), 146–57.

Macleod, Roy M. 'Statesmen Undisguised.' *American Historical Review*, LXXVIII (1973), 1386–405.

McCord, Norman. 'Implementation of the 1834 Poor Law Amendment Act on Tyneside.' *International Review of Social History*, XIV (1969), 90–108.

Martin, Bernice. 'Leonard Horner: a Portrait of an Inspector of Factories.' *International Review of Social History*, XIV (1969), 412–43.

Murphy, James. 'Religion, the State, and Education in England.' *History of Education Quarterly*, VIII (1968), 3–34.

Pallister, Raymond. 'Educational Capital in the Elementary School of the Mid-nineteenth Century.' *History of Education*, II (1973), 147–57.

Parris, Henry. 'The Nineteenth-century Revolution in Government: a Reappraisal Reappraised.' *Historical Journal*, III (1960), 17–37.

Paz, D. G. 'The Composition of the Education Committee of the Privy Council, 1839–1856.' *Journal of Educational Administration and History*, VIII, No. 2 (1976), 1–8.

—. 'A Note on the Quarto and Octavo Minutes of the Committee of Council, 1839/40–1857/8.' *History of Education Society Bulletin*, No. 14 (autumn 1974), pp. 54–8.

—. 'Working-class Education and the State, 1839–1849: the Sources of Government Policy.' *Journal of British Studies*, XVI (1976), 129–52.

Pinnington, J. E. 'The Consular Chaplaincies and the Foreign Office under Palmerston, Aberdeen, and Malmesbury. Two Case Studies: Rome and Funchal.' *Journal of Ecclesiastical History*, XXVII (1976), 277–84.

Roberts, David. 'Jeremy Bentham and the Victorian Administrative State.' *Victorian Studies*, II (1958–59), 193–210.

—. 'Tory Paternalism and Social Reform in Early Victorian England.' *American Historical Review*, LXIII (1957–8), 323–37.

Ross, Alexander M. 'Kay-Shuttlewcrth and the Training of Teachers for Pauper Schools.' *British Journal of Educational Studies*, XV (1967), 275–83.

Sanderson, Michael. 'Education and the Factory in Industrial Lancashire, 1780–1840.' *Economic History Review*, second series, XX (1967), 266–79.

Sutherland, Gillian. 'Introduction.' *Studies in the Growth of Nineteenth-century Government*. Edited by Gillian Sutherland. London, 1972.

—. 'The Study of the History of Education.' *History*, LIV (1969), 49–59.

Thompson, David M. 'The Liberation Society, 1844–1868.' *Pressure from Without in Early Victorian England*. Edited by Patricia Hollis. New York, 1974.

Torrance, J. R. 'Sir George Harrison and the growth of bureaucracy in the early nineteenth century.' *English Historical Review*, LXXXIII (1968), 52–88.

Treble, James J. 'The Reaction of Chartism in the North of England to the Factory Education Bill of 1843.' *Journal of Educational Administration and History*, VI, No. 2 (1974), 1–9.

Ward, Gertrude. 'The Education of Factory Child Workers, 1833–1850.' *Economic History*, III (1935), 110–24.

Ward, J. T., and J. H. Treble. 'Religion and Education in 1843: Reaction to the "Factory Education Bill" '. *Journal of Ecclesiastical History*, XX (1969), 79–111.

Watson, R. J. 'Presbyterian Day Schools.' *Journal of the Presbyterian Historical Society of England*, XIV (1969), 67–74.

Webb, R. K. 'A Whig Inspector.' *Journal of Modern History*, XXVII (1955), 352–64.

West, E. G. 'Private versus Public Education: a Classical Economic Dispute.' *Journal of Political Economy*, LXXII (1964), 465–75.

Unpublished studies

Aldrich, Richard Edward. 'Education and the Political Parties, 1830–1870.' M.Phil. thesis, University of London, 1970.

Alexander, J. L. 'Collegiate Teacher-training in England and Wales: a Study in the Historical Determinants of Educational Provision and Practice in the Mid-nineteenth Century.' Ph.D. dissertation, University of London, 1977.

Brose, Olive J. 'How the British State became Involved in Education: the Background of the First Education Grant of 1833.' M.A. thesis, Columbia University, 1949.

Burgess, Henry James. 'The Educational History of the National Society, 1811–1833.' M.A. thesis, University of London, 1949.

—. 'The Work of the Established Church in the Education of the People, 1833–1870.' Ph.D. dissertation, University of London, 1954.

Cameron, Ronald Hugh. 'Lord Melbourne's Second Administration and the Opposition, 1837–1841.' Ph.D. dissertation, University of London, 1970.

Clark, Gail S. 'The Exercise of Power: the Influence of the Civil Service on English Educational Policy, 1919–1939.' Ph.D. dissertation, University of Texas, 1977.

Cosgrove, John. 'The Educational Aims and Activities of Sir Thomas Wyse (1791–1862).' Ph.D. dissertation, University of Manchester, 1975.

Duke, Francis. 'The Education of Pauper Children: Policy and Administration, 1834–1855.' M.A. thesis, University of Manchester, 1968.

Holland, Mary Griset. 'The British Catholic Press and the Educational Controversy, 1847–1865.' Ph.D. dissertation, Catholic University of America, 1975.

Johnson, Richard. 'The Education Department, 1839–1864: a Study in Social Policy and the Growth of Government.' Ph.D. dissertation, Cambridge University, 1968.

Paz, D. G. 'The Politics of Public Education in Britain, 1833–1848: ᾱ Study of Policy and Administration.' Ph.D. dissertation, University of Michigan, 1974.

Roper, Henry. 'The Education Department for England and Wales, 1865–1885: a Study in Legislation and Administrative Response.' Ph.D. dissertation, Cambridge University, 1972.

Smout, Christopher. 'Demographic Crises in Scotland from the Seventeenth to the Nineteenth Centuries.' Paper presented to the Comparative Studies in History Colloquium, University of Michigan, March 1975.

Toms, Vernon George. 'Secular Education in England, 1800–1870.' Ph.D. dissertation, University of London, 1972.

Index

death, 129; mentioned, 52, 113, 149
Whig Party, 6–7, 24–5, 31, 41–3, 108–9
Whitbread, Samuel, 5
Wigram, J. C., 17, 19–20, 34, 66–8
Wood, Charles, 129
Wood, S. F., 63, 137
Working classes, 1, 77, 120, 124

Wyse, Thomas: and Central Society of Education, 69–72; and inspection, 21–2; and origins of Committee of Council, 87–8; mentioned, 39, 66, 77, 128

'Young gentlemen', 63–8, 76, 91–2 131, 135, 137, 162 n. 12